A Catholic Reading Guide to Conditional Immortality

A Catholic Reading Guide to
Conditional Immortality

The Third Alternative to Hell and Universalism

Robert Wild

RESOURCE *Publications* • Eugene, Oregon

A CATHOLIC READING GUIDE TO CONDITIONAL IMMORTALITY
The Third Alternative to Hell and Universalism

Copyright © 2016 Robert Wild. All rights reserved. Except for brief quotations in critical publications or reviews, no part of this book may be reproduced in any manner without prior written permission from the publisher. Write: Permissions, Wipf and Stock Publishers, 199 W. 8th Ave., Suite 3, Eugene, OR 97401.

Resource Publications
An Imprint of Wipf and Stock Publishers
199 W. 8th Ave., Suite 3
Eugene, OR 97401

www.wipfandstock.com

PAPERBACK ISBN: 978-1-4982-9727-1
HARDCOVER ISBN: 978-1-4982-9729-5
EBOOK ISBN: 978-1-4982-9728-8

Manufactured in the U.S.A.   OCTOBER 17, 2016

Note: the views expressed in this book are entirely those of the author and should not be taken as representative of the views of Madonna House.

To those in the Protestant tradition who suffered loss of reputations and positions for reintroducing this teaching into the Christian world

What profit is there for us in pride? What has boasting in wealth brought us? All these are transient—like a shadow— like a ship passing through the moving waters, whose trace, the path of its prow, is not found once it has passed.

WIS 5:8–9

How great the mercy of the Lord, his forgiveness of those who return to him! The like cannot be found in men, for not immortal is any son of man.

SIRACH 17:24–25

How can man be immortal who in his mortal nature did not obey his Maker? By no other means could we have attained to incorruptibility and immortality unless we had been united to incorruptibility and immortality.

IRENAEUS OF LYON

Irenaeus' argument, in a sentence, was this: To be deprived of the benefits of existence is the greatest punishment, and to be deprived of them forever is to suffer "eternal punishment."

LE ROY EDWIN FROOM

Whoever believes in me, even if he dies, will live, and everyone who lives and believes in me will never die.

JOHN 11:25

Permanent annihilation is a novissimum. That is because it is an instance, perhaps the clearest possible instance, of a condition without a future novelty. An annihilated creature whose annihilation is permanent and irreversible has no future at all, novel or otherwise, and therefore has entered a novissimum in the full and proper sense. For a creature to be annihilated is for it to come to nothing, to move ad nihilum…and eventually to arrive there.

PAUL GRIFFITHS

There is no injustice in the eventual withdrawal of life from those who have no fitness for its endless perpetuation.

EDWARD WHITE

If the image and likeness of God become completely dimmed and the divine light ceases to shine, the torments of hell will cease and there will be a final return to non-being. Final perdition can only be thought of as non-being which no longer knows any suffering.

NICHOLAS BERDYAEV

Man was not originally created for death; the natural *possibility* of immortality was implanted in him.

SERGIUS BULGAKOV

Contents

Permissions | xi

1	Introduction and Definitions	1
2	Scripture	17
3	Tradition, Ancient and Modern	44
4	Philosophy 1	73
5	Philosophy 2	97
6	Hell Recycled	119
7	Catholic Teaching	142

Afterword | 175
Bibliography | 181
Subject Index | 187

Permissions

PERMISSION GRANTED FROM WIPF and Stock Publishers www.wipfandstock.com for quotations from Christopher M. Date, Gregory Stump, and Joshua W. Anderson, eds. *Rethinking Hell, Readings in Evangelical Conditionalism.* (Eugene, OR: Cascade, 2014.)

Permission granted from Ignatius Press for quotations from Hans Urs von Balthasar, *Dare We Hope That All Men Be Saved?* Translated by David Kipp with Rev. Lothar Krauth. (San Francisco: Ignatius, 1988).

Permission granted from HarperCollins Publishers for quotations from N.T Wright, *Surprised by Hope* (New York: HarperCollins, 2008).

Permission granted from Taylor & Francis Books UK for quotations from Joel Buenting, ed. *The Problem of Hell* (Farnham, England: Ashgate Publishing Ltd, 2010).

Permission granted from Orbis Books for quotations from Anthony Kelly, *Eschatology and Hope* (Maryknoll, New York: Orbis Books, 2006).

Permission granted from the Catholic University of America for quotations from Joseph Ratzinger, *Eschatology. Death and Eternal Life* (Washington, D.C.: Catholic University of America Press, 1988.)

Permission granted from Baylor University Press for quotations from Paul J. Griffiths, *Decreation. The Last Things of All Creatures* (Waco, Texas: Baylor University Press, 2014).

Permission granted from Review and Herald Publishing Association for quotations from Leroy Edwin Froom, *The Conditionalist Faith of Our Fathers. The Conflict of the Ages over the Nature and Destiny of Man. 2 Vols.* (Washington, D.C.: Review and Herald Publishing Association, 1965-66.)

Permissions

Permission granted from Holy Cross Orthodox Press for quotations from Nikolaos Loudovikos, *A Eucharistic Ontology: Maximus the Confessor's Eschatological Ontology of Being as Dialogical Reciprocity* (Brookline, Mass: Holy Cross Orthodox Press 2010).

1

Introduction and Definitions

THIS BOOK IS WRITTEN for those who know little or nothing about Conditional Immortality (CI), and especially for my Catholic sisters and brothers. However, scholars and those already knowledgeable about this topic might find some new material from Catholic theology. Also, if you have read only a book or two on CI, you may find this *Guide* a helpful survey of some past and recent literature.

My publisher asked the question: "What makes your book different from others presently on the market?" I answered: "It's a brief introduction to the topic of CI aimed especially at Catholics. I know of no other such book available." My experience is that this subject is almost totally unknown among Catholics.

On several occasions my Catholic friends have asked me what book I was presently working on. When I replied, "*A Catholic Reading Guide to Conditional Immortality,*" I was met with a total lack of comprehension. Likewise, a Catholic theologian friend of mine who has been teaching theology for forty or fifty years asked if I was working on another book. When I responded in the same way I was met with a look of total bewilderment. I must admit that I was somewhat surprised that as a Catholic theologian of long-standing he had never heard of CI. He was somewhat more familiar with Universalism (U) since this topic has recently come into the Catholic academic world due to Balthasar's book.[1]

In my research for this present book I have not come across a great deal of material in Catholic theological literature on CI. Sometimes there were scattered references, but there were hardly any extensive treatments (except for one author whom we shall come to shortly, Paul Griffiths). On the other hand, CI has received an enormous amount of study in the past two centuries on the part of Protestants. A majority of my references,

1. Balthasar, *Dare We Hope?*

therefore, must of necessity come from Protestant studies. They have written many books on this topic; a fair number of ministers have lost their positions and reputations for teaching CI; and conferences have been held on the topic. A great deal of material is also available on the internet. However, CI remains relatively unknown to Catholics, and it seems to many Catholic theologians as well.

A striking contemporary example of this lack of Catholic awareness is the document "Some Current Questions in Eschatology" issued by the Catholic International Theological Commission (1992).[2] When I started reading this document I was hoping for some comments on both U and CI since these are "current eschatological questions." However, I was surprised and somewhat disappointed that these two theological views were never mentioned at all, much less treated to any extent. The document treats the nature of the soul, but such reflections on this topic were not in any definite way connected with the question of the *immortality* of the soul which figures very prominently in the conditionalist position. And so the purpose of the present *Guide* is to present to people—perhaps especially to Catholics—1) an introduction to CI, 2) to mention some of the literature available, and hopefully 3) to stimulate the reader's own further personal study. This is the briefest of introductions, but it will, I believe, present the main themes of the discussion concerning CI.

CI is not being presented in this book as a dogma or teaching of the church, but as one of the *possibilities* of the fate of those who continue to resist God's will. In theology, such theories are called *theologumena*, opinions which are neither dogmas nor heresies. Often, as with teachings such as Limbo in the Catholic Church, they may achieve—even for centuries—*church doctrine status but not dogma*. Some conditionalists present CI not simply as a speculative theory but as a certitude, and as the obvious teaching of Scripture. It is not "heretical" to believe in CI, but in this presentation I stop at the *possibility* of CI as an alternative to both hell and Universalism.

Definitions

Leroy Edwin Froom

Leroy Edwin Froom was the former Professor of Historical Theology at Andrews University. In 1965–1966 he published his monumental two volume

---

2. *Some Current Questions.*

Introduction and Definitions

study *The Conditionalist Faith of Our Fathers*.[3] In its 2,476 pages he documents the majority of conditionalist views from the Jewish and intertestamental period up to about 1962. He covers both Testaments, the Fathers of the Church, the mediaeval period, and the modern eras in both Europe and America. I will frequently be referring to him, especially concerning authors from the nineteenth century. I will note some significant Catholic writers not included in his study.

The major conclusions about CI, repeated countless times in the authors Froom treats, are: 1) eternal punishment, in the sense of conscious pains that last forever, is not in the Scriptures; 2) Scripture teaches that the unrepentant soul will be *completely destroyed*; 3) *innate human immortality* is not a teaching of the Scriptures but comes from the Alexandrians (Clement, Origen) via Plato; 4) when this doctrine of the *natural immortality of the soul* was accepted, the human person was thought to be immortal, and the teaching of eternal conscious punishment followed, that is, hell; 6) this doctrine was propagated especially by Augustine, and became the traditional teaching in the Western Church, in both Catholicism and Protestantism.

Besides meticulously giving excerpts from several hundred authors on the question of innate immortality vs. the scriptural witness of immortality as a gift through faith in Jesus Christ, Froom offers, at the end of each section, a list of authors, dates, places, Christian churches of the author, views, and a brief summary of the teaching of that particular period. The bibliography and subject index are exhaustive. It is thus an invaluable and handy guide to the history of CI. I was impressed by the extent of Froom's treatment and his obvious conviction of this teaching. I was often struck by the courage of the Protestant clergy who had risked reputations and positons in order to defend this view. I respectively dedicate this book to them.

My research of Catholic authors on eschatology is not exhaustive by any means, so I cannot say if Froom's research has been used by some of them. I can say, however, that I am not aware of the use of Froom's research by any of the Catholic authors I have consulted. Reading his Index confirmed for me the almost total lack of awareness of CI on the part of Catholic philosophers and theologians. There has always been an enormous amount of Catholic philosophical and theological writing down through the ages, and recent centuries are no exception. And yet, in Froom's summaries at the end of each section, there are only a handful of Catholic authors listed

---

3. Froom, *Conditionalist Faith*.

as addressing CI; and their contributions are quite brief. Because Froom has been objective in cataloguing the research, it seems true to say that there has been very little creative thought and study published on the part of Catholics on this topic. Over and over again the point is made that the Catholic Church has by and large maintained the position of the innate immortality of the soul which, conditionalists contend, has led to the teaching about hell. Thus, Froom did not find much in favor of CI to report among Catholic authors. I shall make special note of some of the exceptions.

For the above reasons I put "Catholic" in my title to especially draw the attention of Catholics. As I believe my *Guide* will show, teaching the natural immortality of the soul is still very common in the Catholic world, and the normal understanding of most Catholics. As well, Catholics are generally unaware of the complexities of the debate about CI, or even aware that this is one of the theological *alternative destinies* for those who persist in resistance to the Father's will. Despite the enormity and completeness of his study, Froom admits that CI has been and still is a minority view. The purpose of my book is to make this view more widely known so people can make an informed opinion about it.

Adaptation

I am not a professional philosopher or theologian. This "lets me off the hook" as far as appearing to be any kind of authority on the matters involved! I am more of a compiler, a researcher. As well, I am not presuming to present the final arguments for these questions (there probably aren't any), but merely to make known some of the pertinent responsible literature available. Every Christian age has its main theological interest, and ours is eschatology, the Christian doctrine of the last things—death, judgment, heaven, and hell. It is a vast topic. I confine myself to the subject in the title. Because of this limitation it may be helpful to say specifically what topics I am *not* going to treat. If I do treat them, it will only be as they are related to CI. (Another word that authors use instead of CI is *annihilation* (A). Although, specifically, CI denotes what makes A possible, for my purposes these words will often be considered as synonymous.)

I will not be treating the topics of death, the "intermediate period" between death and the final resurrection, purgatory, heaven, final judgement, or the resurrection of the body. The "last thing" I will be mostly considering in regards to CI is hell. My approach will be to *adapt* the many pro and con arguments connected with hell *to support CI*.

For example, many descriptions are given about the pain and suffering of those "in hell." I will use such descriptions to describe what people go through who are "on the way"—not to hell but to a *state* that is hopeless, a *state* where God withdraws their existence *in accordance with their own wishes* not to continue to follow his plan for them. The arguments for the everlasting nature of hell can be used for the everlasting nature of A: the former is conscious suffering lasting forever; the latter is the total removal of existence. This adaptation is legitimate because most of the argumentation about hell—except the scriptural—is speculative and philosophical, and this approach can also be used for CI.

Choosing not to Survive

"Annihilation," as I've mentioned, is a word often used by authors in discussions about CI. I have decided, generally, not to use it myself (though I may on occasion), because both CI and U are trying to restore a better image of God other than a God who condemns any of his children to everlasting conscious pain. As we shall see, similar arguments are brought against a God who would "annihilate" one of his children as in CI. Is not such a God *also terrible*? We shall be considering this argument. It seems to me, however, that the comment I briefly made above, that God *complies* with the person's decision to no longer love him, is a better way of conceiving God's action than that he "annihilates" one of his children. Practically, of course, it amounts to the same thing—the removal of the person's existence. But conceiving this action as respecting the person's will, even though contrary to God's, is a less unloving way, I believe, of considering the Father's "reluctant" decision. As we shall see, a significant turning point in the modern speculation about hell is that it is not a punishment from God unilaterally imposed but an acceding to the person's desire to no longer love God. God is in the business of saving people not destroying them. One of God's essential considerations on our behalf is to respect our freedom, and thus the possibility of a tragic end.

Another word used less frequently for annihilation is "elimination." Both words, however, put the emphasis on God's action. This has validity, of course, since only God can withdraw existence: no one can take herself or himself out of existence. Nor, it will be argued, is annihilation a *natural consequence* of a person's intransigence: sin cannot reach a zero limit, resulting in annihilation.

But there is another word that seems more appropriate than either annihilation or elimination—"survival or non-survival": a person decides not to continue to *survive,* and so God accedes to the person's wish. This word clarifies better that the removal of existence is a *mutual affair* and not solely an imposition by God. Again, the result is the same—the person goes out of existence— but God's acceding to a person's wish not to survive seems a more suitable way of conceiving God's action. And this withdrawal of existence is not unjust since existence was a perfectly free gift in the first place. God does not owe us continued existence if we refuse to accept the purpose of existence.

The Immortality of the Soul

I will spend a fair amount of time presenting the conditionalist arguments *against the natural immortality of the soul,* since this philosophical theory is at the heart of their understanding as to why the scriptural teaching of "destruction, passing out of existence" changed to everlasting conscious suffering. Their contention is that the soul is *capable* of immortality— "immortable"— but not naturally immortal from the beginning of its existence. Their position is that the soul must make a final decision for God. This decision effects passage from the "spirituality" of the soul to its "immortality." These two states are not the same but they are often identified in philosophy. If people do not make such a definitive decision, God can withdraw their existence. It is the opinion of conditionalists that the person is immortal when God grants the gift of immortality *as a result of the absolute acceptance of his will in Christ.* But it is possible also for those who never knew Christ. Every person has the potential to make a definitive decision for God, even if she or he understands God differently from the Christian revelation. Only after such a decision does the person truly become immortal.

The main questions connected with CI to be considered are: 1) is it scriptural? 2) is it compatible with church teaching and tradition? 3) is one capable of making such a final decision that eventually leads to God's withdrawal of existence? 4) is God's act of such a withdrawal compatible with his love and mercy?

Introduction and Definitions

Some Modern Opinions

In my previous *Guide to Universalism* I had a brief section on some opinions against CI. I quoted John Hick: "This is a very dubious doctrine of Christian theism."[4] I also cited the authors of *Victory* who hold that this doctrine "rather than preserving the unregenerate in hell, God extinguishes their existence altogether. Rather than allow them to eternally suffer the effects of alienation [from God], God puts them out of their misery, thereby annihilating them as an act of mercy. Our arguments succeed in showing that God need not annihilate them in order to spare them the grim consequences of freely chosen alienation from Him."[5] A third scholar I quoted, Harmon, counsels reverent scepticism about CI, and suggests that some who hold that position show "an inadequate appreciation for the role of tradition and Scripture."[6] The intent of the present *Guide* is to offer counter arguments to these and many other objections to CI.

The Decreation of Paul Griffiths

In my *Catholic Reading Guide to Universalism* I took Hans Urs von Balthasar's book *Dare We Hope That All Men Be Saved?* as a kind of format for my presentation. He put forth many arguments that he believed could justify such a hope. I then presented similar arguments from other sources to bolster his positions.

For this present *Guide* I will be taking the study of the Catholic theologian Paul J. Griffiths *Decreation, The Last Things of All Creatures*,[7] as a quasi-format for my presentation. I was not aware of his book when I wrote my *Guide to Universalism*. I choose him now because he is one of the few Catholic authors who treats A in any comprehensive way. One of the main purposes of my *Guide* is to introduce you to Paul Griffiths' theology about the last things. His book is quite extraordinary. He develops dimensions of Catholic eschatology that I have not found anywhere else. It's a book I highly recommend in considering annihilation as an alternative to hell.

---

4. Wild, *Guide*, 146.
5. Ibid.
6. Ibid., 148.
7. Griffiths, *Decreation*. He is presently Warren Chair of Catholic Theology at Duke Divinity School.

I first came across Griffiths in his article on "Purgatory" in *The Oxford Handbook of Eschatology*.[8] I will be quoting some of his positions; and then, as I did with Balthasar, bolster his views for A using other sources. As his subtitle indicates, he treats the whole spectrum of eschatology which, as I mentioned above, I do not. I chose Griffiths' book because he argues that the complete annihilation (he prefers this word) of human beings is *possible:* "Can human creatures have annihilation as their last thing? The speculative position entertained and argued in this section is that they can, and that this is both logically and practically possible."[9] As with U, I limit my subject of CI to the *possibility* of the withdrawal of existence and not to any definitive or absolute conclusion that this is how the fate of some people *will* happen. "But doctrinal definitiveness on those matters entails nothing about whether any humans or angels have an inglorious last thing [annihilation]."[10]

We shall see that annihilation (CI), understood as the withdrawal of the person's existence, was a consistent opinion among the Apologists and the Apostolic Fathers, the first Christians to give answers for their faith. CI became a minority opinion— not to say considered a heresy!— only later on. We shall see that throughout the Christian tradition it has always had its advocates, and occasionally some very great authorities. This first Christian explanation concerning the final fate of the unrepentant is having a renewal in recent times.

In this book I am going to take the position of a Christian conditionalist and present arguments mostly from that point of view. I will follow Griffiths who argues that there are only two *novissima* or final states for human persons, annihilation or heaven. Besides, then, rejecting "hell" as a possible fate, I will also, for the purposes of this book, not consider U since conditionalists also reject it for reasons we will be considering. All the argumentation presented will be to allow the reader to hear predominantly the position of the conditionalists. Thus, it will not be an attempt at a *comparative study* but, decidedly, a presentation of the conditionalist positions.

If you are considering obtaining another book on this topic I suggest *Rethinking Hell*, Readings in Evangelical Conditionalism.[11] Presently it is

---

8. Griffiths, "Purgatory."
9. Griffiths, *Decreation*, 191.
10. Ibid., 12.
11. Ed. Christopher M. Date, *Rethinking Hell*.

the best book which gives a contemporary—and not an overly academic—treatment of the various aspects of this topic.

The Main Issues

A few general definitions concerning the main issues will set the stage for our future considerations.

Is the soul which survives death naturally immortal, as in the Greek view, or is this a condition dependent upon one's ultimate choice for the Father's will? Most Christians believe that the soul is naturally immortal; CI emphasizes its natural *mortality,* albeit it's being "immortable." Many proofs are given on either side of this question. However, all agree that God, since he has created everyone out of nothing, also has the power to deprive them of existence, whether "naturally immortal" or not. This is one crucial point to keep in mind throughout our discussion: whether the soul is naturally immortal or not *does not resolve the question of A.*

As we shall see, the discussion concerning CI revolves particularly around three questions: 1) is annihilation *scriptural*; 2) can one make a *final decision* that determines one's ultimate fate; and 3) is it *in conformity with God's nature* to withdraw a person's existence? These questions are similar to the difficulties about the legitimacy of hell. Belief in the natural immortality of the soul, the conditionalists argue, has led to the belief in hell: if unrepentant people are naturally immortal, they will live forever in *eternal torment.* As we shall see, the two major contemporary proponents of A, Froom and Fudge, hold that the immortality of the soul is not scriptural but comes from Plato's philosophy, that is to say, from paganism.

Annihilationism

Theopedia

"Annihilationism is the belief that the final fate of those who are not saved is literal and final death and destruction. It runs counter to the mainstream traditional Christian understanding of hell as eternal suffering and separation from God. In contrast to the more traditional view, which holds that the wicked will remain conscious in hell forever, Annihilationism teaches that, whether or not God may use hell to exact some conscious punishment for sins, he will eventually destroy or annihilate the wicked completely, leaving only the righteous to live on in immortality."[12]

Emmanuel Petavel

Dr. Emmaueal Petavel, a Swiss theologian, was the foremost exponent of CI in the nineteenth century. His wrote two books pertinent to our subject, *The Extinction of Evil: Three Theological Essays*, and *The Problem of Immortality*. Froom calls *The Problem* "unquestionably the most far-reaching single piece of Conditionalist literature to appear in the nineteenth century";[13] and Petavel "the best-known Continental Conditionalist of the century, and materially influenced the thought of his time."[14] Petavel, therefore, is the most important of modern conditionalists. We will be seeing more of his teaching in chapter 2, but here is his basic position:

> The traditional belief takes for granted that the soul of man is absolutely imperishable. Now the Scriptures, though they teach us that all men are *capable* of immortality, speak nowhere of essential immortality apart from communion with Jesus, the Christ. The philosophic theory of the indestructability of the human soul is utterly foreign to the religion of the Bible. Not only does Scripture entirely abstain from using the expression "immortal soul," so constantly recurring in modern phraseology, but it repeats on every page, sometimes in one form of language and sometimes in another, that immortality is not a natural gift, but something to be acquired; a privilege to be conferred upon believers only; a prize to be gained after a brave and earnest struggle; that eternal life is the special reward of those who "by patient continuance in well doing seek for glory and honor and immortality."[15]

Leroy Edwin Froom

> *Conditionalism* is the Christian doctrine that immortality, or everlasting life, is offered to man only upon God's terms and conditions. *Immortal-Soulism*, on the other hand, holds that man was

12. www.theopedia.com/Annihilationlism.
13. Froom, *Conditionalist* II, 605.
14. Ibid., 602.
15. Petavel, *Extinction*, 48–49.

created with a soul, which has a separate existence from the body, and that it is innately and indefeasibly immortal. Conditionalism believes that the man who does not accept God's conditions for life will be ultimately deprived of life, totally destroyed. Immortal-Soulists, on the other hand, believe that the man who disobeys God and persists in his rebellion will be cast into an eternally burning hell-fire, where he will be tormented forever, since his soul cannot die.[16]

Edward Fudge

Edward Fudge's book, *The Fire That Consumes* (1982), is a ground–breaking presentation of CI which has jump-started the modern debate. I quote from one of his more recent presentations (2000).

"Today, as a growing host of evangelical (and other) scholars bear witness, the evidence for the wicked's final total destruction (rather than the traditional view of unending conscious torture, which sprang from pagan Platonic theories of the immortal, indestructible soul), is finally getting some of the attention it demands. Because nearly all of us have completely skirted the relevant material on this subject far too long, I would like to present a concise summary against the case of tradtionalism's conscious unending torment, and at the same time the case for the total, ultimate, everlasting extinction of the wicked."[17]

Clark H. Pinnock

This author wrote the article on A in *The Oxford Handbook of Eschatology*. He was one of the foremost proponents of CI.

> The term Annihilationism derives from the Latin *nihil*, 'nothing,' and points to the destruction of entities. In Christian theology it designates the views of those who hold that the finally impenitent wicked will cease to exist after (or soon after) the last judgment. The position is usually accompanied (though it need not be) by belief in conditional immortality, to wit, while human beings are not naturally immortal, the faithful among them will be given eternal life as a gift, while the finally impenitent will fall into

---

16. Froom, *Conditionalist II*, 19.
17. Fudge, "The Final End of the Wicked," *Rethinking*, 30.

non-existence after the judgment. Their fate and condition are not thought to comprise a stage of everlasting conscious torment but to issue in an extinction of being.

> Annihilationism then is a term designating theories which contend that human beings may pass or be put out of existence altogether. The theories fall into three classes, depending on whether they hold that souls, being mortal, cease to exist at death (pure mortality); or that souls, being naturally mortal, persist only temporarily unless immortality is given by God (conditional immortality); or that, since souls are naturally immortal, they persist in existence unless destroyed by a force working on them from without (annihilationism proper).[18]

Pinnock's first category—pure mortality—is not considered a possibility for the purposes of this study. His second category is the general view of CI. The third view considers immortality a natural condition. Of great importance for my presentation are the following comments of Pinnock.

> Even if we were created immortal, our immortality could be canceled. God is free to eliminate the finally impenitent wicked if he chooses. Even an immortal soul is no match for the power of God, who can reduce even it to nothing. In most cases, Conditionalism is the basis of the belief in Annihilationism though the latter does not require it. God may remove our immortality at the judgment with the result that we perish. In earlier centuries, it was thought that removing immortality would require an extraordinary act of God. Therefore, the destruction of the wicked was seldom entertained as a possibility. But today, we are more likely to think (given the doctrine of the resurrection) that conservation in existence rather than elimination is what requires special divine action.[19]

Everyone would agree that God can annihilate a person whenever he wishes. Even if people believe the soul is naturally immortal, God could still annihilate it if the person does not choose to do his will. Some kind of absolute decision for the Father's will is necessary. With such a decision the person is established forever in her journey towards God on the road to paradise. God foresees that the person will never change such a decision. The person is then made, by God, immortal, and this is not natural but is a gift following upon one's ultimate decision for God, which he respects.

---

18. Pinnock, *Handbook*, 462.
19. Ibid., 468.

Introduction and Definitions

Stephen Travis

The following extract is taken from Travis's book *Christ Will Come Again: Hope for the Second Coming of Jesus*. His biblical exegesis results in CI.

> We must say something about the debate between "eternal punishment" and "conditional immortality." If pressed, I must myself opt for the latter. The case for eternal punishment rests primarily on belief in the immortality of the soul, the requirement of divine justice that the sins of this life should be appropriately punished in the next.
>
> Supporters of "conditional immortality," on the other hand, argue as follows. First, immortality of the soul is a non-biblical doctrine derived from Greek philosophy. In biblical teaching man is "conditionally immortal"—that is, he has the possibility of becoming immortal if he receives resurrection or immortality as a gift from God. This would imply that God grants resurrection or immortality to those who love him, but those who resist him go out of existence.
>
> Secondly, biblical images such as "fire" and "destruction" suggest annihilation rather than continuing conscious existence.
>
> Thirdly, New Testament references to "eternal punishment" do not automatically mean what they have traditionally been assumed to mean. "Eternal" may signify the permanence of the result of judgment rather than the continuation of the act of punishment itself. So "eternal punishment" means an act of judgment where results cannot be reversed, rather than an experience of being punished forever.
>
> Fourthly, we must recognize that such New Testament language is picture-language. This, of course, does not remove our responsibility to take it very seriously, but it indicates that we should be very cautious about pressing such language into service in defense of eternal punishment.
>
> Fifthly, eternal torment serves no useful purpose, and therefore exhibits a vindictiveness incompatible with the love of God in Christ.
>
> Finally, eternal punishment requires that we believe in heaven and hell existing forever "alongside" each other. It seems impossible to reconcile this with the conviction that God will be "all in all" (1 Cor 15:28).[20]

---

20. Travis, *Rethinking*, 46–47.

Kendall S. Harmon

Harmon is not a conditionalist but gives his own understanding to some of the views of the conditionalists.

> Conditional immortality strictly speaking, refers only to the view that all men and women are created mortal but that for those who respond to the gospel the gift of eternal life is given. There are two different understandings of individual eschatology which have been attached to this Conditionalist label, the first of which I call *conditionalist uniresurrectionism*. In this view man is naturally mortal and immortality is given through the gospel only to the righteous in the next life; the wicked who do not respond to Christ are not resurrected since death is their judgment.
>
> The second approach, which is the far more dominant type in terms of its influence and the number of its adherents, I call *conditionalist eventual extinctionism*. This group argues that both the wicked and the good are resurrected, and that the wicked suffer God's judgment until they are finally extinguished, the punishment being proportionate to their sin.
>
> Both these Conditionalist views are to be distinguished from *immortalist eventual extinctionism*, a perspective which says that men and women were created immortal, but that after the resurrection of both the good and the unrighteous, the latter are annihilated after a period of suffering.[21]

Joel Buenting

"An increasingly popular reply to hell is to opt for the annihilation of the damned. "Annihilationism" denotes a family of views according to which God actively destroys (or simply allows) sinners to terminate their existence in hell. According to one version of this view, physical death represents the cessation of conscious life and the termination (or "annihilation") of existence. According to a second version, sinners experience hell but at some point can terminate their existence and commit "metaphysical suicide."[22]

---

21. Harmon, "Case Against," 196–97.
22. Buenting, *Problem*, 2.

Introduction and Definitions

Jonathan Kvanvig

"What the annihilationist view denies is that any person exists in hell. Instead, hell is a term that denotes what becomes of a person whom God literally annihilates."[23]

Paul Griffiths

Immortality

He notes the treatment of the last things in *Lumen Gentium* of Vatican II (Nos. 48-51) which we shall see later, and then says:

"Should the question of whether affirming the soul's immortality be taken to mean that it is a necessary feature of souls that they cannot die in the sense of coming to nothing, entering the last thing of annihilation; or whether it might be taken to mean that souls need not die, but may. To say that the soul is immortal is to say that it is not necessarily mortal; or to say that the soul is necessarily not mortal. We should not go further than the weaker position: that the soul is possibly not mortal."[24]

Definition of Novissimum

> *Novissimum*, therefore, means 'newest' or 'freshest' or 'youngest.' To call something—some state or condition of a creature— 'newest' is exactly to say that there will be no newer state or condition to follow. If, then, a creature has a *novissimum*, it has a last thing in the sense of a condition or state after which there is no novelty, no new and different state or condition yet to come.
>
> Permanent annihilation is a *novissimum*. That is because it is an instance, perhaps the clearest possible instance, of a condition without future novelty. An annihilated creature whose annihilation is permanent and irreversible has no future at all, novel or otherwise, and has therefore entered a *novissimum* in the full and proper sense.[25]

---

23. Kvanvig, *Problem*, 68.
24. Griffiths, *Decreation*, 47–48.
25. Ibid., 7, 15.

St. Bernard of Clairveau

Simon Tugwell, OP, quotes from a sermon of St. Bernard: "This is the second death, which is always slaying without ever completing the slaughter. Would that they could die and not go on dying forever."[26] Could Bernard's plea, "would that they could die and not go on dying forever," be a desire on his part—or even a theologomenon—for annihilation instead of hell?

All the above definitions will be helpful to keep in mind as we proceed to expand on the pro and con arguments concerning CI.

---

26. Tugwell, *Human Immortality*, 169–70.

2

Scripture

CONDITIONALISTS CONSIDER SCRIPTURE THE main argument for their position. Both Petavel and Froom present very compelling scriptural evidence attesting to the *destruction* of the unrepentant rather than to their eternal conscious suffering.

Kronen and Reitan

God's Final Victory by Kronen and Reitan is one of the most exhaustive studies *advocating* U. Because of their predominantly philosophical focus there is only a very brief scriptural section which they claim supports their position. I begin with their critique because of their scriptural opposition to CI, although this is not their main focus. We will examine how their position and that of others stands up to the CI arguments in the Scriptures. They rightly note that "so many Christians have favoured some version of the doctrine of hell over any version of universalism because they have believed Scripture clearly teaches this doctrine of hell."[1] (To repeat my approach in this book: I will consider arguments against a scriptural teaching on hell as scriptural arguments *against A as well*.)

The authors consider one Michael Murray's theology of the plain sense of Scripture to be "the most plausible variant of a scriptural defence of hell; and if acceptable, it would essentially render our arguments in later chapters irrelevant."[2] This is quite an admission of the power of Murray's argument. Murray's approach, then, if accepted, would be a most convincing objection to the conditionalists as well as to the universalists. I am mostly interested in Murray's scriptural methodology and the authors' call for a

---

1. Kronen and Reitan, *Victory*, 48.
2. Ibid.

biblical hermeneutic which is relevant to any scriptural "proofs" for a certain teaching. What follows is a brief paraphrase of this debate.

Murray claims that there are some Scripture passages that are absolutely undebatable. On the other hand, Kronen and Reitan argue that there must be a biblical hermeneutic because some passages are often at odds with other passages. What we need is a "thread that binds everything together."[3] The authors agree that there are some passages with a very plain sense that support hell; they also argue that there are many more passages that support U. The authors conclude that the thread, the core message of Scripture, is that we are saved through Christ's redemptive work. Controversies between the teaching of hell (read A for my purposes) or U cannot be resolved by simply quoting isolated texts. "In short, Christian doctrine is not 'lifted' straight from the text of Scripture. Rather, it emerges out of theological reflection on an encounter with Christ that is mediated through Scripture, but which cannot—and must not—be identified with the 'plain sense' of each scriptural text. Careful philosophical reflection is an important part of that respectful, critical appropriation of the Christian theological inheritance. In the rest of this book, we aim to use this philosophical approach to argue, in effect, that a universalist reading of Scripture coheres best with core Christian principles."[4]

Other authors also seek to find a thread, a core message, in Scripture, as a method of interpreting isolated passages. Gregory MacDonald (Robin Parry) calls it "the contours of a grand theological narrative."[5] His book is based on the thesis that U is part of this narrative. Conditionalists would contend that part of *their* grand theological narrative is that the end of the unrepentant is annihilation. They believe that it is possible that some may not attain their destiny. They base this tenant of their narrative on the countless scriptural texts which speak of the death and destruction of the sinner. They contend that these and other such words literally mean total destruction, that is, A. Much of Christian tradition has misinterpreted these words under the influence of Greek philosophy. Their grand narrative, therefore, does not rest on only a few isolated verses of Scripture, as universalists often seem to imply, but on very many texts that teach not eternal conscious suffering but utter A. The rest of this chapter in my book

---

3. Ibid., 59.
4. Ibid., 65–67.
5. MacDonald, *Evangelical*, 7.

can be seen as an essential part of the "grand theological narrative" of the conditionalists.

I noted beforehand that neither school of thought presumes to have any *proof* either that all will be saved (universalists), or that some have already have been annihilated (annihilationalists). The grand narrative of the conditionalists hold that it is *possible* that some will never attain the beatific vision; the universalists contend that it is *not possible* anyone will ever be lost. Each claims, of course, that the scriptural narrative, thread, core message, supports *their* view.

Is "Hell" in the Scriptures?

At the very heart of the conditionalist argument is that the doctrine of everlasting conscious suffering— the majority traditional teaching about hell— is *not* taught in the Scriptures. Their contention is that such a teaching is a later projection into the Scriptures of the Greek (Platonic) philosophical idea of the immortality of the soul. The final answer to the question of the fate of the unrepentant must come from Scripture. And Scripture teaches not everlasting conscious suffering as a final punishment but A, the withdrawal of existence. For the first witness of the Scriptures on this topic we turn to the ground-breaking book of Froom. And, yes, for every passage for which he argues a conditionalist interpretation, someone else, somewhere, argues for a traditional understanding of hell. However, as noted, I am not interested in giving a comparative presentation in this *Guide*. I confine myself to the conditionalist arguments. Froom is very much indebted to Percival, as we shall see.

The Old Testament

I give here, very briefly, the basic OT arguments of the conditionalists about the destiny of the unrepentant: it is not eternal torment but A.

Often the scriptural phrase that we were "created in God's image and likeness" is given as a proof for innate immortality: God is immortal, and if we are in his image and likeness, well, we also are immortal. Froom gives the convincing argument that God is also omnipotent, omniscience, and so on, but we are not. Therefore God's essential attributes cannot simply be applied to us. He pointedly states that the main deceit of the devil in the garden was that we would not die, that is, that we would be immortal. He considers the Genesis account as the "throbbing heart of all that follows in the conflict over the destiny of man."[6]

The scriptural terminology about the fate of the unrepentant is basically about *destruction.*

"The writers of the Old Testament seem to have exhausted the resources of the language at their command—the Hebrew tongue— to affirm the complete destruction of the intractable sinner. The major Hebrew verb roots (such as destroy, perish, consume, cut off, burn up) are literal, and are used to signify the total extinction, or excision, of such animate beings."[7]

Froom then lists seventy or eighty references in Scripture which use such words.

"It will be observed that in this vast array of Scripture passages there is uniform testimony as to *utter destruction—* without a single statement implying Eternal Torment for the finally impenitent wicked. The notion of Eternal Torment came out of paganism, as a corollary to the postulate of the universal Innate Immortality of the soul."[8]

He goes through an exhaustive treatment of texts, interpreting them as *final destruction.* Edward Fudge is of the same opinion:

"Is the OT silent concerning the wicked's final fate? Indeed it is not. It overwhelmingly affirms their total destruction. It never affirms or even hints at anything resembling conscious unending torment. The OT uses about fifty different Hebrew verbs to describe this fate, and about seventy figures of speech. Without exception they portray destruction, extinction, or extermination. Not one of the verbs or word-pictures remotely suggests the traditional doctrine."[9]

In the Old Testament the abode of the dead is not regarded as a place of torment. "Sheol is the common fate of all mortals. The wicked have no reason to expect to leave Sheol in most of the Old Testament. The righteous, however, do, for they know and trust in the living God. That hope is stated explicitly a few times, but it pervades the Old Testament. As far as the destiny of the wicked in concerned, Sheol is not a final word. The Old Testament does not say much about the end of the wicked."[10]

---

6. Froom, *Conditionalist I*, 29.
7. Ibid., 105.
8. Ibid., 111.
9. Fudge, *Rethinking,* 31.
10. Fudge, *Fire,* 85.

Froom says that "the Old Testament uses 50 different Hebrew words to describe the final fate of the wicked and notes that they all signify different aspects of *destruction*. Such verbs are buttressed by figurative or proverbial expressions which also speak "everywhere and always of the *decomposition*, of the breaking up of the organism and final cessation of the existence of being— never that of immortal life in endless suffering."[11]

"Psalms and Proverbs repeatedly affirm the moral principles of divine government. The wicked, however proud of their boasts today, will one day not be found. Their place will be empty. They will vanish like a slug as it moves along. They will disappear like smoke. Men will search for them and they will not be found. Even their memory will perish."[12]

A few examples from Ps 37 (New American Bible):

v. 2. Like grass evil doers wither quickly; like grass plants they wilt away.

v. 9. Those who do evil will be cut off.

v. 10. Wait a little, and the wicked will be no more; look for them and they will not be there.

v. 20. The wicked perish; the enemies of the Lord, like the beauty of meadows they vanish, like smoke they disappear.

v. 22. The accursed will be cut off.

v. 28. . . .when the unjust are destroyed, and the children of the wicked will be cut off.

v. 34. You will gloat when the wicked are cut off.

v. 35, 36. I have seen ruthless scoundrels, strong as flourishing cedars. When I passed by again, they were gone; though I searched, they could not be found.

> The historical books of the Old Testament take us another step. Not only does God declare what He will do to the wicked; on many occasions He has shown us. When Sodom became too sinful to continue, God rained fire and brimstone from heaven, obliterating the entire wicked population in a moment so terrible it is memorialized throughout the Scripture as an example of divine judgment.
>
> The inspired declarations of the prophets combine moral principle with historical fate. The prophets speak to their own times, but they also stand on tiptoe and view the distant future. A day is coming, they tell us, when God will bring an end to all He has begun. Good and evil will be gathered alike to see the

---

11. Froom, *Conditionalist I*, 106.
12. Fudge, *Fire*, 95–96.

righteousness of the Lord they have served or spurned. Again there will be fire and storm, tempest and darkness. The slain of God will be many—corpses will lie in the street. Nothing will remain of the wicked but ashes.[13]

Between the Testaments

The Apocrypha (Tobit, Sirach, Baruch, Judith, First and Second Maccabees, the Wisdom of Solomon)

This body of literature called the Apocrypha, revered as canonical by Catholics, often used by the ancient church, and sadly ignored by most Protestants, stands between the divine revelation of the Old Testament and the fanciful imagination of some of the Pseudepigrapha. On the fate of the wicked this literature overwhelmingly reflects the teaching of the Old Testament. The wicked will not escape God's judgment. They will surely die. Worms will be their end. They will pass away like smoke or chaff, or burn up like tow. The righteous may hope for a resurrection and blessed life with God, but the wicked will have no part in that.[14]

The Pseudepigrapha. The Sibylline Oracles, the Dead Sea Scrolls, and the Testament of the Twelve Patriarchs.

"It is also absolutely clear that the pseudepigrapha literature thoroughly documents the older view of the sinner's total extinction as one Jewish opinion current during the period 200 BC–AD 100. This doom is frequently accomplished by fire and is usually preceded by a period of conscious anguish and suffering. In looking for a time when sinners will perish from the face of the earth and never again be found, these writers repeat the frequent testimony of the Old Testament."[15]

Because of this unquestionable range of opinion [in the Intertestamental literature] which can be so thoroughly documented, we cannot presume a single attitude among Jews at the time of Christ

13. Ibid., 116–17.
14. Ibid., 132.
15. Ibid., 154.

on this subject. We cannot read Jesus' words or those of the New Testament writers with any presuppositions supposedly based on a uniform intertestamental opinion.

We must deny categorically the common assumption that Jesus' hearers all held to everlasting torment. We must not assume that Jesus endorsed such a view simply because He nowhere explicitly denied it. We are free to examine the teaching of the New Testament at face value and to determine the meaning of its terms according to the ordinary methods of proper biblical exegesis. The literary and linguistic background for this exegesis includes the Apocrypha and the Pseudepigrapha, but rising high and towering over it all we see the inspired revelation contained in the Scriptures of the Old Testament.[16]

The New Testament

Even the most liberal scholarly methods of gospel criticism have to conclude that Jesus said a great deal about the terrible fate awaiting those who reject God's mercy. He spoke of exclusion from the kingdom, the severity of wrongdoing, the destruction of unrepentant sinners—and He taught that opportunity to repent was cut off at death. Try as one might "it is impossible to eliminate sayings of Jesus which give terrible warnings as to the possibility of loss and exclusion." (A.M. Ramsey) Even a study of the goodness of God must include these facts if it is candid and true to Scripture. In his excellent book of that title, John Wenham notes that Jesus "spoke often of hell. . . .In sheer number these statements are inescapable. In intensity they are fearful. We are here faced with the ultimate horror of God's universe, before which we stand aghast, longing to escape, but as in a nightmare unable to move. We cannot escape, for we know *who* said these things, we know his tenderness, we know the authority of his words and we know that this is the language (be it more or less symbolic) which *he* regarded as best suited to describe the price of impenitence. It is Love who speaks like this; it is God himself."[17]

Does the teaching of Jesus and the NT writers require us to expect the conscious unending torment of the wicked? Not unless we

---

16. Ibid.
17. Ibid., 155–56.

ignore the entire OT background to the NT vocabulary involved, then proceed to give to the NT language later definitions imported from pagan Platonic philosophy during the centuries following. Both the OT and NT clearly teach a resurrection of the wicked for divine judgment, the fearful anticipation of a consuming fire, irrevocable expulsion from God's presence into a place where there will be weeping and grinding of teeth, such conscious suffering as the divine justice individually requires, and finally, the total, everlasting extinction of the wicked with no hope of resurrection, restoration, or recovery.[18]

Some New Testament Scriptural Texts

The New Testament passages dealing with final punishment are the main argument of the conditionalists. To see some of these passages listed altogether emphasizes the conditionalist position. Most conditionalists would agree that U simply does not adequately explain this pervasive emphasis on the *possibility* of some kind of final and tragic end of the unrepentant. I simply wish to emphasize the sheer number of statements the Lord makes about the terrible fate awaiting those who reject God. When you read the following gospel passages, try to see them with conditionalist eyes.

Matthew

Matt 3:10, 12. "The ax is already at the foot of the trees, and every tree that does not produce good fruit will be cut down and thrown into the fire. His winnowing fork is in his hand, and he will clear his threshing floor, gathering the wheat into his barn and burning up the chaff with unquenchable fire."

Matt 5:20. "I tell you that unless your righteousness surpasses that of the Pharisees and the teachers of the law you will certainly not enter the kingdom of heaven."

Matt 7:13-14. "Enter through the narrow gate. For wide is the gate and broad is the road that leads to destruction, and many enter through it. But small is the gate and narrow the road that leads to life and only a few find it."

Matt 7:19. "Every tree that does not bear good fruit is cut down and thrown into the fire."

---

18. Fudge, *Rethinking*, 34, 42.

Matt 7:23. "Then I will tell them plainly, I never knew you. Away from me you evildoers!"

Matt 8:11, 12. "I say to you that many will come from the east and the west, and will take their places at the feast with Abraham, Isaac and Jacob in the kingdom of heaven. But the subjects of the kingdom will be thrown outside, into the darkness, where there will be weeping and gnashing of teeth."

Matt 10:28. "Do not be afraid of the one who can kill the body but cannot kill the soul. Rather, be afraid of the one who can destroy both soul and body in hell."

Matt 12:31–32. "The blasphemy against the Spirit will not be forgiven. Anyone who speaks...against the Holy Spirit will not be forgiven, either in this life or in the age to come."

Matt 13:30, 40–43. "As the weeds are pulled up and burned in the fire, so it will be at the end of the age. The Son of Man will send out His angels, and they will weed out of His kingdom everything that causes sin, and all who do evil. They will throw them into the fiery furnace, where there will be weeping and gnashing of teeth. Then the righteous will shine like the sun in the kingdom of their Father."

Matt 13:48–50. "This is how it will be at the end of the age. The angels will come and separate the wicked from the righteous and throw them into the fiery furnace, where there will be weeping and gnashing of teeth."

Matt 18:8–9. "If your hand or your foot causes you to sin, cut it off and throw it away. It is better for you to enter life maimed or crippled than to have two hands or two feet and be thrown into eternal fire. And if your eye causes you to sin, gouge it out and throw it away. It is better for you to enter life with one eye than to have two eyes and be thrown into the fire of hell."

Comments about Scriptural Arguments

Petavel

I introduced Petavel in chapter 1. The proponents of the different views about hell, CI, and U interpret scriptural texts in keeping with their theories. The most convincing argument of the conditionalists, however, is the sheer number of texts supporting their position if taken at their face value without all the allegorizing and mysticism. Here is an example, from Petavel, of such a broad scriptural argument:

What a contrast there is between Scripture and Universalism! Peter speaks of the salvation of the righteous as being accomplished "with difficulty." Paul says that we are to "work out our salvation in fear and trembling." In the Universalist system salvation is inevitable; it cannot fail of accomplishment. That system would make it appear that the bible was written in order to tranquilize the impenitent, and that God had given his Son to the world in order that whosoever believeth *not* on him should be saved! Paul weeps over those "whose God is their belly," who, as he says, will in the end be destroyed: "whose end is perdition." What can come after the end? Universalists would bid the apostle dry his tears, for even perverted disciples are not truly lost; their destruction will be the renewal of their being. Thus to destroy and save become synonymous terms.

The wrath of the Lamb, spoken of in the Apocalypse, will be only a supreme effusion of tenderness for the benefit of obstinate sinners. Jesus urges us to "strive to enter in at the strait gate"; he tells us that the broad way leadeth to destruction. The Universalists, however, say: "No, that way also leads to life; longer but easier than that narrow way, it leads to the same end. Jesus threatens with a fire that can "destroy both soul and body in Gehenna"; but all may be reassured, the threat is impossible of execution, the soul is absolutely imperishable, and "doomed to salvation." According to Universalism, the tares cast into the fire become wheat; the withered vine-branch recovers its foliage in the flames. The sinner is not the blackguard and half-consumed "brand" that is "plucked" from the burning; he is the incorruptible diamond which, having fallen into the mud will certainly one day come forth thence with undiminished value.

It has never yet been explained how Jesus could have said of Judas that "it would have been good for that man if he had not been born," if a blessed eternity was sure to follow his chastisement, however much that might be prolonged, it would have been an advantage for that man to have been called into existence.

It is impossible to eliminate from the Scriptures the irrevocable sentences, the irreparable ruins, a sin against the Holy Spirit, a sin that will not be forgiven, "neither in this world nor in that which is to come," a sin unto death for which it would be useless to pray, a severity of God which will cause him to cut off even the branches that had been grafted into the good olive tree. "God is not to be mocked." The God of the gospel is a "consuming fire" that will "devour the adversaries"; not their sins only but their very persons.[19]

Petavel on Eternal Punishment

Most Christians who believe in hell understand it as punishment and pain that continues forever in a temporal sense such as we know here in this life: suffering years and years and years without end— eternal. Essential for the arguments of both U and CI is that this is not what the scriptural word "eternal" means. I turn to Petavel who was the outstanding conditionalist of modern times. His understanding of "eternal" is accepted by all conditionalists and is repeated many times in their writings. (It is confirmed by the outstanding modern study of Ilaria Ramelli.)[20] I will omit Petavel's references.

In his Introduction to Petavel's book *The Extinction of Evil: Three Theological Essays*, Oliphant presents the author's teaching on "eternal." "The reader of the following pages will, we trust, be convinced that, upon grounds of interpretation, of philosophy, of analogy and of the Christian consciousness alike, it is not its endless conscious torment, but its final dissolution and cessation that is meant by the ultimate death of the soul. It is the doctrine of this book that the "living soul" of which the Scriptures speak can perpetuate itself as a living soul only by conforming to the law of God and of its own spiritual nature. That it can be eternalized in sin and disorder is believed to be a theory full of subtlety and mischief."[21]

And now we turn to Petavel himself.

> It is true that Christ threatens the sinner with everlasting punishment. Those who have neglected his poor and afflicted brethren shall go away, he says, into everlasting punishment. But, with regard to the word here translated "everlasting" and in the very same verse rendered "eternal," we must observe that, when it qualifies an act, eternity is not always the attribute of the act itself, *but applies to the result of the act* (emphasis added). Thus, in the epistle to the Hebrews, Jesus is said to have obtained "eternal redemption," eternal in its results, although the act of redemption was accomplished in one day on the cross. In the same epistle we read of "eternal

19. Petavel, *Problem*, 299–301.
20. Ramelli, *Apokatastasis*.
21. Petavel, *Extinction*, 33–34.

judgment," where evidently the effects alone of the judgment are to be eternal. In the Epistle of St. Jude, Sodom and Gomorrha are quoted as permanent witnesses of divine vengeance, the prey of "eternal fire." The waters of the Dead Sea cover the site of these guilty cities, but the fire which consumed them was eternal as to its effects, because it destroyed them forever. In the same way "eternal" punishment spoken of in the above-quoted passage from St. Matthew is to consist in a gradual destruction, which will be irremediable.

This use of the term is not unknown in modern phraseology. We find it in the expression "an eternal" farewell, meaning a last and solemn adieu. In a similar manner the punishment spoken of by Christ will be final and supreme. "May it not, in its measure, be reckoned an infinite punishment, should God please to doom man, who was by nature a candidate for immortality, to total annihilation, from whence he should never be suffered to return to life. (Witsius).[22]

Listing, as I have above, some of the many passages of the Lord in regard to a kind of tragic end of the sinner, is to emphasize the force of the conditionalist argument.

Catholic Biblical Commentaries

John L. McKenzie, SJ

In the *Jerome Biblical Commentary*, a much-used reference work by Catholics, gospel verses about the fate of the wicked are not interpreted in terms of the everlasting punishment of hell or, for that matter, interpreted at all. The most specific exegesis is on Matt 18: 8–9: "*eternal fire*: This, says McKensie, and "the Gehenna of fire" are derived from Jewish literature; and the image in turn is derived from Isa 66:24. "Gehenna" (Gk *geenna*) refers to the ravine south of Jerusalem which in ancient times was the place where rubbish was burned. Into this the bodies of the enemies of Israel are thrown here."[23]

The same McKenzie, in his *Dictionary of the Bible* says, at the end of his article on Gehenna—and this would apply to all the biblical statements on Gehenna and Hell: "These passages suggest that the apocalyptic imagery

---

22. Ibid., 50–51.
23. *Jerome Commentary*, 43:126–27.

of other NT passages is to be taken for what it is, imagery, and not as strictly literal theological affirmation. The great truths of judgment and punishment are firmly retained throughout the NT, and no theological hypothesis can be biblical which reduces the ultimate destiny of righteousness and wickedness to the same things; the details of the afterlife, however, are not disclosed except in imagery."[24]

This comment applies as well to the conditionalists who interpret all passages about the ultimate destiny for the unrighteous as annihilation. That is their right, of course, as interpreters, to give their opinions, as long as they agree that in the Scripture we are only dealing with *imagery*. The scope is open for other interpretations.

Garrigou Lagrange, OP

Lagrange was one of the foremost Thomistic Catholic scholars of the twentieth century. As a traditionalist he simply interprets all texts of wrath and destruction in Scripture in terms of hell—everlasting personal suffering. Even such a great scholar as Lagrange, in his treatment of hell, simply assumes that this is the interpretation of all such texts. For example, he cites Isa 66:15–24, "Their worm shall not die and their fire shall not be quenched, and they shall be a loathsome sight to all flesh," and then he states: "All commentators see in this text an affirmation of the last judgment, and under a symbolic form that of eternal hell."[25] "This is the doctrine already announced by the great prophets and in particular by Isaias. From the time of these prophets to the Apocalypse the revelation about eternal hell fire never ceased to become more precise, just as the doctrine of eternal life became more precise."[26] He interprets all other texts in the same way, without any distinctions or qualifications.

Harold E. Guillebaud

Guillebaud (1888–1941) was a biblical scholar who translated the bible into Kirundi, a dialect of Rwanda. He was, therefore, very learned as regards biblical words and their meaning. The following excerpts are from

24. McKenzie, *Dictionary*, 300.
25. Lagrange, *Life Everlasting*, 78.
26. Ibid., 82.

his book, *The Righteous Judge,* where he speaks about the general trend of bible teaching.

> Penal suffering certainly forms a part of bible teaching about the doom of the lost, but there is no statement that this suffering will continue forever. The main emphasis in the texts that speak of fire is on the destructive rather than the tormenting effects of the fire. The Greek word rendered "burn up," like its English equivalent, is a strong word implying total destruction, and chaff is utterly destroyed by fire. It is the destruction of what is worthless that the imagery suggests not endless torment of living beings. The view is that "eternal fire" inflicts a punishment that is eternal because it finally destroys. The main emphasis [is] on the destroying and consuming function.
>
> In the Epistles, future punishment is almost invariably referred to in terms of death and destruction. There is no suggestion in these passages that the suffering will be everlasting.
>
> The general trend of the bible teaching is that those whom God condemns at the final judgment will be separated forever from him, and sentenced to a very awful "second death." But just as in the language of this world a "terrible death" means a death accompanied by suffering and horror, but yet is quite definitely the end of life, so the texts supply no reason why the second death should not be the end of existence. The weight of the evidence has been against everlasting torment rather than for it.
>
> A frequent comment in the discussions about the last things is that the Scripture is ambiguous, and we can't really prove anything too definitely by it. A certain Dr. Beet makes this assertion that "as between endless torment and the ultimate ending of existence, the teaching of the Bible is ambiguous." He holds that "God has not seen fit to reveal to us clear and certainly what the ultimate fate of the wicked will be, beyond the fact that it will be irretrievable and utter ruin." There are definite reasons that show that the use of [the words life and death] in the New Testament, as applied to future punishment, is not so vague and indeterminate as Dr. Beet supposes.
>
> The terms "life and death." Put together these three facts: (a) There is no statement in the Bible that all men are immortal, but on the contrary a definite statement that only God has immortality; (b) There are many express statements that eternal life is the gift of God through Jesus Christ; (c) Paul says that "the wages of sin is death." Surely the natural suggestion of these three facts taken together is that death means not only the deprivation of a happy

existence, but what it naturally should mean in human language, the end of existence. In other words, death is not merely neutral; it has a strong bias in the direction of the end of existence.

The doctrine of endless torment is by common consent so dreadful that only a deep conviction that the teaching of the Bible cannot honestly be explained otherwise can make it possible to believe that God could punish so. Such a doctrine cannot be accepted at all as a mere "perhaps." If there is doubt, the doubt must be resolved on the side of the more merciful theory.[27]

Note that this learned author believes annihilation is *more merciful* than eternal punishment. This is also one of the main points of discussion concerning this question.

The Wrath of God

Conditionalists base their strongest arguments on Scripture. I believe both conditionalists and universalists would agree that reason has a place in the interpretation of Scripture, but ultimately reason/philosophy cannot be the deciding factor in these questions of our ultimate fate. One of the main arguments of conditionalists concerns their scriptural understanding of the wrath of God.

Robin Parry

Robin Parry, one of the foremost of contemporary universalists, acknowledges the importance of the wrath of God for this discussion. He quotes a definition of wrath from Chris Marshall with which I believe conditionalists could agree:

> [Wrath] designates God's fervent reaction to human wickedness. [It is] God's refusal to tolerate, compromise with, or indulge evil. Wrath is not a chronic case of ill temper on God's part but a measured commitment to act against evil and injustice in order to contain it and destroy it. It is not so much a matter of direct, individually tailored punitive intervention as it is a matter of measured withdrawal of his protective influence and control, a refusal to intervene to stem the deleterious effects of human rebellion.[28]

---

27. Froom, *Conditional II*, 807–14.
28. MacDonald (Parry), *Evangelical*, 135.

Conditionalists could welcome Marshall's definition. Note, Parry says God desires to *destroy* evil; and he "refuses to intervene" in the person's harmful perseverance. These arguments can be applied to A very well (although Parry might not agree.) Evil is destroyed, not allowed to continue forever, when one's final personal intransigence leads God to withdraw his "protective influence."

Parry points to Rom 1:18–32 as a fundamental New Testament reference to this kind of wrath. We read there the frequent phrase "God handed them over" to their various sins. Especially significant are vv. 5–8: "By your stubbornness and impenitent heart, you are storing up wrath for yourself for the day of wrath and revelation of the just judgment of God, who will repay everyone according to his works: eternal life to those who seek glory, honor, and immortality through perseverance in good works, but wrath and fury to those who selfishly disobey the truth and obey wickedness."

Parry comments: "God's wrath is revealed from heaven when God gives people up to pursue their self–destructive sinful desires. The wrath *is* God's letting them slide down the path to destruction."[29] Parry then proceeds to give one of the scriptural principles for understanding the wrath of God: "God's presence in the present is a foretaste of the same phenomenon that some will experience in the future."[30] Again, conditionalists could welcome this statement.

Stephen T. Davis

However, it is not my concern to present how Parry uses this understanding of the wrath of God to prove U, as he does. I am concerned as to how conditionalists understand the wrath of God; and I believe Parry's understanding is close to theirs. I turn to Stephen T. Davis's article, "Hell, Wrath, and the Grace of God." While he argues for the consistency between God's love and the *existence of hell*, his arguments can also be applied to A.

> God's wrath is simply God's opposition to hatred of, and dissatisfaction with, human disobedience. Grace is the willingness on God's part to treat us better than we deserve. Christians are used to the idea that *the grace of God is our only hope*. It is equally true that the *wrath of God is our only hope*. God's wrath shows the human race that some acts are morally right and some are morally wrong.

29. Ibid., 135–36.
30. Ibid., 136–37.

> If it were not for the wrath of God, we might sink into the pit of moral and religious relativism. People know that normally there are consequences for wrongdoing.
>
> How then are God's wrath and grace related? The answer is that both are aspects of God's nature. But they are not conflicting or opposed attributes. Love and kindness are intrinsic and essential attributes of God, while God's wrath only emerges as a result of human disobedience. Along with God's wrath, God's justice and grace equally constitute the moral equilibrium of the world.
>
> [Why are people in hell?] I believe they are in hell because they choose to be there. People are not sent to hell kicking and screaming against their wills. Unfortunately, some people choose to live their lives apart from God, harden their hearts, and will continue to say no to God after death; some will doubtless do so forever. Allowing them to live forever in hell is simply God's continuing to grant them the freedom that they experienced in this life to say yes or no to God. I hold that people who continue voluntarily to choose hell (even if we grant that they will always be offered the option of repenting and being promoted to hell) will not be sensible. Their hatred of God will have overcome them.[31]

I contend that Davis's arguments for the possibility of hell can also be used for A. It is also relevant for our discussion to mention briefly his comment *against* A.

> I do not think Scripture supports Annihilationism. Some biblical texts can be interpreted along these lines, but the theory makes moral sense only in juxtaposition with the traditional view of hell. That is, it does seem better for God to destroy the wicked than subject them to eternal torture. But given the view of hell that I am working with, that point is not nearly so obvious. Would the wicked themselves prefer Annihilation to hell? I doubt it.
>
> Let us return to the idea that God's grace is our only hope. We deserve to be condemned, but out of love for us, God forgives us and saves us. If our salvation is a matter of grace alone, then one implication of that idea is worth noting. The point is this: if hell is inconsistent with God's love, as universalists always maintain, then our salvation, i.e., our rescue from hell, is no longer a matter of grace. It becomes a matter of justly being freed from a penalty that we do not truly deserve. So in the end, the argument that hell

---

31. Davis, "Hell, Wrath," 92–93.

is inconsistent with God's love overturns the Christian notion of grace.[32]

I believe Davis would also agree that, yes, God's wrath begins in this life (using Parry's line of thought), but that our experience in this life is that God often allows his wrath *to continue unabated.* People commit suicide; terrible atrocities continue unto death; and many die with utterly immoral lives. If God's wrath continues unabated in this life, is this not an argument— using Parry's approach— that *such wrath can continue in the next life, leading to hell or A?* Isn't this basically the problem of evil: why doesn't God intervene to stop evil? Answer: because of his wrath which, according to Davis, is also part of his nature in the face of human resistance and disobedience.

Balthasar on the Possibility of a Final Choice in the Scriptures

Balthasar is very definite that the *possibility* of a final refusal of the Father's plan is the *scriptural witness.* "Dogmatic Universalists" deny that this possibility can be shown from the Scriptures. This implies that they depend more heavily on their philosophical arguments. It's very significant for the thesis of the conditionalists that Balthasar is on their side in holding to the scriptural truth of the *possibility* of making a final fateful decision.

Balthasar is considered by many to be the greatest Catholic mind of the twentieth century. I so consider him myself. Thus, his opinion on this most important debatable point lends tremendous weight—as I am arguing here—to the possibility not of hell (to which *he* applies this possibility) but to CI, to which I apply his views and those of other *infernalists*. (Balthasar uses this term for those who believe in hell.)

The first proof of his position on this point is his insistence that he is not a universalist in the sense of believing ultimately everyone *will be saved.* He stops at hoping. If Balthasar is not a universalist, his theology is open, then, to being a conditionalist. However, in my limited acquaintance with his writings, I have not come across any treatment of A.

Throughout his book *Dare We Hope?* there are definite comments about the possibility of making a final choice. Although the book is meant to argue the case for the possibility of universal salvation, along the way he must give the alternate view—that a final decision against God is possible.

32. Ibid., 101–02.

First, then, I turn to the remarks in *Dare We Hope?* which emphasize the *possibility* of an ultimate choice.

"Could God's love one day lose its patience, with the result that he would be forced to proceed on the basis of sheer (punitive) justice? The answer was yes, certainly."[33]

He was criticized for this book by those who thought he "hopes hell empty (what an expression!)." He responded that people who were against such hoping think that "he who voices such a hope advocates the "universalist redemption" (*apokatastasis*) condemned by the Church—something that I have expressly rejected: we stand completely and utterly *under* judgment, and have no right, nor is it possible for us, to peer in advance at the Judge's cards. How can anyone equate hoping with knowing?"[34]

"Jesus Christ [gave] us enough light to enable us to have hope in God plus a sufficiently serious warning that we must take account of the real possibility of forfeiting our salvation."[35]

> The question, to which no final answer is given or can be given, is this: Will he who refuses [his love] now refuse it to the last? To this there are two possible answers: the first says simply Yes. It is the answer of the infernalists. The second say: I do not know, but I think it is permissible to hope . . .that the divine love will ultimately be able to penetrate every human darkness and refusal. I will draw on several examples to show how the first of these readings interprets the most extreme warnings as implying the factual existence of a full hell.
>
> Everything begins with the inexorableness, inherent in the grace of Yahweh's turning to Israel, of the choice: 'See, I have set before you this day life and good, death and evil. . .blessing and curse; therefore choose life' (Deut 30:15–19). Then follows the long list of blessings and the even longer one of curses. It is of no importance to trace the variations on this basic motif through the whole of the Old Testament.
>
> The individual responsibility of each man before God's throne of judgment (clearly evident since Ezekiel) comes strongly to the fore in the New Testament, above all in the Pauline letters and the Catholic letters. There is still continued talk, in the Old Testament vein, of the day of wrath (Rom 2:5,1 Thess 1:10), of possible damnation (1 Cor 3:11–5), of a two-sided vengeance (2 Thess 1:5–10):

---

33. Balthasar, *Dare We Hope?* 165.
34. Ibid., 166.
35. Ibid., 177.

"Each will receive good or evil, according to what he has done in the body" (2 Cor 5:10).

The truly new element in the New Testament is that the old righteousness of the Covenant becomes concretized into acknowledgment of the ultimate Word of God in Jesus Christ: 'He who is not with me is against me' (Luke 11:23). All the writings of John are interwoven with the crisis (decision, judgment) between Christ as the light and rejection of him as darkness. And this 'Yes' or 'No' transcends the bounds of temporal life; there is a resurrection of life and a resurrection of judgment (John 5:29). This same twofold division runs through all of the First Letter of John.

The absolute decision must be made in one's earthly life; in the hereafter, it will be too late. But it would be pointless to cite still more texts documenting the absolutely required decision about Christ and God's testimony on his behalf.[36]

Balthasar then goes on to cite texts which he says can be interpreted in a universalist sense. "Many [possible universalist] passages could be added here. I do not at all deny that their force is weakened by the series of threatening ones; I only dispute that the series of threats invalidates the cited universalist statements."[37]

As a Jesuit Balthasar wrote commentaries on the Ignatian Spiritual Exercises. He points out that there is a meditation on hell in the Exercises. "The first prelude is the composition, which is to see with the sight of the imagination the length, breadth and depth of hell. With the greatest seriousness, everyone must go through it for himself, for himself alone, placing himself. . .in the consciousness that all those who, 'despite their faith, did not uphold his commandments' (love, of course), condemned themselves to remain forever remote from the eternal love that they rejected."[38] Balthasar points out that St. Ignatius believed in this possibility of "condemning oneself forever."

"All New Testament and theological talk about hell has but one point: 'To bring man to come to grips with his life in view of the *real possibility* of eternal ruin and to understand revelation as a demand of the utmost seriousness.'"[39]

---

36. Ibid., 178–82.
37. Ibid., 186–87.
38. Ibid., 189.
39. Ibid., 198.

> Here we come to deep waters, in which every human mind begins to flounder. Can human defiance really resist to the end the representative assumption of its sins by the incarnate God? If one replies to this confidently and flatly: 'Yes, man can do that' and thereby fills hell with nay-sayers, then the theologians will again have to set up strange distinctions within God's will for grace: there is, then, a 'sufficient grace,' characterized as something that, from God's viewpoint, would have to be sufficient for converting the sinner, yet is rejected by the sinner in such a way that it is actually not sufficient for achieving its purpose; and an 'efficacious grace,' which is capable of attaining its goal. Without my consent, given that I am a free person, nothing can just have its way with me.
>
> To push on any farther into these deep waters is not permitted us. We have to stop at this observation: it would be in God's power to allow the grace that flows into the world from the self-sacrifice of his Son (2 Cor 5:19) to grow powerful enough to become his 'efficacious' grace for all sinners. But precisely this is something that we can only *hope for*.[40]

"Karl Rahner is therefor right when he says: 'We have to preserve alongside one another, without balancing them up, the principle of the power of God's general will for salvation, the redemption of all men through Christ, the *duty to hope for the salvation of all men* and the principle of the real possibility of becoming eternally lost.'[41]

I think Rahner's comment is an admirable expression of a balanced theological view of *novissima*. To return to Balthasar.

> We shall not try here to press these biblically irreconcilable statements into a speculative system. Rather, we shall describe the different responses that historically have been advanced in theology and in the interpretation of the New Testament. None of those attempted responses was formulated hastily. [They do not simply dismiss] the horrifying thought that brothers and sisters of Christ, created by the Father for Christ, who died for them in atonement, may fail instead to reach their final destination in God and may instead suffer eternal damnation with its everlasting pain—which, in fact, would frustrate God's universal plan of salvation. If we take our faith seriously and respect the words of Scripture, *we must resign ourselves to admitting such an ultimate possibility* (emphasis

---

40. Ibid., 208–10.
41. Ibid., 212.

added), our feelings of revulsion notwithstanding. We may not simply ignore such a threat; we may not easily dismiss it, neither for ourselves nor for any of our brothers and sisters in Christ.[42]

Balthasar concludes his book with a word about judgment: "Let us limit ourselves to the truth that we all stand under God's absolute judgment. 'I do not even pass judgment on myself,' as St. Paul says. 'The Lord is the one to judge me. So stop passing judgment before the time of his return. He will bring to light what is hidden in darkness' (1 Cor 4:3ff). Not forgetting St. John: 'We should have confidence on the day of judgment'" (1 John 4:17).[43]

Judgment figures prominently in Balthasar's understanding of the possibility of choosing against the Father's will. He has an extended reflection on this in his "Eschatology in Outline" to which we now turn.

> There is a final question that arises at this point but which, after all that has been said, cannot be answered. How will the Judge behave toward those who come before him as ones who have turned away, who appear in the gospel parables and other *logia* of Jesus as the ones whom he 'does not know,' as the ones who have been 'rejected' and 'expelled' (Matt 22:13) and handed over to the powers of darkness? We do not know. We may ascribe a part of the definitive division of mankind into sheep and goats (as in Matt 25:31–46) to paranesis [catechetical pedagogy]—this is especially clear in Heb 6:4–12—and another part supposedly to the form of eschatological black-and-white painting so common in the Old Testament. But there is still an unsettling residue that cannot be interpreted away. We can only go so far as to say: as Redeemer, God also respects the freedom that God, as Creator, has given to the creature and which gives the creature the freedom to resist God's love. This 'respect' means that God does not overpower, oppress or do violence to the precarious freedom of the creature by the omnipotence of his absolute freedom.[44]

It seems very clear that in the critical debate between the universalists and others of whether or not a person can freely resist God's overtures of grace absolutely with fatal consequences, Balthasar comes down on the side of those who answer yes.

---

42. Ibid., 236–37.
43. Ibid., 253–54.
44. Balthasar, "Outline," 456.

SCRIPTURE

Oscar Cullman

Oscar Cullman was widely known and appreciated in the Christian academic world. In 1955 he delivered the Ingersoll Lecture at Harvard on "The Immortality of Man," which was subsequently printed as *The Immortality of the Soul or the Resurrection of the Dead?* He propounded the theory, repeated many times in Froom, that the Greek conception of the immortality of the soul and the early Christian conception of the resurrection of the body are mutually exclusive. He received a fair amount of "violent hostility" (his phrase) which revealed the unacceptability of this teaching amongst the general Christian population. His book is a significant contribution, from a great scholar, to the arguments of the conditionalists. He is inserted in this Scripture chapter because he said scriptural exegesis was the basis of his study.[45]

"The immortality of the soul is one of the greatest misunderstandings of Christianity. For the first Christians the soul is not intrinsically immortal, but rather became so only through the resurrection of Jesus Christ, and through faith in Him. It is a mistake to read into the Fourth Gospel an early trend toward the Greek teaching of immortality."[46]

Cullman contrasts the death of Jesus and Socrates. Socrates doesn't fear death because death sets him free from the body. "Jesus shares the natural fear of death. Death for Him is not something divine: it is something dreadful. This is really *the last enemy of God*. Nothing shows better the radical difference between the Greek doctrine of immortality of the soul and the Christian doctrine of the Resurrection. He must indeed be the very one who in His death conquers death itself. He cannot obtain this victory by simply living on as an immortal soul, thus fundamentally *not* dying. He can conquer death only by actually dying."[47]

> Furthermore, if life is to issue out of so genuine a death as this, a new divine act of creation is necessary. And this act of creation calls back to life not just a part of the man, but the whole man—all that God had created and death had annihilated. For Socrates and Plato, no new act of creation is necessary. For the body is indeed bad and should not live on. And that part which is to live on, the soul, does not die at all. Belief in the immortality of the soul is not belief in a revolutionary event. Immortality, in fact, is only a

---

45. Cullman, *Immortality*, 6.
46. Ibid., 15, 17.
47. Ibid., 21–22.

> *negative* assertion: the soul does *not* die, but simply lives on. Resurrection is a *positive* assertion: the whole man, who has really died is recalled to life by a new act of creation.[48]

"The spirit...is the great power of life, the element of the resurrection; God's power of creation is given us through the Holy Spirit. This power of life is at work in all members of the community. We are already in the state of resurrection, that of eternal life—not immortality of soul: the new year is already inaugurated. The body, too, is already in the power of the Holy Spirit. Death has already been overcome (death, be it noted, not the body); there is already a new creation (a new creation, be it noted, not an immortality which the soul has always possessed) and the resurrection age is already inaugurated."[49]

> One could ask...whether the New Testament does not assume, for the time after Easter, a continuity of the 'inner Man' of converted people before and after death, so that here, too, death is presented for all practical purposes only as a natural 'transition.' There is a sense in which a kind of *approximation* to the Greek teaching does actually take place, to the extent that the inner man, who has already been transformed by the Spirit (Rom 6:3), and consequently made alive, continues to live with Christ in this transitional state, in the condition of sleep. This continuity is emphasized especially strongly in the gospel of John 3:36, 4:14, 6:54, and frequently. Here we observe at least a certain analogy to the "immortality of the soul," but the distinction remains none the less radical. The fact that even in this state the dead are already living with Christ *does not correspond to the natural essence of the soul* (emphasis added). Rather it is the result of a divine intervention from outside, through the Holy Spirit, who must already have quickened the inner man in earthly life by His miraculous power.[50]

Cullman's last statement answered a question I had: if we are already immortal here on earth *through faith*—"has eternal life" (John 6:54)—through the gift of the Holy Spirit, isn't death a simple transition as it was for Socrates? Cullman says yes, there is a "certain analogy" here. But the difference is that Socrates believed in the natural immortality of the soul which simply continued after death. For us immortality is not natural but a gift through faith—"he who believes in me will never die" (John 11:26).

48. Ibid., 26.
49. Ibid., 34.
50. Ibid., 55–56.

But our transition into eternity—if we have chosen for Christ and received the gift of immortality— *is* continuity with the next life on the other side of death.

Cullman also raises the question: Can this gift of the resurrection of both body and soul once obtained through union with Christ *be lost*? Theoretically, what God has given as a gift can be taken away. This is the Christian understanding of "immortality." But can the immortality which is natural to the soul in the Greek sense be lost? The Greeks would say no. And this is why when this concept was projected into the Scriptures, "eternal punishment" was born: the soul will always be immortal even in its rejection of God.

Kendall S. Harmon

Harmon offers arguments against CI, especially refuting Edward Fudge. Harmon is concerned that disbelief in hell will foster U, even if people don't know this theory. Or, ignorant of U, they will simply believe everyone will go to heaven. Very few people, however, know about the other option—A.

Harmon says we need a reverent scepticism about A, even though it has a long and distinguished tradition of many of the finest minds in Christendom. Yes, there is an inadequate appreciation for this tradition. Philosophically it is agreed that God can destroy or preserve creatures, but what does Scripture say? CI is not scriptural. You cannot base Christ's words on intertestamental literature either, as Fudge does. Harmon also disagrees with Fudge's NT exegesis, with his interpretation of the final doom: "For Fudge, God's final sentence *begins* with banishment, *continues* with a period of conscious suffering, and *ends* with destruction. In fact, not a single New Testament passage teaches exactly this sequence: destruction dominates while punishment and exclusion fall into the background."[51]

Harmon comments on various gospel passages: "All four of these passages use different images to point to the same horrible reality: God's eschatological judgment on the impenitent. These images are intended to have the same referent *not* different referents—it is not that there is penal suffering and *then* annihilation —but that destruction, darkness, exclusion, not being known, agony and punishment are all windows through which to see the same truth."[52]

51. Harmon, *"Case Against,"* 213.
52. Ibid., 214.

Harmon then gives the following opinions that, in my view, could easily refer to annihilation as well.

John Donne: "Hell is the everlasting absence of God and everlasting impossibility of returning to his presence."

N. Berdyaev: "Hell is the state of the soul powerless to come out of itself, absolute self-centredness, dark and evil isolation, i.e., final inability to love."[53]

"I don't know who you are" is eschatological exclusion from Christ's presence. Not being known by God is a third and final element of hell. "I do not know you." But those who are lost remain unknown to God . . .not only are they banished from his presence, not only are they given over to themselves, but they also are not known by God and *they know that they are not known*, for Christ has looked them in the eye and told them."[54]

Gerry Beauchemin, *Hope Beyond Hell*.

This book is basically a strong argument for U. I mention it here because the author only treats very briefly the scriptural positions of the conditionalists which, as I've mentioned, are the basis for their doctrine. His book was revised in 2016 but he is either unaware of the enormous amount of study in Petavel, Froom, and Fudge in opposition to his scriptural view, or has chosen not to engage in a comparative study. Since I seek to convey the very convincing case presented by the conditionalists for their understanding of death and destruction in the bible as A, I simply give Beauchemin's brief explanation of such texts as an example of the on-going interpretation of these texts in terms of eternal suffering. In this sense Beauchemin is on the side of the conditionalists, but he does not interpret them as possibly leading to A: he is a universalist.

He rejects the term "Universalism" because he defines it as "all beliefs are equally valid."[55] He rejects this view (which, by the way, is not the common understanding of U.) He defines it thus: "Christ's blood propitiates the sins of the whole world. This is universal propitiation. Every knee will bow in sincere worship of Jesus Christ. This is universal worship—"Christian"

---

53. Ibid., 220–21.

54. Ibid., 222–23.

55. Beauchemin, *Hope*, 232.

Universalism."⁵⁶ He is a universalist according to the more common understanding of this term today.

But I am interested, only briefly, in his scriptural understanding of the texts interpreted otherwise than by the conditionalists.

> Death and destruction is thought by most Christians to refer to an eternal hell of suffering or to a state of annihilation. Thus, they are understood to be a permanent state. Often in Scripture, two statements are made side by side that together shed greater light on a given theme. Consider 1 Cor 1:19; Rom 2:12; 14:15; 20–21. Here *apollumi* is used in the same sense as "set aside" or "bring to nothing." Scripture is clear that all are judged including unbelievers who have sinned without law. Thus to "perish" here cannot be utter annihilation, for judgment must follow. [He quotes more Scripture.] In all the above, whatever is meant by death and destruction, it cannot be unending torment or annihilation. What gives God greater glory: annihilation or restoration?⁵⁷

In summary, the conditionalists hold that the words in scripture describing the end of the unrepentant—death, the way of death, destruction, perish, blot out, blown away as chaff, and many others—are to be taken literally as the end of existence and not as "eternal" suffering.

---

56. Ibid.
57. Ibid., 36–37.

3

Tradition, Ancient and Modern

The Early Tradition

THE BASIC ARGUMENT OF the conditionalists from tradition is that their position was the earliest of those who defended the faith in the first centuries—the Apostolic Fathers and the Apologists. Their main argument is the unity of Scripture with this earliest apologetic.

The Apostolic Fathers

Clement of Rome, Ignatius of Antioch, the author of the Didache, the Epistle of Barnabas, Hermas of Rome, Polycarp of Smyrna, Papias, the Letter to Diognetus, and the Homily of Clement.

As I frequently mention this *Guide* is not a scholarly work, purporting to give the latest research on topics. Thus here I simply give the view of one of the foremost conditionalist scholars—Froom— on his study of CI in these Apostolic Fathers. He and many other conditionalist scholars claim that it is irrefutable that the Apostolic Fathers were conditionalists. These fathers are usually placed in the first half of the second century. I will omit Froom's references.

Clement of Rome (d. 100)

Clement never speaks of the immortality of the soul, either in thought or in phrasing, nor of eternal punishing. Clement did not believe that the wicked either possessed immortality by nature or should ever obtain it. And when Clement discusses that death which is the ultimate fate of the wicked, he clearly states that they will ultimately be deprived of all existence and become nonexistent. He does not refer to merely spiritual death in sin, or of endless life in everlasting misery.

Again and again Clement uses the terms "perish" and "destruction" as the equivalent of "punished with death" for the fate of the wicked. He frequently quotes from the Old Testament—the New Testament was not yet assembled—citing how "transgressors" are to be "destroyed from off the face of the earth"; and God will "blot out" even their name from under heaven. That was Clement's belief. Clement clearly believed that immortality was conditional, to be bestowed on the righteous only.[1]

Ignatius of Antioch (d. 107)

Froom acknowledges (along with other scholars) that some Letters of Ignatius may not be genuine. I will present several which are generally considered to be authentic.

To the Ephesians

"In chapter eighteen Ignatius alludes to the provision of the cross as being "to us salvation and *life eternal*." And in chapter nineteen he tells of "God himself being manifested in human form for the *renewal of eternal life*. Then in chapter twenty he interestingly refers to "breaking one and the same bread, which is the *medicine of immortality*, and the antidote to prevent us from dying, but [which causes] that we should *live forever* in Jesus Christ. Ignatius holds that "immortality" and "eternal life" for the righteous are the exact opposites of "perishing" for the wicked."[2]

To the Magnesians

At the very outset of the epistle to the Magnesians he speaks of Christ as "the constant source of our life," and he adds, concerning

1. Froom I, 766–67.
2. Ibid., 770–71.

the "unbelieving" and those Christians "not in readiness to die into His Passion," that "His life is not in us." In chapter ten he makes the unequivocal statement, "For were He to reward us according to our works, we should cease to be." This comports with Ignatius' message to the Ephesians, that when the sinner is rewarded according to his deeds, he will then cease to exist. Thus there will be an end of all things— except of those who partake of the proffered life in Christ.[3]

"That is the burden of Ignatius' testimony. His continuing theme is the *gift of life and immortality for the saved in Christ.* He is utterly silent in regard to any Innate Immortality of the soul or anything akin thereto. Instead, the declarations of these separate treatises are a unit in setting forth immortality and incorruptibility as conferred in, and only through, Christ."[4]

The Didache (c.120)

The Didache or The Teaching of the Twelve Apostles, one of the most important of the early documents, is a manual for baptismal instruction. It portrays the two ways of life and death, characteristic of the sub-apostolic age. "In essence, the 'way of life' leads to readiness for the last events—the Second Advent, the resurrection, and the eternal kingdom. In contrast the 'way of death' leads to the final destruction of the impenitently wicked. There is no admixture of Jewish Philonian or Greek Alexandrian philosophy, and nothing remotely resembling the later Innate-Immortality-of-the-soul concept either in phrase or thought, or its later common corollary, the Eternal Torment of the impenitent. "There are two ways, one of life and one of death; but a great difference between the two ways. Many shall be made to stumble and shall perish; but they that endure in their faith shall be saved.[5]

---

3. Ibid., 771.
4. Ibid., 773
5. Ibid., 775–77.

Epistle of Barnabas (c.140)

"1. In the entire epistle Barnabas does not once hint, either by phrase or thought, that man has an innately immortal soul.
2. He never once states or infers anything about endless suffering or torment for the wicked. On the contrary, they are to die, perish, be destroyed, blown away as the chaff and eaten by moths.
3. He speaks of the sleep of the dead, the coming of the Lord, the resurrection and endless life of the righteous and definitive retribution of the wicked. Dr. Edward Beecher admits that "what Barnabas says may be understood of the annihilation of the wicked."[6]

Froom's Summary of the Apostolic Fathers

"From the beginning to the end of them [the Apostolic Fathers] there is not one word said of that immortality of the soul which is so prominent in the writings of the later fathers. Immortality is by them asserted to be peculiar to the redeemed. The punishment of the wicked is by them emphatically declared to be everlasting. Not one stray expression of theirs can be interpreted as giving any countenance to the theory of restoration after purgatorial suffering. The fire of hell is with them, as with us, an unquenchable one; but the issue is, with them as with Scripture, "destruction," 'death,' loss of life."[7]

Petavel on the Apostolic Fathers

"The apostolic Fathers never speak of a native immorality; an immortal life is in their view the exclusive privilege of the redeemed. The punishment of the rejected consists in a gradual destruction of their being, which finally becomes total. This punishment is called eternal, as being definitive and irremediable; we have already shown in the Scripture this use of an adjective, qualifying not the momentary action but the permanent results of the action. Neither do the Apostolic Fathers speak of a universal salvation. They teach that the unquenchable fire will consume its victims. In a word, they all with one accord appear to be Conditionalists."[8]

6. Ibid., 783.
7. Ibid., 801.
8. Ibid., Petavel, *Problem*, 229–30.

The Apologists

Justin, Arnobius, Tatian, Theophilus, Irenaeus, and Lactantius.

Froom holds that the Apologists were all conditionalists before the views of U and Hell were formulated. We will consider the three most important Apologists, Justin, Irenaeus, and Arnobius.

Justin Martyr (106–65)

Justin was the first of the Christian apologists whose works have come down to us. Brian Daley, SJ, referring to Justin's teaching, simply states that "the wicked will be punished in eternal fire. Sinners will receive back the same bodies they now have in order to undergo eternal punishment. Justin almost invariably describes this punishment as eternal fire."[9] Daley doesn't go into other possible meanings of "eternal."

Froom comments that Justin speaks of "everlasting punishment" but not of unending conscious suffering, or punish*ing*. It is only by assuming that *aionios* means endless, instead of "for the age," that the thought of eternal punishing can find sustaining support."[10] He then lists ten citations from Justin's works (some cited by Daley but interpreted otherwise), and says:

> These ten citations are impressive. But it is in this immediate connection that Justin explicitly declares that, when the fires have done their work, the wicked then "shall cease to exist." That is too explicit for misunderstanding. And in equally strong and definite language Justin stresses the inseparable fact that they will be punished only "so long as God wills them to exist and to be punished." The inescapable conclusion is that it then ceases. Theirs is therefore a *terminable* existence. At the end of the period determined by the will and justice of God, the punishment of wicked souls will cease by the very cessation of their existence. Such is the obvious meaning, for Justin repeatedly denies the inherent, independent, and indefeasible immortality of the soul.[11]

---

9. Daley, *Hope*, 21–22.
10. Froom, *Conditionalist I*, 818.
11. Ibid., 819.

Tradition, Ancient and Modern

Irenaeus (d. 202)

Irenaeus is considered to be the Father of Orthodoxy, "the most renowned champion of orthodoxy in his generation."[12] Among the conditionalists he is considered the foremost second-century contender of their doctrine. Froom's main point is that CI was the dominant teaching of the Christian Church until Athenagoras (c. 127–190), who was the first ecclesiastic to assert innate immortality.

> The treatise *Against Heresies* bears a remarkable testimony to the Conditionalist doctrine of the nature and destiny of man, and its inseparable corollary, the ultimate destruction of the wicked. Irenaeus stood as a bulwark against the Eternal-Torment of the wicked postulate, and Origenism, the universal restoration of the wicked. He seemed to exhaust the expressive vocabulary at his command in denying the immortality of the unsaved. The incorrigibly wicked are consigned to eternal punishment which, he explains, ends in complete cessation of being or existence; and this results in the end of all evil. The chastisement of the wicked will be eternal in its effects, because God's benefits are eternal. His argument, in a sentence, was this: *To be deprived of the benefits of existence is the greatest punishment, and to be deprived of them forever is to suffer "eternal punishment."*[13]

Irenaeus held that man's entire nature was created *for* immortality, but was mortal, and not yet possessed of immortality. He maintained that *unfallen* man, in his first estate in Eden, had to obtain something that he did not at first possess, and failed to obtain. Immortality will be bestowed at the resurrection, with reunion of the believer's body and soul.

To live is to exist; to die to cease to exist. Irenaeus' concept of life is that of the literal sense of existence. And life eternal is never growing old. Never dying the second death, never ceasing to exist. It is Christ, the Prince of Life, who existed before all, who is the source of all life. To live, then, is to exist. Length of days for ever and ever, or unending existence, is set forth as identical with immortality and incorruptibility. Believers are the children of the resurrection, through which they will obtain the life now pledged to them. Immortality is now in promise, but not as yet in actual

---

12. Ibid., 874.
13. Ibid., 876–77.

possession. Thus the elect are enrolled for eternal life. That, said Irenaeus, is the Christian's glorious prospect.[14]

"Coming specifically to immortality, Irenaeus gives its primary meaning as exemption from death and annihilation; in other words, unending existence. When applied to God it is the absolute, eternal existence of which He cannot be deprived. But Irenaeus repeatedly asserts that immortality was forfeited by man through his transgression, and cannot possibly be the inherent possession of the disobedient. And he asks the unanswerable question, "How can man be immortal who in his mortal nature did not obey his Maker?"[15]

"In various ways and by multiple forms of expression, Irenaeus insists that immortality is a gift conveyed to the believer through the gospel, which provision he interestingly describes as "breathing out immorality" and "vivifying man afresh." "By no other means could we have attained to incorruptibility and immortality unless we had been united to incorruptibility and immortality."[16]

"To the later Origenists, Restoration's future punishment is purgative. After a protracted period the soul sentenced to Hell will allegedly come forth purified and join the ranks of the redeemed. But to Irenaeus, to whom the verdict of the judgment is eternal, the punishment is punitive, and is eternal in its effects. The hideous cruelty of Augustinianism's duration of the punishment is eternal, but its nature is death, destruction, perdition, cessation of being, annihilation— not ceaseless punishing."[17]

"Irenaeus holds that souls will endure as long as God wills the existence and continuance of the saved. It is the Father who imparts continuance forever and ever on those who are saved. He says, "life does not arise from us, nor from our own nature." Such as accept the gift of this provision" shall receive length of days for ever and ever."[18] Froom then has a section quoting many texts from Irenaeus to substantiate the above doctrine.

---

14. Ibid., 879–88.
15. Ibid., 880–81.
16. Ibid., 881.
17. Ibid., 883.
18. Ibid., 884.

Arnobius of Africa (d. 330)

Arnobius is of special significance because he was from the fiery Africa of Tertullian and Augustine who developed the doctrine of hell, and yet he was not influenced by this teaching of his learned countrymen.

> He was the first Latin writer of note to declare clearly the doctrine of the ultimate extinction of the wicked. He taught explicitly that the incorrigibly impenitent sinner is destined, after a due and determined period of punishment, to pass out of existence.
>
> To Arnobius the human soul, with its inherent sin and imperfection, could not of itself be inherently immortal, becoming such only by the grace and gift of God. For the unrepentant unrighteous there must be a second death, a Gehenna of unquenchable fire, which gradually consumes and at last extinguishes the wicked, without leaving any "residuum."[19]
>
> Arnobius clearly distinguishes between the first death and the final death, and declares that in the true, or final death of the wicked there is nothing left behind— absolute destruction after the final death agonies. He warns against the presumption of Innate Immortality. Continuance of life, he holds, is conditional.[20]
>
> Arnobius repeats his contention that souls are of a neutral character, that is, capable of entering into either life or death. But he adds they are "gifted with immortality, if they rest their hope of so great a gift on God Supreme, who alone has power to grant such blessing."[21] Christ was sent by God for this end, that He might deliver unhappy souls from ruin and destruction, souls in a mortal state before He came. The Almighty Master of the world has determined that this should be the way of salvation, this door, so to say, of life; by Him alone is there access. Such is the prize of immortality set before us.[22]
>
> And all this, be it remembered, was not only set forth as Arnobius' faith, but was accepted as sufficient evidence of his Christianity to open for him the gates of Christian church membership. Nor is it to be forgotten that these two views of man [innate immortality and Conditionalism] were both held at the time, and

---

19. Ibid., 919.
20. Ibid., 923.
21. Ibid., 925.
22. Ibid., 926.

that the view of Arnobius, and that of many holding with him, was accepted as equally the Christian view.[23]

Athenagoras (127-190)

My purpose in this chapter on tradition is to present the views of those who believed in CI. We shall not be considering contrary views, especially the two Fathers from burning Africa—Tertullian and Augustine— who were mostly responsible for the full development of hell in the Christian tradition. But if we ask the question, "How did we get to Tertullian and Augustine from the unanimous voice of the ancient tradition," a brief mention must be made of Athenagoras whose treatise *On the Resurrection of the Dead* (187) is considered the major turning point towards immortal-soulism and eternal punishment. His teaching exemplifies exactly the main contention of the conditionalists that Platonism was the cause of the doctrine of hell. Froom has a very detailed eighteen page study of Athenagoras.

Athenagoras was born in Athens, and thus Greek was his native language. In his earlier *Apology* (177) to the Roman emperor Marcus Aurelius, his express purpose was to show the compatibility of Platonism with Christianity. His ideas about the immortality of the person do not occur in this document, but are fully expressed ten years later in the aforementioned treatise on the *Resurrection*. It is a wholly philosophical document in which *he doesn't once mention the resurrection of Christ!* He uses expressions such as "continuance of being in immortality," "God made man of an immortal soul," "wholly incorruptible and immortal," "from the first created immortal," "an immortal nature," "possessed of an immortal soul and rational judgment," and many other similar phrases. For my purposes it is not necessary to go into any further details about his views. The important fact is that "Athenagoras assuredly and openly now taught the innate, inalienable, indefeasible immortality of the soul. And he was, so far as can be determined, the first Christian ecclesiastic so to do."[24]

---

23. Ibid., 927.
24. Ibid., 932–33.

Tradition, Ancient and Modern

The Middle Ages, Non-Christian Witnesses

Averroes (1126–1198)

> Averroes was recognized as one of the outstanding Islamic thinkers of his day. But this peripatetic (follower of Aristotle) created consternation by challenging the Innate Immortality of the soul, thereby becoming a symbol of the concept that both body and soul "ceased to exist when they died." Scholarly historian Peter Bayle says, "He taught the mortality of the human soul, and that man does not have an eternal nature that never dies. The challenges of Averroes as to the traditional immortality of the soul postulate created a panic in Islamic circles. They were, of course, in direct conflict with the Mohammedan concept of a paradise of eternal delights and a hell of endless torment on which the Koran dilates. Averroes was blindly devoted to Aristotle and the Aristotelian doctrine of the soul, more so than to the religion of Mohammed.[25]

Moses Maimonides (1131–1204)

Maimonides was a student of Averroes and is considered one of the greatest Jewish religious minds of Western and Eastern civilisation.

> Maimonides taught that immortality is for the righteous only, with ultimate destruction for the wicked. Those unworthy of life would not live forever, but would be "cut off" and "perish" and the soul would ultimately be extinguished. The worst of all punishments, Maimonides held, is *Kareth*, which means "excision," or complete destruction. It is a death from which there is no return, a ruin which admits of no reparation. Evil men are to be destroyed body and soul. Here are Maimonides' exact words on the fate of the wicked:
> "The punishment which awaits the wicked man is that he will have no part in eternal life, but will die, and be utterly destroyed. He will not live for ever, but for his sins will be *cut off and perish* like a brute. It is a death from which there is no return.[26]

---

25. Froom, *Conditionalist II*, 18–19.
26. Ibid., 23–24.

Sixteenth and Seventeenth Centuries

John Calvin

From Augustine until the sixteenth century Western Christianity pretty much held to the Immortalist-soul theory and its corollary that those who are unrepentant go to hell. Protestantism generally held this doctrine. John Calvin is often considered the major theologian of the Reformation. "It may safely be said that...Calvin was of all the Protestant Reformers the foremost opposer of the doctrine of Conditional Immortality. And with it he was the most ardent Protestant advocate of the inseparable dogma of the Eternal Torment of the non-repentant non-elect. As a consequence, to this day, the most intense advocates of these twin dogmas are Calvinists as a group."[27] A brief quotation from the *Institutes* (Book 3, chapter 25, section 12) will suffice:

"As language cannot describe the severity of the divine vengeance on the reprobate, their pains and torments are figured to us by corporeal things, such as darkness, wailing and gnashing of teeth, inextinguishable fire, the ever-knawing worm. Hence unhappy consciences find no rest, but are vexed and driven about by a dire whirlwind, feeling as if torn by an angry God. How fearful, then, must it be to be thus beset throughout eternity!"[28]

D, F. Walker

D.P. Walker in his *The Decline of Hell, Seventeenth-Century Discussions of Eternal Torment,* gives, for that period, a detailed presentation of growing opinions about the decline of hell and the revival of the theories of U and A. I am only concerned with A. Some of the writers can be found in Froom, but Walker gives a much more detailed historical account of the few he treats that are of special interest to us. I will use Walker for two views of the sixteenth and seventeenth centuries.

---

27. Froom, *Conditionalist II,* 116.
28. Boruff, "Calvin on Hell."

The Socinians

Often in literature on CI the Socinians are mentioned.[29] They were prominent in the late sixteenth and early seventeenth centuries in Poland. Two brief quotes will give a sense of the Socinians belief about our topic.

A certain Calovius, who was not a Socinian, writes to one Martin Ruar who was a Socinian, and the former asks just what the Socinians believe about hell:

> At times your authors talk ambiguously about the resurrection of the wicked: so that sometimes I am inclined to think that they believe in their Annihilationism, or certainly that the reprobate after the resurrection will be annihilated rather than subjected to everlasting torments. Thus, since in Socini's [the founder's] book against Pucci the perpetual dissolution of soul and body is ascribed to Adam as natural, and this is established as necessary through Adam's transgression, only the faithful and pious being liberated by Christ from this necessity. According to his opinion, it certainly seems to follow that the wicked are not liberated from it, and are thus subject to perpetual dissolution and will never be recalled to life.[30]

Then, one Ernst Soner, a Socinian, gives an interesting Socinian account of A:

> [Soner] concedes an absolute right of God as creator to annihilate His creatures ("absolutum Dei imperium"). This right or power has nothing to do with justice, which is restricted to the distribution of punishments or rewards proportionate to bad or good deeds. In Soner's system it is clear that the wicked do resurrect, since God will punish them with finite torments proportionate to their sins, and then annihilate them. This annihilation is not a punishment, though it resembles one in that it is inflicted only on sinners. It is imposed by God's absolute power and is neither just nor unjust; in the same way the eternal life of the blessed is not really a reward, but a free gift. That is to say: both annihilation and eternal bliss are disproportionate to any human, finite sins or merits; their occurrence cannot therefore be due to God's justice.[31]

---

29. Froom, *Conditionalist II,* 86–87; Fudge, *Fire,* 390.
30. Walker, *Decline,* 80–81.
31. Ibid., 85–86.

Is hell unjust? "The best Soner can do is argue that eternal torment would conflict with God's mercy, and that, since all creatures contain some "ray of divine goodness," God could not allow a part of Himself to be forever in evil and misery; whereas, if the wicked are annihilated, this divine ray returns to its source.[32]

Soner's last sentence is a profound insight into the theological "superiority" of A over hell: creatures share in the transcendentals of God—truth, beauty, and goodness; thus God could not allow these to be forever *joined* to an evil state or condition. I consider this one of the most convincing arguments for A over against hell.

Nicholas Malebranche (1638–1715)

Malebranche was a Catholic priest of the Oratory founded by St. Philip Neri. He was an outstanding philosopher of his day—friends and in conversation with Leibnitz. He is still today prominent in the Catholic philosophical tradition. He is not included in Froom's survey because he did not believe in either U or in A. His theodicy mostly concerned the problem of evil. He figures prominently in Walker, however, because he was involved in the philosophical/theological question of how to reconcile people going to hell— which he believed in— with the goodness and love of God. He came up with an ingenious answer to the problem of evil which deserves to be better known in the modern discussion. I have not come across it in recent literature.

He doesn't see the problem/conflict of God's love vs. his justice *in God's nature*, as if God now acts with love and now with justice. He locates the solution in God's *providential means and ends in the guidance of creation*. Walker summarizes; quotes are from Malebranche:

> God's attributes must be manifest in all His acts, but the conflict arises not between attributes but between means and ends. These means shall be as simple as possible. Since God cares more about these means than the end, He can only create and maintain the universe by 'volontes generales', i.e., by a few universal, invariable laws, even if this results in a highly defective creation. Why God should care more about the perfection of the means than that of the ends, unlike someone else making anything, is not explained.

---

32. Ibid.

> In the physical order Malebranche gives the example of rain. Its main purpose is to water crops so that we might have food. Physical conditions where the rain falls may cause floods. The resultant evil is not willed by God, but is merely a consequence of His necessarily producing everything according to simple, unchanging laws, dictated by His Wisdom.
>
> As an explanation of moral evil, that is, of God's permission of sin and the consequent damnation of most of mankind, the theory is more complicated and less convincing. Malebranche compares the incidence of rainfall to that of grace, which is often given to those who are too hardened to profit by it, or who do not persevere to salvation, and is sometimes apparently refused to those whom it might save. Many of the places are not well-cultivated fields and it may happen to miss some fertile places. This rain of grace produces only a small crop of saved, little wheat and many tares.
>
> God's justice consists in evaluating every being according to its natural perfection or imperfection, and in punishing or rewarding any being which respectively falls below or rises above its place in the hierarchy. "A man whose affections are disordered through bad use of his freedom is brought back into the Order of Justice which God owes to His divine perfections, if this sinner is miserable in proportion to his disorders. Thus God can only be good within the limits of His justice; He is infinitely good to the good.[33]

If I understand Malebranche correctly, when justice becomes his supreme virtue he means God's fidelity to the providential *ends and means pattern* he has established. In simpler terms, Malebranche teaches the rather common notion that we reap the fruits of our actions: if we follow God's providential plan of means and ends, we rejoice; if not, we suffer the consequences of our actions. God cannot act outside of this "just plan of means and ends." I'm sure Malebranche believed in miracles, that God can act outside his normal established ends and means providential plan. But miracles by definition are extraordinary acts of God. There are many objections to Malbranche's thought here, but it seems that locating justice in following God's plan instead of justice competing with other attributes *within God's nature* is a fruitful avenue of exploration.

---

33. Ibid., 203–07.

William Whiston (1667–1752)

To give one example of a conditionalist from Walker's period, I chose Whiston. He succeeded Isaac Newton as professor of mathematics at Cambridge and was therefore an intellectual giant of the period. In 1740 he published his view on hell in *The Eternity of Hell Torments*. He comments on several biblical passages.

> Chaff is burnt up in Utter Destruction. Luke iii,17. These words are very much of a piece with those already cited from Isaiah the Prophet and others. Only they compare the wicked to chaff, which is not laid up in garners, as wheat is for its preservation, but entirely burnt up for its destruction. Which is strong against those that suppose the wicked to have their lives preserved on purpose that they may be subject to never ending pains, and plainly implies that their punishment—in the sense of torment— shall end much sooner, by an utter destruction, or what we should call annihilation also.
>
> 2 Thess 1.8–9. *In flaming fire, taking vengeance on them that know not God; and that obey not the gospel of our Lord Jesus Christ, who shall have for punishment a lasting destruction, from the presence of the Lord, and the glory of His power.*
>
> This text is so far from affirming, as is commonly supposed, that the wicked shall, at the last day, be preserved in being, in order to suffer the enduring everlasting torments that it rather implies the contrary; that the flaming fire into which they are to be cast at that day, will, in some time, utterly consume them.

There can be no mistake as to Whiston's mature views on the fate of the wicked—their utter destruction—thus clearly expressed. So Conditionalism's permeations were deep in high circles as we come toward the middle of the eighteenth century, and both the predecessor and the successor of Sir Isaac Newton are listed as Conditionalists.[34]

The Modern Period

For the sake of brevity I confine my presentation of the modern period mostly to the latter half of the nineteenth century since Froom says this was "to witness to a new awakening on the various questions involved in Christian eschatology, as well as to see much of the long-standing prejudice

---

34. Froom, II,, 224–26.

removed and a host of advocates rise up whose testimony and influence largely lifted the question of Conditionalism out of the assigned category of heresy. This awakening gave to Conditionalism a recognized place in the Christian doctrine, as well as opening the doors for a widespread investigation and open candid discussion."[35]

Richard Rothe (1799–1867)

Rothe was the principle advocate of Conditionalism in Germany and gave it its most scientific exposition. The concept that immortality is to be *acquired* forms the foundation of the Rothe system—and Rothe was called "the most powerful dogmatician of our [nineteenth] century. Back in 1870 he had written: "It is no longer maintained that the human soul possesses immortality by virtue of a supposed simplicity of substance." Rothe also reached the conclusion of the ultimate extinction of the personality of the wicked, as did many other Continental theologians. But Rothe held that the duration of the chastisement of a soul would be in proportion to its guilt:

"We are obliged to admit that the sufferings endured in hell by the reprobate will in reality end, but that the end will consist in the destruction of the guilty. This idea is very ancient in the church. . . .This opinion alone seems capable of satisfying all the conditions. It has nothing to fear from contemporary philosophy, for men have ceased to maintain that the human soul possesses a natural immortality."[36]

Edward White (1819–1898)

The movement towards Conditionalism received an unquestionable acceleration from the book by Dr. Edward White, *Life in Christ*, first appearing in 1846.

"More than any other individual in the nineteenth century, White was instrumental in bringing the principles of conditional immortality to prominence."[37] "His conclusions: 1. that man is mortal; 2. that the Fall

---

35. Ibid., 316.
36. Ibid., 593–94.
37. Ibid., 322.

brought the sentence of death; 3. that the supreme object of redemption is to renew in man the divine image, with endless life through union with the life of Christ; and 4. that without Christ man will utterly perish without hope of recovery. White painstakingly turned to the history of the great departure, compassing the Church Fathers, and tracing step by step the disastrous role Platonism has played in it all."[38] "As to the biblical side, it was unreasonable and illogical, he constantly maintained, that four or five obscure passages should set at nought some five hundred clear and explicit texts."[39]

"In 1846 he brought out his first book, *Life in Christ*. In this he sought to rescue a great truth from the obscurity in which it had been largely buried under unscriptural theology, spawned, as he put it, by the pagan concept of man's inherent immortality. The Bible was fundamentally a revelation of everlasting life, offered to whomsoever will."[40]

In 1882, on the occasion of the thirtieth anniversary of a Chapel he had founded in London, he said: "I protest again, with all my heart and soul and mind, against what appears to us still those two opposite errors, both springing from the common root of faith in man's natural immortality: first, against the doctrine of endless torments to be inflicted in hell on unsaved men, whether civilised or barbarian; and, secondly, against the now popular doctrine of the absolute final salvation of all men, good and bad; as directly contrary both to the letter and spirit of the Christian revelation recorded in Holy Scripture."[41]

"Conditionalism harmonizes Scripture with Scripture as to life and death. It likewise reconciles the sovereignty of God and the freedom of the human will. It recognizes the second death as an everlasting penalty and at the same time the final extinction of evil—not by restoration but by the ultimate cessation of the impenitent. It shows that there is no injustice in the eventual withdrawal of life from those who have no fitness for its endless perpetuation."[42]

---

38. Ibid., 325.
39. Ibid.
40. Ibid., 327, 329
41. Ibid., 331.
42. Ibid., 333–34.

Tradition, Ancient and Modern

William Gladstone, Prime Minister of England (1809-1898)

Gladstone is well known for his political achievements but few know that he was also a serious student of theology. Even though he was not a professional theologian he studied the works of the nineteenth century on the subject under consideration. His summary will serve as a good example of the prevalent views in that century. It is taken from one of his last books.

1. That the natural immortality of the soul is not taught in Scripture.
2. Neither is it commended by the moral authority of *always, everywhere, and by everyone* acknowledged. [Vincent of Lerins]
3. Neither is it affirmed or enjoined by any of the great assemblies [General Councils] of the undivided church, or by any unanimity, actual or moral, of Decrees and confessions posterior to the division of the church into East and West.
4. The immortality of the soul is properly to be regarded as. . .a gift or endowment due to the Incarnation of our Lord.
5. If we set out from the belief that Christ both reveals and gives immortality, which is exemption from death, and is life without end, it is plain that the first application of this doctrine is to the righteous.
6. In regard to future punishment, it is plain that great differences of opinion have prevailed at different periods of the history of the Church, the first centuries presenting a view of a different colour from that which may be said to have prevailed over others from about the time of St. Chrysostom and St. Augustine.
7. It does not appear safe to apply the term traditional theology to the largely developed opinions of later ages on future punishment, as compared with the more reserved conceptions of an earlier period.
8. There can be no such thing as suffering, of whatever kind, through eternity except by God's departing from a principle of justice.
9. The ordinary and principal description of the future state of the unrighteous is that conveyed in the word death. This word in its ordinary signification bears the sense of an extinction or cessation of some kind. It might mean cessation for the wicked of life itself.
10. The popular definition of death. . .takes away from death that idea of cessation and extinction: it adds an idea of suffering, amounting

largely to misery and torment, which the original sense of the word in no manner contains.

11. It [Restitutionism (U))...strikes at what all believers in a future state consider as the grand and central truth of the subject, this, namely, that we are living in a state of probation....But under Restitutionism all idea of essential quality as a distinctive mark disappears, and therefore all idea of genuine probation.

12. The notion of Universal Restitution is, then, not supported by Scripture, or by Christian tradition, or by any sound philosophy of human nature.

13. The metaphysical doctrine of a natural indefeasible immortality of the soul, as an immaterial substance, has come, unawares and gradually to reckon, or be assumed, as a doctrine of Faith, and no longer as only a philosophical opinion.

14. The central and final stronghold of believers is faith in the infeasible and universal justice of the Divine Being.[43]

Henry Constable (1816–1891)

"Constable came to be regarded as one of the outstanding British champions of conditional immortality of the century."[44] "He reached the unwavering conclusion that neither eternal misery nor Universal Restoration is taught in Scripture. That immortality is for God's redeemed alone became his profound belief, with eternal death or destruction for the lost."[45] "All the expressions of Scripture used concerning future punishment are not merely unsuitable but they are positively false if applied to the Eternal Torment or Universal Restoration theories. The Scripture illustrations are fatal to both views."[46]

"Thus it was that the three basic theories of future punishment became established in the church, ever after to continue in relentless conflict. And in the battle between opposing concepts of the ultimate extinction of evil *versus* the eternal existence of evil, Origen erred fatally as to the means

43. Ibid., 636–37.
44. Ibid., 339.
45. Ibid., 337.
46. Ibid., 342–43.

of extinction. His false premise "compelled him to promise life where God had threatened death."[47]

"But Constable closes on the biblical note of the ultimate "termination of evil." It will have an end. "It is not *from* eternity, and it will not be *to* eternity." "Eternity of evil," declares Constable, is "not a doctrine of the bible." "Evil is a thing of time, and is not an essential part of the constitution of God's universe." Thus he likewise disposes of Tertullian Augustinianism. This leaves the ultimate and utter destruction of sin and sinners as the truth.

The truth of Conditional Immorality and the ultimate, utter destruction of the wicked goes back to Christ and the apostles. The other two theories were later innovations, and clearly not apostolic. Constable's is a classic argument."[48]

Frederic William Farrar (1831–1903)

Farrar was neither a conditionalist, a universalist, or an original thinker about our theme. I mention him here because conditionalists must be very grateful to him for his *courage* in preaching his famous sermon against the traditional understanding of hell. As Froom put it: "No such sermon had ever been heard in the venerable [Westminster] Abbey in its six long centuries. Moreover, it contravened a popular belief in fifteen centuries' standing. It created a tremendous stir [1877] on both sides of the Atlantic."[49] Farrar related the contents of his sermon in this way:

"I had to repudiate a doctrine which had been more or less universally preached by the majority of Christians for fifteen hundred years. I knew that to do so was an act which would cost me dear. I knew that during six centuries of the history of the present Abbey it was probable that no sermon had been preached which even greatly modified, much less repudiated with indignation, that popular teaching about hell which seemed to me a ghastly amalgam of all that was worst in the combined errors of Augustinianism, Romanism, and Calvinism."[50]

In his preaching and writings he outlined the same arguments we have been considering. What is somewhat different about Farrar is that, although he absolutely repudiated hell, he doesn't seem to have found his

47. Ibid., 346.
48. Ibid., 347.
49. Ibid., 404.
50. Ibid., 406.

way to an alternative. He received many positive and negative responses to his views. One that struck me was this: ""You have spoken out what nearly every one of us secretly thought."[51]

It's possible that this has become true for the majority of Christians today. The main purpose of my two *Guides* is to rescue people from intellectual doldrums concerning the final state of Christians. If they reject hell they may, without too much study, choose one of the two possibilities in our tradition—U or CI. Farrar can serve as a kind of "patron saint" of those who have repudiated hell but still wonder and are uncertain about the alternatives. Now *he* knows! But we are still pilgrims, and must be satisfied with possibilities. My *Guides* are attempts to provide some guidance.

Frederick Ash Freer (1837-1917)

Freer was not an original thinker about CI but he is noted for his great contribution to the spread of this teaching. He translated what we have seen is considered the most fundamental book on CI in the nineteenth century, Petavel's *The Problem of Immortality*. He is one of those behind the scenes persons to whom huge debts are owed. He also wrote a biography of Edward White. He expressed the summation of White's views thus: "From the Conditionalist point of view, therefore, it is evident that the restitution of all things when God shall be all in all may be attained by the elimination of all uncongenial elements, the destruction of all impenitent human beings."[52] "And sagely he further states that Conditionalism is a synthesis which sets the various doctrines of the gospel in their true light and their just relations."[53]

Emmanuel Petavel

Petavel's book, *The Problem of Immortality*, totals 597 pages. His study is probably the most comprehensive ever written on this topic. I imagine it has become a kind of bible for conditionalists. An outline of his chapters, and a brief description of its contents, will serve as a good over-all vision of the various aspects of the immortality question treated throughout my

51. Ibid., 407
52. Ibid., 624.
53. Ibid., 625.

present *Guide*. Each chapter of Petavel's book is very detailed and profound. I quote here the thesis he is attempting to prove in each chapter. It will serve as an excellent presentation of his book.

Chapter I. State of the Question. Immortality is a problem that demands a dogmatic study. It has been too little recognized. Conditionalism is a return to the primitive Gospel.

Chapter II. Immortality as Viewed by Independent Science. Biology and comparative physiology, geology and palaeontology, and, indeed, all that is included in the term experimental science, fails to supply any proof of the immortality of the soul.

Chapter III. Immortality According to the Old Testament and in Judaism. In the Old Testament, death always indicates cessation of functions. The doctrine of the unconditional immortality of the human soul is neither taught nor assumed in the Old Testament.

Chapter IV. Immortality According to the New Testament. The immortalization of man by means of faith in Jesus Christ is the principal aim of the New Testament writings.

Chapter V. Jesus Christ is the Only Source of Immortality. Justification and sanctification by the Holy Spirit unites us to Christ, and man again becomes capable of immortalization.

Chapter VI. Baptism and the Lord's Super, Symbols of Immortality. Baptism is the symbol of a new birth. The Lord's Supper is an emblem of the sustenance of the new life symbolically conferred in baptism.

Chapter VII. The Second Death or Future Punishment. Sin, a guilty revolt, tends towards the subversion and suppression of the conditions of human existence. The supreme punishment will be the deprivation of all faculties.

Chapter VIII. Conditional Immortality in the Writings of the Earliest Fathers of the Church. Barnabas, Clement of Rome, Ignatius, Hermas, Polycarp, the Didache, Justin, Tatian, Irenaeus, Theophilus of Antioch, Clement of Alexandria, Arnobius. [All were conditionalists]

Chapter IX. The Deviation of the Churches, and the Doctrine of Compulsory Immortality in an Eternal Hell. The corruption of the traditional dogma [CI] explained by the infiltration of heathen dualism.

Chapter X. The Theory of Universal Salvation. Its anti-biblical character. False notion of divine Fatherhood. Fearful dangers of an excessive optimism.

Chapter XI. Examination of the Principal Arguments Adduced against Conditionalism and in Support of the Traditional Dogma. That the indefensible immortality of individual souls is taught implicitly, if not explicitly, in the Bible.

Chapter XII. Harmonies and Benefits of the True Biblical Teaching. As an evangelical synthesis, it [CI] bears the character of a theodicy, and it places in their true light several doctrines generally misunderstood: the notion of God, predestination, and man; the Christological notion and salvation, and eschatology.[54]

At the conclusion of his other book, *The Extinction of Evil*, Petavel outlines thirty-six objections and responses to A, and gives his CI arguments. It would be difficult to find a better summary of the conditionalist position and the objections that continue to be advanced. These are the issues discussed by the various schools of thought about the fate of the unrepentant. (Some of the replies are shortened for convenience; and for the same reason I've excluded some of the objections and replies.)

Objection I. Does not the saying that a certain sin "shall not be forgiven in this world or in the world to come," imply eternal suffering?
  It implies eternal punishment, not eternal suffering. The gradual death of the sinner, which is consummated in the world to come, is the remediless punishment of this unpardonable sin.

Objection II. The predictions which foretell eternal punishment may convey the idea of limited duration in the Old Testament; but when quoted in the New Testament they predict absolutely endless suffering.
  This assertion rests only upon the assumption of man's natural immortality, a doctrine equally foreign to both the New and the Old Testaments.

Objection III. Jesus repeatedly threatened sinners with terrible punishment.
  Utter destruction, preceded by the protracted pangs of the second death, is indeed a terrible punishment.

---

54. Petavel, *Problem*, xv–xviii.

Objection IV. *Kolasis aionios* and *zoe aionios* (Matt xxv. 46) imply the equal duration of the punishment and of the reward.

As the final extinction of the sinner constitutes the punishment, this punishment, in its effect, is really of equal duration with the blessedness of the redeemed. The endless extinction of those who once had life, and might have had it for ever, is just as perpetual in duration as endless life.

Objection V. As man was created in God's image, he must be as immortal as God Himself.

Although man was created in God's image, he is not omnipotent, and possesses neither omniscience nor omnipotence. There is therefore no reason for concluding that he must necessarily live forever. Man has been placed by the so-called orthodox doctrine upon too lofty a pedestal; he is no "partaker of the divine nature," *except through regeneration* (2 Pet i. 4). (emphasis added)

(This quote from 2 Pet has always been one of my scriptural proofs for the immortality of the soul. But Petavel clarifies that this is *only through regeneration*)

Objection VI. Nothing is ever annihilated in nature; atoms always retain their identity.

We do not deal with atoms, but with human beings. For them, complete destruction and disintegration is practically annihilation. Might we not be justified in terming a soul dead which had utterly and for ever lost even one of its essential faculties; for instance, individual consciousness?

Objection VII. The word "annihilate" is not Scriptural.

The question is not whether this term…has an exact counterpart in the language of the Bible. What we maintain is, simply, that the bible teaches, in the plainest and most emphatic terms, that the end of the hopelessly impenitent is their final and complete destruction.

Objection VIII. *Kolasis* means mutilation, not annihilation.

Yes, but successive mutilations would ultimately put an end to the mutilated creature. If you sever the parts of a whole, the whole as such no longer exists.

Objection X. The parables of our Lord all teach eternal suffering.

We ask for an instance. The parable of the rich man and Lazarus...says nothing of the duration of the flames of Hades.

Objection XI. Man could never have invented the doctrine of everlasting torment.

Facts appear to contradict this assertion: actuality to possibility is a valid consequence.

Objection XII. There are many mysteries in religion in general, and in eschatology in particular.

It is generally admitted that the fate of the wicked is among those things which are revealed.

Objection XIII. The declaration of Jesus Christ is "their worm dieth not, and their fire is not quenched."

This imagery is reproduced *liberatim* [freely] from the Old Testament. It is confessedly hyperbolical in the Old Testament, and is equally so in the New, being used in both cases to represent total, hopeless, and final destruction.

Objection XV. This view will convert no one to the truth of Christianity.

This remains to be proven; but it is certain that the traditional doctrine [of hell] is a stumbling-block in the path of many.

Objection XVI. We do not see that the destruction of the proud and ambitious begins here upon earth.

Their very pride and ambition are essentially a darkening of their reason; hence we have the expressions "puffed up with pride," "intoxicated with ambition,"...and they lead to the ruin of all the proud, great and small.

Objection XVII. The devils begged Jesus not to *destroy* them. Therefore, for them at least, there is no annihilation.

Precisely the reverse. The demons would not have asked not to be destroyed unless they feared such a punishment.

Objection XVIII. Moral beings cannot be destroyed.

Why not? A *moral* man means a man whose morals are good. This is all, we believe, that can be included in the term moral being.

Objection XIX. The torments of hell would be useless if they were not eternal. One cannot conceive of a being created for the purpose of being slowly consumed.

Still less can we conceive of a being created to be eternally tortured. Most things on earth end by gradual decay.

Objection XX. The destruction of the wicked would tend to show that God was mistaken in creating them.

> It is rather the eternal existence of evil and evil doers which would appear to be irreconcilable with the wisdom of the Creator.

Objection XXII. There is one passage where Paul speaks of eternal suffering, *olethron aionion* (2 Thess 1.9).

> Not eternal suffering, but "eternal destruction," the word used by Plato for annihilation. This verse represents the wicked as being destroyed for ever; they shall never return from the nothingness into which they pass (compare Ps. xcii.8).

Objection XXVI. An impenitent sinner will be tempted to give himself up to evil if he has no other punishment to fear than extinction.

> The fact is that traditional theology still lingers in the train of barbarous legislation, when insisting on interminable tortures and considering annihilation as a penalty of little weight. Indeed, the doctrine of the destruction of the wicked possesses more deterring influence than the traditional doctrine can exert; while it is free from one drawback, and has a special advantage of its own: it represents a God justly severe but not merciless, and it appeals to the instinct of self-preservation, one of the most powerful, though not one of the noblest, impulses of human nature.

Objection XXVII. If the soul can be dissolved like the body, it must be material.

> The Bible teaches that certain souls shall be destroyed; but how that shall be, we are not told, any more than we are told how souls are born and formed.

Objection XXVIII. The progress made by this doctrine does not establish its truth.

> No; but it obliges us to examine the proofs on which it rests.

Objection XXIX. This doctrine diminishes the value of the merits of Jesus Christ and the work of redemption.

> We reply that this doctrine, far from detracting from the merits of Christ's work, adds to them. It is more specifically divine to give life eternal than merely to save from pain. If sin entailed everlasting torments, the atonement was not so much an act of grace as of equity; so that the love manifested in the sacrifice of the Redeemer would seem to lose something of its spontaneousness, and conse-

quently of its moral value. As to the fruits of the work of redemption, they consist in the preservation, to an innumerable multitude of human beings, of an existence which had been forfeited, and in the magnificent gift of incorruptibility and eternal bliss.

Objection XXX. The most powerful preachers have proclaimed eternal torments.

> Great preachers often make great mistakes. Besides, all is not false in the traditional doctrine which we are opposing. The afterlife of the sinner, future retribution, a place of misery. . .are elements of truth which have unfortunately been used in promoting error.

Objection XXXI. This doctrine is calculated to lesson our anxiety for the salvation of souls.

> On the contrary, it enkindles it, inasmuch as it sets forth with more clearness and certainty terrible punishment which threatens the guilty. When it calls upon the sinner, and startles him with the cry of "Fire! Fire!" it appeals to Scripture, as well as to logic and to a universal law.

Objections XXXII. The words of Jesus Christ are intended to inspire salutary terror.

> Professor Barlow: Basically he argue that the threat of eternal punishment can easily lead people to think that eventually they will get off, because no amount of private sin can justly render him liable to infinite punishment. And the voice of conscience within him, in spite of every theologian, loudly proclaims that the Judge at whose bar he is about to stand, is just. Feeling then, and rightly feeling, that the infinite sentence would be unjust, and being at the same time told by our popular theologians that he is sure of either eternal hell or heaven, it is easy to see how hope may spring up within him, and how he may bring himself to believe that, as God is surely just and hell eternal, and as bad as he may be, he does not deserve *eternal* punishment, he may be admitted to heaven after all.
>
> (I find this a very convincing argument that probably many people use: eternal punishment is against the love and mercy of God, therefore everyone will be saved. If U is on the rise, it is partially due to the impossibility of justifying hell.)

Objection XXXIII. "Hell cast into the lake of fire." (Rev xx. 14) Hell here is *Hades*, or the intermediate abode. *Eternal hell* is not destroyed.

In Revelation the Beast is cast into the lake of fire, then Hell and Death. Now the Beast, Hell and Death, are abstract or symbolic, being incapable of suffering. What can be the meaning of such creatures being cast into the fire, if not the total suppression of the rebellion, the baneful influence and the blasphemy which they typify: in short, the END of moral evil?

"The last enemy that shall be DESTROYED is death," says St. Paul. But death and hell destroyed then will commence the new and final state of the universe, and "God shall be all in all"; that is to say, in all who have survived unto that day.

Objection XXXV. Sin committed against an infinite Being deserves infinite punishment.

Were this objection well founded, we might reply that the sinner's punishment is infinite, inasmuch as it deprived him of immortality, which is infinite in duration.

Objection XXXVI. It is written, "For our God is a consuming fire." Let us fear to weaken the force of such a declaration.

This passage supports our theory. What God consumes ceases to exist; and herein lay the miracle of the burning bush, which burnt and was not consumed; while of the wicked it is written "the wrath of the Lord consumed them as stubble."[55]

(A reminder that this is the text Fudge chose for the title of his ground-breaking book *The Fire That Consumes*.)

Paul Tillich

Paul Tillich was one of the outstanding Protestant theologians of the twentieth century. He is a significant modern witness to the view of *natural mortality*. This statement is from his famed *Systematic Theology*:

"Estranged from the ultimate power of being, man is determined by his finitude. He is given over to his natural fate. He came from nothing, and he returns to nothing. He is under the domination of death and is driven by the anxiety of having to die. This, in fact, is the first answer to the question about the relation of sin and death. In conformity with biblical religion, it

---

55. Petavel, *Extinction*, 147–73.

asserts that *man is naturally mortal. Immortality as a natural quality of man is not a Christian doctrine,* though it is possibly a Platonic doctrine."[56]

John Macquarrie

John Macquarrie (1919-2007) was an Anglican theologian. Timothy Bradshaw, writing in the *Handbook of Anglican Theologians*, described Macquarrie as "unquestionably Anglicanism's most distinguished systematic theologian in the second half of the 20th century." His understanding of hell is in terms of annihilation. He says: "If heaven is fullness of being and the upper limit of human existence, Hell may be taken as loss of being and the lower limit. This utter limit of Hell would be annihilation, or at least the annihilation of the possibility for personal being. We utterly reject the idea of a Hell where God everlastingly punishes the wicked, without hope of deliverance."[57]

---

56. Quoted in Froom, *Conditionalist II*, 924.
57. Quoted by Kvanvig, *Destiny*, 43–44.

4

Philosophy 1

AS WE HAVE SEEN, one of the essential arguments of the conditionalists is that the teaching of the natural immorality of the soul is not in Scripture: it's a Platonic theory that eventually led to the doctrine of hell with its consequence of everlasting punishment. As good scholars they do not deny the use of philosophy in an attempt to understand Scripture, but they are loath to allow philosophy in any fundamental way to determine the scriptural meaning. They contend that this is precisely what has happened concerning the final states of people after death. Although philosophy as the "handmaid of theology" has always been strong in the Catholic tradition, Balthasar offers this caution:

" He [Balthasar] affirms philosophy's unique contributions to human understanding, which can and ought to be factored into the theological project, but these contributions always fall flat because they are disconnected from the dynamism (and humility) of a living relation to biblical revelation that authentic Christianity provides (and requires). Tragically, the attempts that come closest to the truth [Platonic?] are usually the most dangerous, because they are the most presumptuous (Icarus and his wings): precisely because they are so sure of success, they fail most fundamentally to grasp the humility of God who humbles himself in taking the form of man.[1]

No doubt, conditionalists would apply this caution to the insertion of Platonic teachings into the Scriptures.

---

1. Martin, *Hans Urs von Balthasar*, 119.

Philosophers of the Nineteenth Century

For the purposes of my *Guide,* a few philosophical pros and cons of the modern period will be sufficient. Petavel, in his classic *The Problem of Immortality,* has a chapter on philosophical approaches to CI in the latter part of the nineteenth century. I quote three of his authorities. They are probably unfamiliar to us but they were renown in his day.

Renouvier (1876)

> There is no doubt that the hypothetic notion of an indefinite preexistence of souls, in whatever form it may appear, as well as that of an unlimited duration of all souls, ought to be condemned; it is evident that souls appear at one moment and disappear at another. We have distinctly declared ourselves opposed to the idea of real being who on account of a pretended right inherent in their substance could demand for themselves an eternal existence.
>
> If therefore we speak of the soul as a substance, it is only in this relative sense: that in the world that is to be, which we are studying, it is a relatively stable centre of divergent and convergent actions; and by this we do not mean that it is an element not subject to conditions, which would thereby be assured of eternal duration. On the contrary, it has only a conditional position.
>
> It has its beginning when the creative power, which alone is unlimited by conditions, confers existence upon it; it comes to an end when that existence is taken from it. There is then nothing to prevent us from making the general assertion that souls are mortal; but it is at the same time possible that a perishable soul might yet not perish, and that being conformed to the ideal, it might enjoy a perpetual existence to which in itself it has no right. If in the development of spiritual life there is formed a personality of such value as to deserve an indefinite existence, we may well believe that such an existence would be maintained. If, on the contrary, there is nothing in the soul rendering it worthy of that individual permanence, the conclusion is inevitable that it is destined to perish.[2]

I find this philosophical explanation one of the most accurate as to the possibilities of the soul after death.

---

2. Petavel, *Problem,* 69–70.

M. Secretan (1815)

Evil must come to an end, the spirit of God must pervade all things. But how? The dead-lock in which we find ourselves between two solutions equally contrary to the needs of the conscience is the result of their common supposition of an essential immortality of the individual spirit. This doctrine, which the whole Church has accepted, and popular theism (known as spiritualism and natural religion) has carefully maintained, comes to us from Greek philosophy, and we are not absolutely obliged to receive it.

In fact, the difficulties involved in the doctrine of a pardon unaccompanied by repentance, and a constrained liberty [U], and in that of an eternity of evil [hell], will be avoided if we admit, with a school of thought now making itself heard, that impenitent sinners are to be destroyed, either in natural death or after further trials. Without here examining which of these three doctrines accords best with the texts to which they all appeal, it seems to us that the third escapes from the moral impossibilities against which the two others have been shattered, and they are perhaps not more ancient.

Moreover, the third is very naturally justified by analysis. Moral evil is in fact not simple deprivation of being, as it has been represented by a theology too abstract and too prompt in its conclusions, but evil is not without relation to non-existence; it is a movement of the being towards non-being; a tendency toward self-destruction. A created being, a derived being, wishes to place himself or keep himself away from the basis and source of his being; such is the common character of all forms of evil. By virtue of its definition, evil seems to tend towards its own extinction, its own annihilation. Thus the consideration of evil in itself leads us to the same conclusion as the study of the divine perfections, "The wages of sin is death." We therefore incline towards an immortality to be won.[3]

Ott (1888)

How, then, is to be avoided the antimony produced on the one hand by the necessary and definitive exclusion from the kingdom of heaven of the individuals who do not wish to become worthy

---

3. Ibid., 72–73.

and capable of entering it, and the perpetual sufferings supposed to result from that exclusion, and on the other hand the justice and goodness of God, who cannot doom even the greatest criminal to iniquitous punishment?

A good deal of attention has of late been paid in Protestant circles to an hypothesis which seems to solve this grave problem in a plausible manner, the hypothesis of conditional immortality. It is supposed that only those souls that have become worthy and capable of future life will enjoy the gift of immortality, and that the others will either come to an end with the body and be definitively annihilated, or else will not die until they have suffered the punishment of their misdeeds, but will all the same be annihilated after having paid their debt to divine justice.

Evidently these souls would not be able to bring any reproach against God. He gave them being, that is to say, a condition better than non-existence, and granted to them many passing enjoyments, as well as the promise of eternal felicity under certain conditions; they have absolutely refused submission to those conditions, and, doing evil, they have incurred the penalty of the law, and have borne sufferings not exceeding those which they themselves have caused. They die at last because they have not been willing to enter into the only combination in which it was possible for them to live. The justice and the goodness of God are thus equally satisfied, and the general plan of the world attains full realization. Unless all should be saved, and not one will, should be found to be perverse enough to be finally struck out of the book of life, this solution seems in fact to be the best answer to the difficulties of the question.[4]

William E. Hocking (1873-1966)

Hocking was an outstanding American philosopher of the twentieth century. His major area of expertise was the philosophy of religion. He gives a very imaginative view of the "immortability" of the person.

> In my own view, this is the case: survival of death is a possibility but not a necessity of destiny. We have begun this present existence without our prior consent.... If there were a soul in whom living had bred a genuine aversion, through conscious cultivation

---

4. Ibid., 74–76.

of a distaste for life—if there were such a soul—*I cannot think it doomed against its will to go on.*

Or, what is more imaginable, if one became determined to deal with this life as a unique and completed whole, coinciding with the career of the body, satisfied to define himself as the rational animal ending in nothing—I can hardly think survival a necessity for such a soul (though I suspect in most who profess this attitude subconscious countercurrents which may eventuate in an agreeable disappointment!) In any event, the quality of the human self, as I conceive it, is *not immortality but immortability, the conditional possibility of survival.*[5]

I don't know if Hocking was influenced by the conditionalists of his day, but his use of the word "immortability" is exactly the view of the conditionalists as regards one of the qualities of the nature of the soul.

Josef Pieper (1904-97)

Pieper was an acknowledged and popular Catholic Thomistic philosopher whose books continue to be widely read. In his short book *Death and Immortality* we turn especially to chapter 7 "Immortality—of What?" and chapter 8 "Indestructibility and Eternal Life." He attempts to give the proper Catholic understanding of "the immortality of the soul" based on St. Thomas. All Catholics may not agree with his position but, if I understand him correctly, conditionalists could accept his conclusions. It is not necessary for the purpose of this book to present Plato's views on immortality in any detail; but briefly, Pieper holds that

> Plato himself, however, is no Platonist. At any rate, in the late dialogue *Phaedrus,* when he launches on what seems a wholly fresh approach to the question of "in what sense a living being is termed mortal or immortal," he suddenly ceases to speak of the soul alone. "We think," he says "of a living being, spiritual and physical at once, but both, soul and body, united for all time." Plato himself, therefore, here concedes that it is a catachrestic [misuse], inadequate, use of language to call the soul "immortal." The established phrase "immortality of the soul" is misleading, inasmuch as, strictly speaking, only the man but not the soul can die or not die. Hence it would be better to speak of the indestructibility of the

---

5. Froom II, 925.

soul, or its imperishability—as the great teachers of Christendom in fact always do.[6]

What, then, is meant by the imperishability of the soul?

"That is perishable which possibly cannot be; that is imperishable, *incorruptibile*, which cannot possibly not be." Thus Thomas Aquinas in his commentary on Aristotle's *Metaphysics*. This, certainly, is a clear enough statement. But can the human soul really be called imperishable in such a sense? When we read in Spinoza's *Ethics* that "our mind is eternal," and when Goethe calls mind "a being of entirely indestructible nature," both are saying that the soul is imperishable. That by definition it is of such a nature that it cannot possibly not be. Nevertheless, it is quite clear that Thomas Aquinas would passionately reject any such mode of thinking and speaking."[7]

> One who considers the universe, as well as body-soul-man himself, as *creatura*, as having proceeded from the absolute, existence-determining will of the *Creator* and thus having received its being from this creative source—one who takes this view cannot possibly regard such existence, summoned forth from the void, as so inherently stable that there can be no thought of its reversion to nothingness. A creature is by definition incapable of maintaining itself in being by its own powers. To be sure, we likewise cannot take the step into nothingness by our own powers, no matter how much we may long to do so. In fact we are, in a sense that must be taken very literally, *incapable of not being*.
>
> Nevertheless, the fact remains: "Created beings could return to nothingness as they emerged from it— provided that pleased God." (Aquinas) For no one but the Creator could revoke and undo the act of creating. In view of the infinite debasement of Creation by historical man, that undoing might even be an act of *justice*—such a thought is not altogether alien to the Christian tradition.[8]

"The arguments, therefore, must show persuasively how the human soul is ultimately independent of the body and that on the basis of its being, or more precisely, on the basis of that aspect of its being which is perceptible to us, it cannot be included in the obvious dissolution of the body. Quite a few of the "classical" arguments do in fact advance this thesis. Their cue

---

6. Pieper, *Death*, 104–06.
7. Ibid., 107.
8. Ibid., 108–09.

words differ: "simplicity," "immateriality," "spirituality," "supertemporality," and so on."[9]

I call the reader's attention to two statements in Pieper's comments: first, that God can annihilate a person and this is "*not altogether alien to the Christian tradition*"; and second, are the last words quoted in the above text to be equated with "immortality"? The conditionalists would say no. And, when we come to Pieper's closing statements, I believe he also agrees. But first we turn to his preferred proof for the "spirituality" of the soul.

"As far as I am concerned, the most persuasive argument derives from the "*capacity for truth.*" It can be found in one form or another, incidentally, throughout the whole range of the tradition from Plato and Augustine to Thomas Aquinas. No one can perceive the force of this argument unless he "sees" that cognition of truth, however it makes use of the physical senses, is essentially a process independent of all material concatenations."[10]

This is a very traditional and common argument for the existence of a faculty able to produce concepts beyond the material. It can be found in numerous philosophies, and even in modern books on Intelligent Design.[11]

So Pieper gives his proof for the *spirituality* of the soul as the "capacity for truth." But is this the same as the "immortality of the soul" in his view? I may misunderstand him, but in his concluding statement he seems to say *no*. He makes a distinction between the *capacity for indestructibility and immortality (Resurrection)*. They are not the same. Here are his closing words:

> Western theology has in fact said: because ultimate bliss also means the actual perfection of the blessed, and because the soul does not possess the perfection of its nature, not even the godlikeness it is capable of achieving, except in conjunction with the body—therefore the indestructibility of the soul seems actually to require the coming Resurrection.
>
> This would signify, however, that the overcoming of death had not taken place yet, as indeed this same theology tells us. For there is also the Resurrection for the Judgment (John 5:29). Still less can that overcoming consist in the mere indestructibility of the soul. But since on the other hand what exists "by nature" (that is, "because of the Creation") is always primary and is the basis for every other divine gift that may be accorded to creatures, therefore, if the soul were not "by nature" indestructible there would simply

---

9. Ibid., 114.
10. Ibid., 114–15.
11. Varghese, *Wonder*, 163–68.

be nothing and no one able to receive the immortality which truly conquers death, that gift for which the sacred tradition of mankind has devised countless names: Perfect Joy, Eternal Life, Great Banquet, Crown, Wreath, Peace, Light, Salvation—and so forth.[12]

I believe conditionalists could agree with this final statement. Pieper makes a distinction between an indestructibility that the soul has by nature and the "immortality which truly conquers death." This indestructibility is what the conditionalists call the "immortableness" of the soul— it is capable, by nature, *to receive* the gift of the Resurrection, immortality. The soul naturally possesses something that makes it *capable of immortality.* (Hocking's "immortability.") Pieper calls this quality "simplicity," "immateriality," "spirituality," "supertemporality."

The Problem of Hell, A Philosophical Anthology[13]

This is a fairly recent (2010) and extremely important book for our topic. As the title indicates, Buenting's book is about hell. Hell, in my *Guide*, is not considered as an option. But, as I've mentioned several times, I am going to use the arguments for and against hell and apply them to annihilation. For example, eternal conscious punishment is against the goodness and love of God. Right: the love and goodness of God is also against annihilation. One cannot make an absolute decision about one's eternal fate. Right: one cannot make an eternal decision that would eventuate in annihilation; and so on. Especially will I apply descriptions of the state of those "in hell" to the state of people on their way *ad nihilum*, to annihilation. Arguments against hell will provide very good arguments against A. The authors of all these articles offer intricate philosophical explanations of their positions. Space only allows me to give some of their conclusions, and to convey to the reader that a great deal of intellectual effort is being expended in our times on all these questions about the *novissima*.

To begin, it may be helpful to present Buenting's survey of the topics and authors treated in this Anthology: 1) universalism, that ultimately everyone will be saved (Talbot); 2) why annihilation is not philosophically tenable (Brown and Walls); 3) people are in hell against their will (Barnard);

---

12. Pieper, *Death*, 117–18.

13. Buenting, *Problem*. If you are only buying a few books I would also recommend this one as far as philosophical studies on our topic is concerned. Be prepared for some heavy thinking!

4) people can escape hell when ready (Buckareff and Plug); 5) some people will continue to reject God forever (Davis); 6) since God knows beforehand who will be damned, God can never be completely free from moral culpability for damnation (Knight); 6) no person warrants infinite punishment (Kershnar); 7) an acceptable doctrine of hell must be based on Scripture, tradition, or a revelatory experience (Cain); 8) the *value of persons* must be the standard for deciding ultimate fate (Sickler) ; 9) there is "no non-problematic version of the doctrine of hell" (Kronen and Reitan). We will only look briefly at the articles most relevant to our topic, and apply theose insights to annihilation.

Thomas Talbott, "Grace, Character Formation, and Predestination unto Glory"

Talbott is one of the foremost universalists of our times. He argues from St. Paul that grace will ultimately win over the resistance of all creaturely wills.

> Paul taught that God's grace is utterly irresistible in this sense: However free its recipients might be to resist it in certain contexts, or even to resist it for a substantial period of time, they are not free to resist it forever. For the end, at least, is foreordained. In Paul's own words, 'For those God foreknew [that is, loved from the beginning] he also *predestined* to be conformed to the likeness of his Son" (Rom 8:29). But if some end, such as a person's eventually being conformed to the likeness of God's Son, is predestined or foreordained, then that end cannot be avoided forever. So it looks as if a good moral character is, according to Paul, wholly a work of God within and not something for which the morally virtuous are entitled to credit themselves. Once we have emerged as individual centers of consciousness and rational agents, God can nonetheless transform our perspective, and perhaps even instantaneously, in a perfectly rational way; he need only grant us a direct "face to face" encounter with himself, thereby providing compelling evidence for both his existence and the bliss of union with him. God always has a trump card to play, namely the revelation of his own being that guarantees from the outset his ultimate victory over sin and death.[14]

---

14. Talbott, "Grace," 25–26.

One of the main differences between the universalists and the conditionalists is whether or not people can make final decisions which eventuate in eternal separation from God. Talbott says no, they cannot.

In Near Death Experiences people often relate how they are *overwhelmed* by a loving Presence and *freely* give themselves to this totally accepting and non-threatening Being. These experiences can rightly be taken as an example of what Talbott is proposing as a "face to face encounter." However, it still doesn't follow that it is *never possible to resist this Presence;* and we do not, as a matter of fact, hear from *everyone's experience,* since only the few return.

Raymond J. VanArragon, "Is it Possible to Freely Reject God Forever?"

This argument between conditionalists and universalists as to whether or not a final free negative choice is possible is not a problem between conditionalists and infernalists (a label some use for those who believe in hell): both believe such a choice is possible. Conditionalists, however, believe the result of such a choice is not hell but God withdrawing existence. The arguments VanArragon presents for the possibility of rejecting God I apply to conditionalists who would thank him for his work! What follows is a brief summary of his main position. I paraphrase; the quotes are from his article.

Is it possible to freely reject God forever? This may mean an alienation from God but not necessarily a painful one. Rejecting God is acting in a way contrary to God's will. Such an action must be sufficiently rational, informed, and not causally determined by anything. It doesn't seem possible that a person can make a free choice where "forever" is part of the content since one can never know all the implications of such a choice. However (and here is an argument the conditionalists can use), VanArragon says it is possible for someone to make a choice which has the consequences of rendering her unable to freely accept God in the future. He gives the example of an addict taking that final responsible dose that puts her over the edge: she has some awareness that this will cause enslavement, and she makes such an act. We can do likewise on our journey to our final fate.

To freely reject God is to act in a way that goes against God's will where performance of that action is sufficiently rational, sufficiently informed, and not determined by God, nature, or desire. Moreover, given the broad way that we will understand the notion of rejecting God, freely doing so is possible for a person who is of a non-Christian religious persuasion, or is actively ignoring God, or does not even believe that God exists. It is sufficient that the agent has some sense of right and wrong, a sense that matches up at points with what God commands and forbids, and that at a point of matching up the agent freely does what she recognizes is wrong.[15]

VanArragon then presents his main considerations. "Now what would it be to freely reject God *forever*? There are two possibilities: first, to do so might involve making *one* critical choice (or a finite series of choices); and second, it might involve making an endless series of choices."[16]

I am not really concerned with his arguments about the second choice. That refers to the possibility of people "in hell" making such choices forever. I am concerned with his first possibility since it would apply as well to the conditionalist position: Is it possible for a person to make a decision at a certain time, or in a series of decisions, that determines one's final end?

VanArragon is not exactly in support of the conditionalists here:

> I grant that it is difficult to defend the possibility of the first kind of rejection, where only one free choice (or a finite series) is made. The main obstacle to the freedom of such a choice, as I see it, is ignorance. An appropriate degree of knowledge and awareness is a necessary condition for free choice; but it seems doubtful that anyone who chooses to close the door on God forever will have a sufficient grasp of what she is rejecting; and even more doubtful that she could appropriately comprehend the monumental character of her choice.
>
> Indeed, it seems likely that no human being can freely choose something where the consequences extend forever, where the "forever" is part of the content of the choice—simply because none of us can adequately grasp what that would mean. If so, then anyone who chooses something forever is not making a free choice, in so far as she lacks adequate knowledge of what she is choosing. The choice to reject God forever in the first way, then, seems non-free: such an agent could not have the requisite knowledge of which she is choosing. For that reason I shall leave this possibility aside."[17]

So it doesn't seem that VanArragon is helpful philosophically for conditionalists in this matter of being able to reject God forever. However, he adds something that conditionalists might agree with.

---

15. VanArragon, "*Possible*," 31.
16. Ibid., 32.
17. VanArragon, "*Possible*," 32.

It is worth noting, however, that even if it may not be possible for a person to make one free choice to reject God forever, it may be possible for her to freely make some choice which has the consequence of rendering her forever unable to freely accept God. For instance, a person may freely choose to perform some evil action; this may be the choice that finally solidifies her character for evil and prevents her from desiring what is good. Such a situation may be similar to that of a drug addict who crosses the threshold into uncontrollable addiction. By freely choosing to partake of the drug one more time, the addict enslaves herself to it.

Similarly, the person who essentially enslaves herself to sin—and even does so permanently—may not have chosen such enslavement—but she may nonetheless bear some blame for her predicament in virtue of the fact that she should have known that by liberally doing what was wrong she was courting catastrophe.[18]

Some of VanArragon's arguments of the possibility for a person to continue "sinning forever" can be applied to the conditionalist position.

Infernalists hold that people in "hell" are sinning forever. Is this possible? VanArragon says yes. Some object that this is not possible because eventually the person will realize the disastrous consequences of her choices and desist. VanArragon counters that we often choose what we know will be harmful for us. And not all sinful acts have obvious harmful consequences. Such objections do not necessarily stop people from choosing against God's will. In this life people continue on while acting against God's will. It could be the same after death: it could simply be a condition similar to this life.

Would God intervene to prevent a person from continually sinning and end up alienated from him forever? Some argue that God would not allow this. God would do whatever is necessary to remove ignorance to such resistance. VanArragon argues that God would certainly not in any way take away a person's freedom; he would respect that person's freedom. It is not essential that God intervene to prevent a person making a final choice. But God may have good reasons for respecting such a choice: the person might change the direction of her choice; her temporary enslavement could then be lifted; God could give some new experience that could effect a free change. But such interventions on God's part may not necessarily work.[19]

---

18. Ibid., 32–33.
19. Ibid., 33.

The freedom [caused by such interventions] may help to preserve the point of the person's continuing existence. And that could give God reason to do it, enabling the sinner to *freely* reject God forever rather than drift into eternity with her ability to do so completely extinguished. And here we have a way that God could actually facilitate a sinner's perpetual rejection of him—not a malicious way, but instead a way that enables a person to carry on a meaningful existence—by preserving the freedom and autonomy that could otherwise be eliminated by sin. *I have tried to demonstrate that it is possible to freely reject God forever.* (emphasis added) To reject God forever is to alienate oneself from God forever, and thus to defend this possibility is to defend the Christian doctrine of eternal hell.[20]

This article of VanArragon is the most convincing philosophical argument I've read for the *possibility* of a final decision against the Father's will. Moreover, he leaves the door open to use his argumentation for annihilation, for he doesn't define what hell is: "It has been no part of my aim to establish what hell is actually."[21] A conditionalist could use VanArragon's profound justification for the possibility of making a final fateful decision and theorize that the result is annihilation and not hell. "[People] may conclude that a mere defense of the possibility of freely rejecting God forever is the best we can do, and that much about the doctrine of hell is bound to remain a mystery to us."[22] Yes, "hell" is ultimately a mystery, but the theory of annihilation can be respected as one of the possible answers to this mystery.

Catholic Positions on a Final Decision

Ratzinger on the Hypothesis of a Final Decision

I interrupt my presentation of the authors in Buenting to insert this opinion of Ratzinger on the above question treated by VanArragon. Ratzinger, not unsurprisingly, comes down on the yes side of the possibility of a final rejection of the Father's will since he holds the traditional doctrine of hell. His comments occur in a section called "The Judgment" in his book *Eschatology, Death and Eternal Life*.

---

20. VanArragon, *Possible*, 42–43.
21. Ibid., 43.
22. Ibid.

> Christ inflicts pure perdition on no one. In himself he is sheer salvation. Anyone who is with him has entered the space of deliverance and salvation. Perdition is not imposed by him, but comes to be wherever a person distances himself from Christ. It comes about whenever someone remains enclosed within himself. Christ's word, the bearer of the offer of salvation, then lays bare the fact that the person who is lost has himself drawn the dividing line and separated himself from salvation. We can rightly conclude that in the final analysis man becomes his own judgment. Christ does not allot damnation. Instead, man sets limits to salvation.
>
> It is in this context that, by way of coda, we must reflect on the so-called "hypothesis of a final decision." L. Boros states: "In death, the first fully personal human act becomes possible. And so death is the ontologically privileged place of emergence into consciousness, of freedom, or meeting with God, and of a decision about eternal destiny."
>
> In all probability, the dominant motive behind the development of this thesis was the sense that the fragile, and often and in many ways shadowy freedom we know during earthly life, is too feeble and limited to support the weight of an everlasting and irreversible destiny. Is it not true that, for a judgment which is to hold throughout eternity, a different freedom would be required from that which we experience elsewhere?
>
> Admittedly, the traditional view thought overmuch in terms of one particular moment in time. The truth of a man that judgment renders definitive is that truth which has emerged as the fundamental orientation of his existence in all the pathways of his life. In terms of the sum total of decision out of which an entire life is constructed, this final direction may be, in the end, a fumbling after readiness for God, valid no matter what wrong turnings have been taken by and by.
>
> Or again, it may be a decision to reject God, reaching down into the deepest roots of the self. But this is something that only God can determine. He knows the shadows of our freedom better than we do ourselves. But he also knows of our divine call, and unlimited possibilities. Because he knows what human weakness is, he himself became salvation as truth, yet without stripping himself of the dignity that belongs to truth.[23]

The novelty of Boros' opinion had to do with the *time* of making a final decision: it does not occur in the time of our "shadowy freedom" but in a moment in our passing when "a different freedom would be required."

---

23. Ratzinger, *Eschatology*, 207–09.

However, both Ratzinger and Boros believe that a "decision to reject God eternally" is possible, whenever it may be made.

The Catechism of the Catholic Church

The Catechism's statement about mortal sin expresses the Church's belief in the possibility of an ultimate fatal decision:

"Mortal sin is a radical possibility of human freedom, as is love itself. It results in the loss of charity and the privation of sanctifying grace, that is, of the state of grace. If it is not redeemed by repentance and God's forgiveness, it causes exclusion from Christ's kingdom and the eternal death of hell, *for our freedom has the power to make choices for ever, with no turning back*. (emphasis added) However, although we can judge that an act is in itself a grave offense, we must entrust judgment of persons to the justice and mercy of God." (no. 1861)[24]

To return to the authors in Buenting's *The Problem of Hell*.

Claire Brown and Jerry Walls, "Annihilationism: A Philosophical Dead End?"

Walls is one of the foremost defenders of hell. As the title indicates, the authors set out to give philosophical arguments *against* annihilationism, the position that people who do not repent will, by the power of God, cease to exist. The authors believe that a critical philosophical approach to annihilationism has been lacking, and they seek to remedy that. They will contend that annihilation is philosophically unmotivated. (I presume this means it cannot be philosophically substantiated.) This article contains some penetrating arguments *against* annihilation. What follows are the views of the authors unless otherwise indicated by brackets. We begin with their outline of the arguments of the conditionalists.

The main positions of the conditionalists (another name for those who hold for annihilation) are: immortality is a condition dependant on repentance; non-existence is the natural consequence of persistent sinning (the corruption argument); annihilation is more in keeping with God's nature than hell; continued existence of sinners in hell is incompatible with Christ's final victory.

---

24. *Catechism of Catholic Church*, 456.

That impenitence leads to annihilation is not a traditional understanding and needs caution. Traditionally sinners lack a fullness of being but it doesn't mean that they lack their substantial form, or that their absolute existence will be lost. Evil and serious damage to our willing and intellectual faculties do not naturally or necessarily lead to non-existence. "The corruption argument thus faces serious problems. It works only if sin is capable of corrupting persons so much that their cognitive and volitional capacities become irreparably damaged to an extreme degree."[25]

My comment. Conditionalists would hold that it is possible to approach such an extreme degree, but it cannot "naturally" result in annihilation: only God can annihilate. There is no "natural deterioration" that leads to one's destruction, but it can lead to an irreparably damaged state. Any final destruction and annihilation is always an *act of God*: only God who has created can remove from existence. The person always continues in existence, however much she abuses her powers. But God can decide, at a certain point, that the person is confirmed in resistance "to an extreme degree," and there is no point in sustaining her existence. But only God can withdraw existence: there is no "natural process" that leads to annihilation.

However, the descriptions of the person on the way to annihilation, which the authors deny is possible, can be used by the conditionalists to describe people who have arrived at the point when God decides annihilation is appropriate. For example: "Sin is capable of completely and irreparably destroying a creature's capacity to know particular sorts of truths. On such a view, sin is capable not only of leading us to false beliefs, of making us bad thinkers, or even of damaging our cognitive abilities to such an extent that we cannot know God or good without grace; sin must also be capable of damaging us so severely that we lose our epistemic capacities for the relevant knowledge."[26]

Conditionalists would say that this can also describe a person's extreme deterioration when God decides that a point of no return has been reached and there is no hope for the person's change of attitude. Universalists would argue that there is never such a state of hopelessness for the person: God's grace will eventually overcome all resistance. This is, to repeat again, the major point of disagreement: conditionalists say that such a final irremediable act of a person *is possible*. Then the result is not eternal punishment but annihilation. This is the major dividing line between the two positions. Of

---

25. Brown and Walls, "Annihilationism," 53.
26. Ibid., 52.

course, both answers are philosophical speculations. Conditionalists insist that the answer must come from revelation, and that this is the scriptural testimony.

The authors continue with the question of whether annihilation is conformable with God's moral perfections. (They specifically "bracket" comparing annihilation with U as regards compatibility with God's love. There would be no contest here: surely to ultimately save everyone would be preferable to annihilating anyone.)

According to the annihilationists, annihilation seems more in keeping with God's goodness since no one suffers eternally as in "hell." Such a fate is unjust. The annihilationist position faces the same problem: it also is everlasting punishment in that it lasts forever. Is this also not an infinite punishment? In this discussion there are also milder views of hell being proposed. Would these not be more acceptable than annihilation? The authors quote a syllogism of Kvanvig in his book also entitled *The Problem of Evil*, which they call "the rational suicide argument for annihilation."[27] They will use this for one of their arguments against A. I present only three of the points.

K1. Some of the wicked will attempt post-mortem suicide.

K5. God would never attempt to interfere with someone attempting post-mortem suicide if that person were acting rationally.

K7. If God does not interfere with a person's attempted post-mortem suicide, that person will be annihilated.[28]

> Many of the unsaved may well wish to be annihilated, but if they have no recourse to methods that are perceived to result in non-existence, they will be unlikely to attempt to annihilate themselves. But God's allowing people to reject his love by no means commits him to satisfying their every preference, including whims for their own non-existence.
>
> It is another matter altogether to think he should give his creatures the prerogative to decide whether they shall be related to him at all. God settled that matter when he chose to create us in his image. God did not need our permission. . .to create us, and he does not need our permission to sustain us in existence. The 'freedom' to decide whether or not we exist is simply not a

---

27. Ibid., 57.
28. Ibid., 53.

freedom that we have any good reason for believing God ever does or will offer anyone.[29]

According to the Hellenists, God gives us the freedom to so choose. Therefore, he can give us the freedom to desire to cease to exist.

Another argument often used by the conditionalists is that an eternal hell is a kind of metaphysical dualism, a "kingdom" of resistance where God's reign is eternally not complete. On the other hand, if every one of the unrepentant is annihilated then no one will eternally remain in rebellion against God. (This is a frequent argument of the universalists as well.)

> First, we should note that a person can rebel against God while recognizing God's authority. Such a person will recognize divine authority but resent it. To put the point somewhat differently, if the rebellious in hell continually resent God and reject his love, it does not follow that they have defeated either God or his love: they have simply rejected his love in a way that allows God to demonstrate his unending mercy in continuing to offer love to them.
>
> If the rebellion of the lost does challenge God's supremacy, it is a problem that annihilation does not solve. How is God's reign any less supreme than it would be if the rebellious were to cease to rebel only by ceasing to exist? When one thinks that in order to reign supreme God must annihilate some of his creatures, one's conception of supremacy has gone terribly wrong. Annihilation is thus philosophically unmotivated and unless powerful new arguments emerge, or annihilationists can convincingly show that the majority report in biblical interpretation has been misguided, their position is at a dead end.[30]

The conditionalists believe that they have shown that the "biblical majority report has been misguided." They rest their case ultimately on scriptural arguments. I don't think they are much bothered if their position is "philosophically unmotivated"!

Also, people in hell or being annihilated may or may not give any challenge to God's supremacy, but A does remove the example and presence of people who have refused the Father's will. Unrepentant people in "hell" become a permanent "proof" of this possibility of resistance. It would seem more desirable to remove examples of resistance than to have them

---

29. Ibid., 58–59.
30. Ibid., 62.

eternally remain for all to be aware of and be able to still consider resistance *as a possibility for themselves.*

Andrei A. Buckareff and Allen Plug, "Value, Finality, and Frustration: Problems for Escapism"

This article supports U as one of the possibilities. Their thesis has two components: "1) hell exists and might be populated for eternity; and 2) if there are any denizens of hell, then at any time they have the ability to accept God's grace and leave hell and enter heaven."[31] The authors go into detailed arguments about first-order desires and second-order desires. St. Paul's statement in Rom 7:15 is an expression of this two-tiered human fix: "For I do not do what I want, but I do what I hate." People in hell are subject to this condition, but eventually they will be able to choose to do the right thing— desire union with God. This understanding of hell is provided by God out of love.[32]

One obvious objection to this "escapist theory" of hell is that it is not a final condition: traditionally hell is a place you cannot leave. The escapist answer to this is that some people may decide not to accept the grace of conversion and remain in hell forever. God will foreknow who these are and will decide on a day of no return, a day of judgement. So there will be finality for some. "That foreknowledge then allows God to determine the timing of the final event—be it the last day or the final judgment."[33]

What about the objection of U that holds that eventually everyone will be saved? God's ultimate purpose will be frustrated if some choose to remain in hell. The authors' response centers around the issue of a person's freedom: the universalists hold that eventually God will remove all obstacles to a free choice.

> But it is not obvious that such a change can be effected without actually doing violence to the character and will of the agent. Moreover, it assumes that persons would still choose rationally once the change has been effected. But the scriptural data is opaque enough for us to be comfortable in asserting that we cannot be confident about whether or not all persons will be reconciled with God.

31. Buchareff and Plug, "Value," 77.
32. Ibid., 80.
33. Ibid., 88.

Escapism has the resources built into it to satisfy the universalist so long as the universalist is not committed to a predestinarian soteriology. We claimed that a strength of escapism is that universal reconciliation without divine coercion is not merely a logical possibility but may be a likely state of affairs in the eschaton.[34]

I will try to relate this view to A.

Since hell is not an option for conditionalists, I apply what the authors say about people who are "in hell" to those who are still on the way to some final decision. They will only be "in hell" when God foresees that they will not repent. All those "on the way" who remain adamant, whom God foreknows will not accept the grace of repentance, will not remain in hell, since they are not there yet, but will be annihilated. To repeat: I am using Griffiths' position that there are only two *novissima*, annihilation and heaven. The authors of this article allow for the probability of the existence of hell, U, or A! The attractiveness of this theory, then, is that it is open to all of the above, and, who knows, there may be other possibilities!

Stephen Davis, "Hell, Wrath, and the Grace of God"

Davis believes in the existence of hell, its eternity, and that some people can make the final choice leading to this state. God's wrath, understood as God's opposition to human disobedience, is also our *hope*: it is a facet of God's just and holy nature and an eternal necessity. It keeps us from moral relativism. Grace is God treating us better than we deserve. We need to affirm both grace and wrath when thinking about God. These two constitute the moral equilibrium of the world.[35]

Davis agrees with the common modern theological opinion that people *choose* to be in hell. He believes that such a decision is possible forever, and that allowing such choices is consistent with the love of God.

Traditionally, Protestants did not hold to any kind of post-mortem conversion. Davis cites Christ's descent into Hades as an example of such a change. He also quotes Clement of Alexandria in favor of such a post-mortem possibility: "I think it is demonstrated that God being good, and the Lord powerful, he saves with a righteousness and equality which extend to all that turn to Him, whether here or elsewhere. For it is not here alone that the active power of God is beforehand, but it is everywhere and always at

---

34. Ibid., 89–90.
35. Davis, "Hell," 92.

work."[36] Davis accepts this possibility that Christ can save people wherever they are. "This is why I suggest, or perhaps hope, that even in hell people can be rescued. Everyone must have an opportunity to respond positively to God."[37]

Davis then discusses two objections raised by Kvanvig. First, if one opportunity of conversion is possible in hell, then why not many, or even an infinite number? Thus the finality of hell is abolished. Davis accepts this possibility.

Kvanvig's second objection is that post-mortem conversion sounds like a kind of reincarnational theory, akin to an endless cycle of rebirths. Davis outlines the differences between Christian and far-Eastern theories of endless cycles. In the Christian view there are no new lives, no new bodies. It is not guaranteed that there are endless choices: perhaps only one final choice for each person. It is not a matter of karma (growth in better knowledge for one's choice). The Christian theory is based not on knowledge but on *guilt*: people must accept *forgiveness* from God.

Davis concludes with brief comments on A and U. The former is not scriptural; and he doubts that the wicked would prefer annihilation to his view of hell.

As far as U is concerned, he holds that some people will never repent and turn to God. He ends with a humble comment expressed by others writing on these topics: "I do not think we know much about the future life."[38]

In relating Davis's comments to annihilation I would simply say, again, that if people can still make choices of conversion they are not yet in hell as traditionally understood, but *on the way*. And we can't really know if they are given a conscious choice between an eternal hell and annihilation. The final *novissimum* for the unrepentant is not a choice they make but a decision of God as to how to treat such a person. It's possible, of course, that God could make known to them that they will be annihilated if they continue their refusal of grace. I think to be given this knowledge is in keeping with human responsibility: persons would know the consequences of their refusals. In the conditionalist view, hell is not an option as it doesn't exist as a possibility.

36. Ibid., 99.
37. Ibid., 100.
38. Davis, "*Hell*," 101–2.

Stephen Kershnar, "Hell and Punishment"

This is a very important article for my purposes since Kershnar presents deep philosophical arguments *against* eternal punishment. He will argue that his conclusions also hold good for A. Although conditionalists may not agree with his philosophical arguments against annihilation, his views on these questions adds a significant contribution to the discussion to which conditionalists need to respond. His arguments.

It is not possible for a person to go on suffering indefinitely and reach, what he calls, a zero level of well-being. In other words, suffering cannot approach a limit. This is the traditional understanding of hell. Punishment for an action cannot exceed justice. "Justice does not permit God to impose an infinite punishment on some human beings. If God sets up a system where persons suffer greatly for refusing to accept him in their lives, then he punishes them."[39]

In a passage called the "Beneficent-Character Principle" the author says—voicing the views of an objector—that

> if someone [here, God] could provide a benefit to another at no cost to anyone. . .then refusal to do so reflects a defect in beneficence."[40] However, in accord with beneficence, God would then provide a life that is as good as possible, or at least one that does not involve negative infinite well-being. If this is not possible, then a beneficent being like God would annihilate someone rather than consign him to hell. If a person's suffering would in itself make the world a better place, the beneficent thing for God to do would be to annihilate him rather than send him to hell. A different objector might claim allowing people who do not warrant heaven to go there would impose a cost on God. Hence, a beneficent being would again opt for annihilation.[41]

Then follow his arguments *against* annihilation. Even though conditionalists would disagree, the author has provided in his article arguments *for* hell that conditionalists could accept with gratitude and apply them to annihilation!

> Consider annihilation. This occurs when, after earthly existence, God causes some human beings to cease to exist. This conflicts

---

39. Kershnar, "Hell," 119–20.
40. Ibid.,121.
41. Ibid., 121.

with the *Infinite Negative Well-Being Thesis* (hell results in a person having an infinitely negative amount of well-being). Annihilation is just only if God has a right to punish human beings and, as argued above, he does not. In addition, an individual suffers an infinite loss when he is annihilated rather than sent to heaven. If an infinite punishment of a human being is unjust, and for the reason above I think it is, then such a punishment is unjust.

A proponent of annihilation might object that it [annihilation] is a natural end to human existence, except when God intervenes to ensure that someone lives on in heaven. The idea, then, is that God would not wrong anyone because no one has a claim against him that she be kept alive for eternity. The real problem with this account is that it conflicts with the *Beneficent-Character Principle*, that is, the refusal to benefit someone when it has no cost to the benefactor reflects a defective character, in particular a lack of beneficence.[42]

As frequently mentioned throughout this *Guide*, conditionalists would agree that annihilation is our end unless one turns to God and receives the *gift of immortality*. But only God can effect annihilation: it is not a "natural" progression leading to zero. The author's *Beneficent-Character Principle* is simply his own philosophical theory which admits of refutation.

James Cain, "Why I Am Unconvinced by Arguments against the Existence of Hell"

Cain: endless suffering seems to violate justice. "But even here I do not think that it would be an obvious violation of justice. If the suffering resulted from natural punishments [that is, the consequences of our choices], or it arose as a natural reaction to one's awareness of lose, then even suffering of infinite duration might not be unfair if it was not wrong to give such a being immortal life of infinite duration."[43]

A fair amount of the author's argument concerns the *consciousness* of such eternal sufferings. "If there is an afterlife, for all we know there may be modes of consciousness there that are quite different from the way in which we now experience things."[44] Here is one example of his approach: "Consider the possibility that the afterlife might be experienced by some as

---

42. Kershnar, "Hell," 130–31.
43. Cain, "Unconvinced," 139.
44. Ibid., 140.

having a quality somewhat like a moment in which we do not feel a flow of perceptions. If one were experiencing suffering, then over the course of one's afterlife one would experience infinite suffering if the afterlife were endless. Perhaps for some, hell may be a sempiternal, finitely experienced moment of loss that stands in a simultaneity relation with the infinite progression of time."[45] Basically, with a change of consciousness, the author contends that the suffering of hell may be reduced: "There might even be a richness and some goodness for (some of) those in hell that is lacking in this life."[46] Thus the finite nature of suffering makes God's participation in this fate not so terrible.

And what about the problem of relating the permanent separation from God with God's love? The author does not see that the NT provides any strong arguments against hell, nor for U. "The doctrine of hell seems imbedded in the NT, where God's plan appears to include the existence of hell."[47]

This is also a strong argument for annihilation: it argues for a possible fatal outcome for the unrepentant, and that this is grounded in the NT.

---

45. Ibid., 140–41.
46. Ibid., 142.
47. Ibid., 144.

5

Philosophy 2

Jonathan L. Kvanvig and The Problem of Hell

I FOUND KVANVIG'S BOOK on hell very profound. Basically it is an argument *against the traditional view of hell,* or what he calls the "strong view of hell." However, he ultimately attempts to come up with his own theory of hell that avoids the defects of the strong view. Prior to this conclusion he considers several alternatives to the strong view, and one of them is A. I am mostly concerned with his refutation of A. Some of his insights about his "solution" to the problem of hell will also be relevant. The quotations are his; I will mostly paraphrase his comments.

Annihilationism denies that anyone is in hell. "Hell"(H) is another word for annihilation: God literally annihilates people. The problems with A are the same as those with his strong view of hell. Kvanvig is against any penal theory of hell, that is, hell as a punishment. But annihilation simply substitutes "metaphysical capital punishment for metaphysical life imprisonment [H]."[1] The author believes his theory is more merciful than A; his criticisms about A are as follows.

> According to this latter view God need not do anything in order for a person to fail to exist in the afterlife, for no person is intrinsically immortal. Instead, the realm of God's activity is to be found among those in heaven. God makes some persons immortal by intervening in the course of things, which is toward nonexistence. So even though holding that God intervenes to destroy some individuals would be problematic, holding that he merely fails to intervene in order to preserve in existence certain individuals is not problematic.
>
> Just like the significant moral difference in the human realm, between killing and letting die, there is a significant moral

---

1. Kvanvig, *Problem,* 68.

difference between the annihilationist view when it construes annihilation as requiring the active intervention of God to destroy life, and the annihilationistic view when it claims only that God fails to interve,ne so as to preserve life. The first view might be more appropriately thought of as annihilation by way of commission, whereas the second is better put in terms of annihilation by way of omission.[2]

This observation by Kvanvig is at the heart of one of his refutations. However, it's a distinction I believe conditionalists would not have any difficulty in accepting. It does not really affect their theory because one way or another, annihilation happens. Kvanvig's view of hell is that it must be the result of a choice by the person, and not a punishment imposed by God. This is why I preferred the word *non-survival* (above, chapter 1) which puts the emphasis on the person's choice and thus results in God's acceding to that choice. In this sense both kinds of annihilation outlined by Kvanvig are acceptable: by acceding to a person's desire not to do the Father's will, both God's *intervention* to bring that life to an end and his *failure to intervene* to keep a person in existence are the same act.

As I have often mentioned, one of the major questions in eschatology is whether or not it is possible to make a final decision against God. The universalists say no, and therefore everyone will be saved. If I understand him correctly, Kvanvig also will eventually say no, but the result is not U, which he rejects, but *some other form of hell*. Other philosophers would argue that *philosophically* the possibility of such a decision can be demonstrated (Talbott); but both opinions are speculative and arguable.

Kvanvig comes up with his "rationality principle": "If the most significant goods for that person (i.e., those goods judged to be essential for a continued life to be worthwhile) *are rationally thought to be unachievable,* that person should be free to choose nonexistence."[3] "A person could still rationally (although depravedly) believe that nonexistence is preferable to dependence on God."[4]

"Conceived in the starkest terms, the alternative to presence in heaven is nothingness. To choose to be dependent on God is to choose a path that results in presence in heaven, and to choose independence from God is not logically possible. Furthermore, granting such a choice can be justified, so

---

2. Ibid., 68–70.
3. Ibid., 142.
4. Ibid., 144.

there is reason to reject the exile doctrine [hell] because it depends on the view that the value of existence always overrides the important of freedom."[5]

"One might object here that those who choose against heaven need not be wishing for ontological independence from God, but are rather choosing only against submission to the will of God. Such people may not care one whit whether they are ontologically dependent on God as long as they do not have to obey him. Generally people rebel only against submission to God and not to ontological dependence on him."[6]

Conditionalists welcome these arguments, and can use them as part of their philosophy of CD. However, while Kvanvig is perceptive in offering these arguments, they are not conclusive even for him.

"These conclusions, however, do not imply the annihilationist doctrine. We have concluded that the teleological character of hell is properly described in terms of annihilation, but we cannot infer from this claim, as the annihilationists doctrine of hell does, that the objective, substantial character of hell—that is, its mechanical character—is annihilation."[7]

What is the teleological view?

"The teleological view is that there is no independence from God. But it takes *confusion* (emphasis added) to see things teleologically in terms other than either God or nothing."[8] "There is no guarantee that such confusion can be eliminated. Also, there remains the question of what God is to do with them."[9] "The teleological account of hell just presented does not require that God grant all wishes for eternal separation from himself."[10]

Another of Kvanvig's arguments against A is as follows.

"Omissions are easier to justify than commissions. So even if omissions in cases of rational suicide are justified, commissions in the afterlife by God are not, and hence annihilation is not a possibility."[11]

"Continued existence is the result of God's commissions, not his omissions. Hence, if certain omissions are justified in the case of rational suicide,

---

5. Ibid., 146.
6. Ibid., 146–47.
7. Ibid., 147.
8. Ibid., 148.
9. Ibid.
10. Ibid., 149.
11. Ibid., 149–50.

the analogous omission in the afterlife situation has as its immediate and direct consequence annihilation."[12]

At the end of Kvanvig's position on hell he writes: "So the doctrine of hell itself holds no promise that some persons will exist in hell. In addition, although it is possible for persons to have hell as a place of residence or state of existence, it is also possible that those consigned to hell undergo a complete and total eradication of being."[13] So, in the end, Kvanvig allows for the possibility of annihilation—"a total eradication of being."

Kvanvig on "Losing Your Soul"

Eight years later in his book *Destiny and Deliberation* Kvanvig returns again to the subject of annihilation. The annihilationist position (we can equate it here with Kvanvig's "losing your soul theorists") is that one may arrive at a point of rejecting God, and then God accedes to one's wish and removes his sustaining power of existence. Arguments are bandied back and forth on whether it is possible for the person to arrive at such a state; also, descriptions are given about what this journey psychologically would look like. In a fascinating section entitled "On the Idea of Losing One's Soul" Kvanvig uses the Lord's expression about losing one's soul (Matt 16:26) to philosophize about these questions. He will conclude that philosophically it is *not possible* for a person to come to such a final decision. I paraphrase; quotes are from the author.

The question is whether one can come to a final decision about one's end and no further choice is possible. "The loss of soul theory maintains that, through a series of choices, one can get oneself in a position where one no longer has choices, where all options but one is impossible."[14] "The idea of losing one's soul is a special case of the idea of lost abilities, and the relevant lost ability in the present context is the ability to *choose*. To have lost one's soul is to have lost the ability to choose in favor of God and against whatever focus on self results in the ultimate disaster of losing out on the greatest good of loving God and enjoying him forever."[15]

Kvanvig makes the distinction between what is psychologically impossible and what is *causally* impossible. Psychologically "the process of

---

12. Ibid., 150.
13. Ibid., 159.
14. Kvanvig, *Destiny*, 29.
15. Ibid., 34.

character formation is capable of producing ossification of such hardness as to preclude, perhaps, any possibility of acting out-of-character, but the possibility in question here is psychological possibility. We are familiar with the pronounced effects on behavior by various techniques of intervention, including pharmacological and even shock treatments, to say nothing of natural catastrophes such as the result of a stroke."[16] He is saying that philosophically you can't *prove* that there won't be some other factor that could *cause* a change of decision in the person.

> The most entrenched behavior patterns are casually open to revision even if not psychologically open to such revision. The story told by lost soul theorists is thus weak. It needs a defense of the claim that one's character can be so fixed that it becomes causally impossible to act out of character. The relevant kind of possibility needs to be causal impossibility, and lost soul theorists have provided no clue whatsoever as to how to get from psychological to casual impossibility. I conclude, then, that the inferences needed by lost soul theorists do not sustain the conclusion that losing one's soul is possible or that this possibility implies the loss of freedom central to the lost soul explanation of the finality of Hell.[17]

Kvanvig himself offers this reflection about the meaning of losing one's soul that he rejects but that conditionalists would welcome and say is possible.

> Loss of soul theorists claim that what is true of external physical reality is also true of the internal psychological realm. The process of character formation can make it easier to desire the good and the right, but it can also make it easier to resist. As the process continues. . .the end point toward which the process is headed is one where the patterns of desire and preference have become hardened to the point that any desiring or preferring is impossible.
>
> The loss of soul theory results from applying this general idea to the afterlife itself. Regarding the greatest good possible for human beings, the experience of Heaven, we may conceive of the situation in which a hardening of desire and preference has occurred to such an extent that the choice of Heaven is no longer possible. To be in such a position is to have lost one's soul. In that situation, there is nothing one can do or choose to decide or intend, including no sequence of choices that would make possible

---

16. Ibid., 39.
17. Ibid., 39–40.

> the experience of Heaven. That option, because of what one has become, is foreclosed forever. One has lost one's soul, and in losing one's soul one has become a person for whom Hell is eternal and the final Judgment final in terms of something persons do to themselves.[18]

To repeat, Kvanvig says this is a philosophical proof of the possibility of making a final decision from a psychological point of view, but not casually. Conditionalists might reply that it's impossible to give a philosophical proof for possible causal factors to change one's behavior, since such casual factors *could be many*. They would say, I believe, that the psychological proof—minus this casual factor— is sufficient: they would welcome it to support their position.

Kvanvig: Was C.S. Lewis an Annihilationist?

Kvanvig first quotes Lewis's comments about the final stage of someone in hell: "What is cast (or casts itself) into hell is not a man: it is "remains. To be a complete man means to have the passions obedient to the will and the will offered to God: to *have been a man*—to be an ex-man or "damned ghost"—would presumably mean to consist of a will utterly centered in its self and passions utterly uncontrolled by the will."[19]

> These last remarks. . . raise an insoluble difficulty for Lewis. This problem concerns Lewis's reasons for rejecting the annihilationistic conception of hell. *Much of what he says suggests the annihilation view* (emphasis added), for he holds that what is in hell are the "remains" of a person. Yet, he believes that annihilation is not possible, for he says,
>
> "Destruction, we should naturally assume, means the unmaking, or cessation, of the destroyed. And people often talk as if the "annihilation" of a soul were intrinsically possible. In all our experience, however, the destruction of one thing means the emergence of something else. Burn a log, and you have gasses, heat and ash. To *have been* a log means now being those there things. If a soul can be destroyed, must there not be a state of *having been* a human soul? And is not that, perhaps, the state which is equally well described as torment, destruction, and privation?"

---

18. Ibid., 31
19. Kvanvig, *Problem*, 121.

Lewis's argument here is that true annihilation of anything cannot really occur. There is always something that has the property of having been what it formerly was, and hence the destruction of the soul cannot amount to literal annihilation. If the soul were literally annihilated, there would be nothing that has the property of having been a soul. Hence hell must be a domain of "remains" of persons, rather than a description of the nonexistence of the damned.

This argument, however, is deeply flawed. For one thing, it is incompatible with the one version of the Christian doctrine of *creatio ex nihilo*, the doctrine according to which God created the universe literally out of nothing. Lewis claims that every change is the change of something into something else, for he claims that there is always the property of having been what it formerly was. Yet, if we suppose a first moment of time at which God created all that existed at that time out of nothing, there is no such property. The initial state of the universe could not have been, consistent with the doctrine of *creatio ex nihilo*, the creation of something that has the property of having been something else at a previous time.

The mistake Lewis makes is that of confusing what can occur according to scientific law...with what can occur in the broader sense of logical or metaphysical possibility. According to the tradition of theism, God is omnipotent, and one of the implications of this doctrine is that God has the power to destroy the entire created order, leaving absolutely nothing in its place, just as he had the power to call what there is into existence out of nothing.

Not only is Lewis's argument against the annihilation view inadequate but also his response to one objection *comes exceedingly close to implying the annihilation view.* (emphasis added) The objection concerns how the blessed in heaven can be truly blessed while some are suffering in hell, and in response Lewis says,

"But I notice that Our Lord, while stressing the terror of hell with unsparing severity, usually emphasises the idea not of duration but of *finality*. Consignment to the destroying fire is usually treated as the end of the story—not as the beginning of a new story. We know much more about heaven than hell, for heaven is the home of humanity and therefore contains all that is implied in a glorified human life: but hell was not made for men. It is in no sense *parallel* to heaven: It is "the darkness outside," the outer rim where being fades away into nonentity."

Yet, if hell does not involve "duration," if it is "in no sense *parallel* to heaven," but instead is "the outer rim where being fades away into nonentity," the most natural view of hell to hold is that it is a metaphorical description of what becomes of a person when God annihilates. Lewis, however, balks at this conclusion. Nonetheless, his language is strongly suggestive of that view, and it is not clear how to reinterpret his language so that the annihilation view can be avoided.[20]

Kvanvig, then, holds that Lewis's position can lead to annihilationism.

John Kronen and Eric Reitan, "Species of Hell"

This is an article (2010) that antedates the authors' later very profound book, *God's Final Victory* (2011) that purports to be their philosophical justification for U. (I referred to their book quite extensively in my *Guide to Universalism*.) In this earlier article they offer arguments that U is more merciful than A. This is manifestly true if one believes in U where there is no final suffering at all. But we are interested in their reasoning which they contend *disproves* A.

In annihilation, as an act of mercy, God puts people out of their misery forever. The authors argue, as universalists, that God can eventually save everyone without violating their freedom. If this is possible, annihilation is not necessary. They offer three objections to the possibility of annihilation.

> Perhaps the annihilationist thinks that God might annihilate creatures who *would* eventually be saved were he to sustain them in being—but why would God make such a choice? It is no act of mercy to deprive a creature of *eternal joy in union with God* for the sake of avoiding merely finite suffering brought on by temporally finite choices.
>
> Perhaps God annihilates some creatures as retributive punishment for sin. If annihilation is motivated by the demands of retributive justice, then what would motive annihilation if these demands have been met on the cross? And if retributive justice demands something less severe than eternal damnation—such as annihilation—would it not follow that the demands of justice do not require an infinite punishment for sin? Rather than annihilating the unregenerate, He could impose a different penalty that enabled them to experience salvation once the penalty that enabled them to experience salvation was paid.

---

20. Ibid., 121–23.

Perhaps, however, the argument is that annihilation is actually more *serious* than eternal damnation, because non-being is objectively worse than existence in a state of even the most total torment. The demands of justice can be met through the creature's annihilation, thereby removing the need for a vicarious Atonement. Does it follow that God would choose the option which expresses His justice but *not* His love?[21]

Freedom

Freedom is one of the major issues in our whole discussion. The authors of *God's Final Victory* state: "In recent centuries, arguably the most significant theological development concerning DH [the Doctrine of Hell] has been a shift away from defending it in terms of God's justice and towards defending it in terms of God's respect for creaturely freedom—God either cannot or will not (for moral reasons) override creaturely freedom on this matter."[22] The arguments for universalism, on the other hand, hold that God can "override" human freedom while still respecting it. But God cannot do this, say the conditionalists. Therefore, not everyone will be saved; that is, there is no *guarantee* that everyone will be saved. The arguments hellenists (I prefer hellenists to infernalists) present for this creaturely freedom I will "recycle" in favor of A.

Universalists' first argument is that God can give an efficacious grace to everyone understood as a grace that converts people without violating their freedom; and it is not morally wrong for God to do this. Using intricate arguments from Aquinas and Talbott, the authors conclude that "God doing this [granting efficacious grace] certainly is *metaphysically* possible, and hence within God's power; and if (as Aquinas maintained) free acts are not random but motivated, it follows that any rational creature presented with the vision of God will freely but inevitable respond affirmatively to the promise of loving union."[23]

However, critics might say that because of a person's bad habits she or he may not be able to "see" God and thus be open to conversion. No, a free act is still possible: "Even if we can decide to block the vision of God by, as it were, deliberately averting our gaze, the notion of the creature as ordered

---

21. Kronen and Reitan, "Species," 179–80.
22. Kronen and Reitan, *Victory*, 127.
23. Ibid., 136.

to God, coupled with God's infinite causal power, seems to entail that it is within God's power to override such resistance." The authors admit that their arguments may not be convincing. Can we ever see God completely? Maybe not. But "what is essential is that the creature be able to experience the divine in a manner suitable to the creature's nature and sufficient to produce an unambiguous appreciation of the reality of God."[24] But isn't the granting of such a grace immoral?

One argument of Aquinas was that God can reveal to the unregenerate that he is their *summum bonum*, and that he can eliminate any affective states that prevent their acceptance of this truth. On the other hand, he held that it is still possible to freely reject God. But the authors of *Victory*, following Talbott, hold that "if efficacious grace involves establishing the conditions for free choice, then, a fortiori, it cannot override free choice."[25]

Walls concedes that if the unrepentant choose to resist grace they are not free. But—and here is the supreme difference about freedom for our purposes: "What Walls rejects is the claim that God could therefore save the damned without overriding their freedom. In brief, Walls looks in turn at both ignorance/deception and bondage to desire and argues that both states could be freely chosen by the damned. Walls thinks their ignorance might be *wilful*, resulting from freely chosen self-deception. We can imagine that someone freely chooses to become a slave to sinful desires because he did not want to exercise the discipline necessary to impose order on his desires."[26]

The authors counter: "It seems unlikely that anyone actually *chooses*— freely or otherwise—to be in bondage to desire. We may still ask why anyone would make such a choice."[27]

Kvanvig on freedom

Kvanvig in a later book *Destiny and Deliberation* offers some of the most penetrating philosophical arguments upholding a person's ability to make a final decision contrary to God's plan. This is what universalists deny, but which is central to the position of the conditionalists and the hellenists. He attacks the universalist position on three different fronts; I will only

---

24. Ibid., 139.
25. Ibid., 142.
26. Ibid., 142–43.
27. Ibid., 145.

consider one. But what I wish to emphasize is that he presents very convincing philosophical arguments *for a person to finally choose against God.* Conditionalists would welcome this significant contribution to this debate.

Against Necessary Universalism

His definition of Necessary Universalism is "that it is impossible that Hell is afflicted on anyone." A common argument of the universalists is stated by Talbott: "As long as any ignorance, or deception, or bondage to desire remains, it is open to God to transform a sinner without interfering with human freedom; but once all ignorance and deception and bondage to desire is removed, so that a person is truly "free" to choose, there can no longer be any motive for choosing eternal misery for oneself."[28] Kvanvig's refutations are very complicated and involved. I simply note his conclusions and one of his simple arguments.

"Talbott assumes that God can correct cognitive errors in [a person] getting him to the point of seeing the truth of certain claims that the wicked often ignore or prefer to avoid. It is not clear, however, that God can do so consistent with assumptions about human freedom."[29]

One of Kvanvig's assumptions he calls the Principle of Alternative Possibilities (PAP), that in order to act freely one must be able to do otherwise. "This assumption of PAP shows why necessary universalism cannot be salvaged by insisting that there are conditions under which a choice for anything but Heaven would be impossible. The assumption that God can correct cognitive errors without threatening human freedom is mistaken."[30]

Mercy and God's Waiting

Everyone agrees that there is something sacred about our freedom. There are countless arguments defending it from any influence that would compromise this sacredness, even from God. One of the basic ancient arguments for the "problem of evil" is that God has given us freedom and will not prevent us from using it, even if it's against his will and our true good. The particular aspect of this problem I address here is why does God allow

28. Kvanvig, *Destiny*, 48–49.
29. Ibid., 49.
30. Ibid.

the harm caused by our misuse of freedom *to go on for so long?* As the dire consequences grow both for us and for others, why doesn't God then put a stop to it? He has respected our freedom, but are there no limits to this respect, to this patience?

I remember reading many years ago an example that has always remained with me.

You are baby-sitting. Let's say the parents told you that Jimmy was to go to bed at 8 o'clock. At 7:45 you begin making tentative suggestions that bed time is approaching. Of course, no reaction from Jimmy. You bring out the cookies as a further enticement. He eats and is quiet. At 8 o'clock you start insisting that he has to go to bed now. The resistance grows. At 8:15 your impatience grows and so does his entrenchment. Finally, at 8:30 you bodily lift him up and take him to bed, close the door and turn out the light, hoping for the shouts to subside.

The author's comment here was to the effect that *we* come to an end of our patience with such disobedience but God does not. He would allow Jimmy to wreck the whole house rather than physically restrain his freedom.

Why would God allow such freedom and consequences? The approach taken here is that suggested by St. Paul, that God *out of mercy* allows time for people to repent and change their ways. (After Jimmy has wrecked the whole house it's possible he might have a change of attitude and be sorry!) Another reason is provided in the parable of the Prodigal Son. After a sufficient amount of time had passed the father could have sent someone to tell the son that his time is up, that he no longer has any place at home, and so don't bother coming back. But the father's approach is to allow the son to experience the full consequences of his actions, to "come to his senses" and, as a result, to *decide for himself* to return or not. One of the arguments of the universalists is that God never gives up on anyone, and it may take eons of time for people to finally accept his grace of conversion. I would like to see this as a time of mercy, and I think conditionalists would also.

After all, it is a momentous decision, isn't it, to decide on one's eternal fate? God's mercy gives the Prodigal Son time to really reconsider his misguided thoughts and actions. God's mercy gives a person time to change. Such continued resistance is causing harm to the person and perhaps to others as well. God allows these harmful consequences in the hope that the person will "come to his senses." It seems that God values our freedom more than the prevention of harmful results. For God, such harmful results are only temporary: his patience will wait for a change of heart.

Others would be aware of this patience of God and praise him for his great mercy. "My thoughts are not your thoughts," says the Lord; and he surely has countless thoughts of which we are unaware! But these are possibly two of his thoughts about why he allows so much harm: he respects our freedom; and he desires that we learn to make the right decisions through the consequences of our actions. We may or may not learn, but he gives us sufficient time to decide.

But—and here again is the great dividing line—will everyone eventually "come to his senses" and accept the Father's will; or is it possible that resistance can be ultimate, a negative *no turning back* state of soul, never "coming to one's senses"? The universalists hold the first position, the conditionalists the second.

Fackre and Divine Perseverance

One aspect of the universalist theory is that after death God continues to approach the unrepentant with grace, and eventually *all will open their hearts and be saved.* In treating the question of how people can be saved who have never heard of Christ or believed in him (known as the soteriological problem of evil), Gabriel Fackre uses the expression "The Divine Perseverance." It is a common opinion that, in this life, "those who do not know Christ can be saved by following their best lights, and those who do so are therefore Christians without knowing it. [Rahner's Anonymous Christian] The Doctrine we are exploring has a temporal as well as an eternal expression. In *this* world, as well as the next, God does not give up on us."[31]

> The evidence from Scripture that hearing, believing and confessing the reconciling work of God in Jesus Christ is integral to personal salvation is overwhelming. John 3:16—"whoever *believes in him*"—is echoed throughout the New Testament. A canonical interpretation of biblical truth searches for the pattern of teaching found throughout Scripture. Here [in John] is a manifest one that supports the inseparability of personal salvation from personal belief, and thus the necessity of hearing the Gospel proclaimed. The divine perseverance will not deny the saving Word to any, and will

---

31. Fackre, "Perseverance," 91.

> contest all the makers of boundaries, *including the final boundary,* "*the last enemy, death.*" (emphasis added)[32]

Conditionalists may not have a problem with this post-mortem conversion theory. They would be open to any and all hope for the salvation of people. The two points they insist upon are that a final negative choice can be willed in spite of the mercy of the divine perseverance; and that this then results in the withdrawal of the person's existence.

Simon Tugwell, OP, on Immortality

The position on immortality of Simon Tugwell, a Dominican priest, is not in the mainstream of Catholic thinking. He writes:

"The Orthodox belief that it is mortality which will put on immortality has to accommodate the obvious fact that our mortality is not immortal. Immortality may already have been given in some sense, but if so it coexists with mortality. Immortality is not something which the soul possesses by right. It is something the whole person has by God's gift of his own Spirit. (Rom 8:10–11)[33]

It's possible to take Tugwell's "immortality. . .in some sense" as referring to the "immortableness" of the conditionalists: a quality of the human soul is that it is *capable of immortality.*

Matthew Levering, Jesus and the Demise of Death

After critiquing several philosophical theories that "death brings an utter end to the human person," and briefly examining some of the scriptural texts that possibly imply a "spiritual" existence after death, Levering concludes:

> Aquinas, however, already recognized that physical processes are thoroughly involved in human cognition. He does not appeal to the spiritual soul as though it were another material principle. Rather, Aquinas posits the spiritual soul both for theological reasons and because otherwise one cannot account for conceptual abstraction from material particulars. If neural processes were all there is, then one would simply be substituting one material

---

32. Ibid., 93.
33. Tugwell, *Human Immortality,* 107–08.

particular for another, rather than knowing the universal in the particular. Sanctification and divination worthy of the name also mandate that we possess a spiritual soul. Otherwise, we face a profound reduction of the scope of human intimacy with God, since no matter how much our neural pathways are transformed, neural pathways do not possess much potential for intimate union with divine spirit.

As we have seen, Murphy argues that "the New Testament authors are not intending to teach *anything* about humans' metaphysical composition." Although I agree that the New Testament authors are not developing anthropological assumptions and claims in their writings, Jesus and Paul affirm that humans undergo bodily death without undergoing annihilation. When Jesus warns about caring for one's soul which humans cannot kill, and when Paul envisions a period of disembodied life with Christ after death, these passages uphold the place of reflection on the spiritual soul within a biblically guided eschatology. Far from being redundant, the doctrine of the soul allows for the New Testament's rich account of graced participation in the divine life, both now and in the life to come. Christian eschatology is right to affirm the doctrine not only philosophically but also biblically.[34]

I was pleased to see that Levering speaks of the "spiritual" soul and not the "immortal soul." At least in the chapter I am referring to he does not get into any discussion of the difference between these two concepts. However, defining what survives death as spiritual is more in conformity with the conditionalist position. Also, when he says that a spiritual soul has "potential for intimate union with the divine spirit," this is another way of speaking about the "immortalizability" of the human spirit, as do the conditionalists.

Richard W. Kropf

Kropf is a Catholic theologian and has been a personal friend of mine for many years. He is a Teilhardian scholar. The conclusion of his brief study, *Searching for Soul: Teilhard, de Lubac, Rahner, and the Evolutionary Quest for Immortality*, coincides with the conditionalists' theory concerning the immortality of the soul. In a few closing sentences Kropf summarizes his position.

34. Levering, *Jesus*, 107.

> If both de Lubac and Rahner are correct, then this raises the question as to whether immortality or survival after death is a natural outcome resulting from the possession of an immortal soul— the Platonic philosophical viewpoint adopted by traditional Christian thought— or even the natural product of human evolution, as Teilhard once seemed to suggest. Rather, must it not be seen as a gift of God, whose "grace" somehow enables the human person to share in God's own Being or undying life? Is this not much more in tune with the thought of St. Paul (1 Cor 15:35–49), where "resurrection" is not seen as the revivification of the material "corruptible body," but rather of its replacement as a "spiritual body" through the power of the same spirit— the Holy Spirit— who raised Christ from the dead?[35]

Soren Kierkegaard (1813-55)

After we have seen some of the philosophical approaches to our subject, I turn to the great Soren Kierkegaard. He was one of the most brilliant Christian thinkers of modern times, and a profound religious psychologist among his other gifts. As far as I know he was not specifically involved in the CI revival of his day. However, in his *Sickness unto Death* he gives a very deep and penetrating description of a person "on the way to nihilum." I do not know his writings in any depth, so I cannot say if he ever envisaged annihilation as a possible outcome of such sickness as he describes. But I believe his following observations can be taken as descriptions of a person on her way to some kind of point of no return in her personal deterioration. Hellenists would say that at that point the person goes to hell; conditionalists would argue that then God accedes to the person's choice of negativity, and annihilates her. Probably Kierkegaard meant to describe a person on the way to *hell*, since this was the traditional doctrine at his time. However, I use his insights to describe a person on the way *ad nihilum*.

For this brief analysis we turn to an article by D. Anthony Storm. What follows is not so much an analysis of *Sickness* as a whole but rather excerpting some descriptions of the sickness and relating them to a person in Griffiths phrase "on the way to nihilum." Quotes are from Kierkegaard.

> All despair is ultimately traced to the despair not to will to be oneself. "To be in despair is not only the worst misfortune and

---

35. Kropf, *Searching*, 19–20.

misery—no, it is ruination." Kierkegaard emphasizes that despair is not necessary, that it was not imparted to us by God. "To despair over oneself is despair to will to be rid of oneself—this is the formula for all despair. The self ultimately can rest only in the one who made it. What is missing is essentially the power to obey, to submit to the necessity in one's life, to what may be called one's limitations. The tragedy is not that such a self did not amount to something in the world; no, the tragedy is that he did not become aware of himself, aware that the self he is is a very definite something." "In order to despair to will to be oneself, there must be consciousness of an infinite self. And this is the self that a person in despair wills to be, severing the self from any relation to a power that has established it, or severing it from the idea that there is such a power."

Kierkegaard next addresses the Socratic definition of sin, which is ignorance. "While this view has merit, that people sin out of ignorance (or stupidity), this Greek concept is inadequate because it cannot explain persistence in sin, only the first sin of its type. The very fact that one repeats a sinful act is proof that sinfulness transcends cognition. Sin has its roots in willing not in knowing. It is not right for dogmatics to claim to grasp the magnitude of sin."

"To despair over one's sins indicates that sin has become or wants to be internally consistent. It wants nothing to do with the good, does not want to be so weak as to listen occasionally to other talk. No, it insists on listening only to itself, on having dealings only with itself; it closes itself up within itself, indeed, locks itself inside one more enclosure, and protects itself against every attack or pursuit by the good by despairing over sin."

The weakness of not willing to be oneself, becomes defiance, since the sinner refuses to admit what he is—sinner. Despairing sin, when it refuses forgiveness, is the most intense sin of all.[36]

I'd like to recommend this book for a profound description of someone "on the way *ad nihilum.*" It seems to me we have in *Sickness* Kierkegaard's reflections on several key issues we have been considering in this chapter. He comes down on the side of *the will being the chief cause of sin, and not intellectual ignorance.* According to Kierkegaard, the Christian philosophy is that sin is basically in the will, and one can be defiant in an ultimate way that can lead to a tragic end. He presents a profound analysis of despair

---

36. Storm, *Sickness*, 1–14.

which lends support *to the possibility of making a final tragic decision.* His positions can be used against the universalists.

Griffiths on Annihilation

I end these two chapters on philosophy with Griffiths because he is the most recent author of all those I have quoted, and because his views will be more understandable after having heard other opinions. I have found very few Catholic authors commenting to any great extent on annihilation in my admittedly limited reading. However, not only is Griffiths one of the few, but he is by far, presently, *the* Catholic author who treats this topic extensively. And more relevant for our study, he sees annihilation as a definite *possibility.* We saw briefly (above) his definition of *novissimum.* We consider now his thinking on the *novissima,* and especially about the *possibility* of annihilation. I paraphrase; quotations are from the author.

He defines *novissimum* as a state or condition after which there is no new and different state or condition. Hell and heaven are creaturely *novissima* in the strict sense. Hell is a failed and inglorious *novissimum.* Those in hell are people who have failed to reach their glory. We do not know if there are any such [who have failed]. Human creatures are capable of both a glorious and an inglorious *novissimum* as the Christian tradition affirmed. Each human creature will inevitably reach one or the other. "Doctrinal definiteness on those matters entails nothing about whether any humans or angels have an inglorious last thing."[37] Perhaps all members arrive at a glorious last end. This is U, and some have affirmed it as a necessary feature of the created order. However, "Christian orthodoxy has not much to say about most of these questions."[38] "Christian tradition is precise and unambiguous in its teaching that some humans and angels consummate the gift of their lives in a *glorious novissimum.*"[39] Some people— canonized saints—are in heaven.

Angelic Last things

His thinking about the annihilation of angels is also relevant for humans. May an angel be annihilated? Yes, there are three axioms:

37. Griffiths, *Decreation*, 12.
38. Ibid., 17.
39. Ibid., 12.

"The first is that the LORD brought angels, like all creatures, into being from nothing, which means that they are, and can be, only as participants in the LORD. The second is that fallen angels fall by their sin, fall as they become sinners. And what their sin amounts to is. . .attempting to extricate themselves from participation in the LORD. And the third is that there is nothing about the fallen angels or about the LORD that requires their failure at the annihilation they constantly and effectively attempt."[40]

Aquinas: Can an intellectual substance be corrupted?

"The dominant answer is the negative. Corruption is contrary to the definition of an intellectual substance, Thomas thinks, which means that intellectual substances are not and cannot be subject to it. If every intellectual substance subsists in its own essence, which is a standard definition offered by Thomas, this is just to say that existing is proper to it, and that it is not dependent upon anything external to it or other than itself for that existence. It follows from this definition that substances of this kind cannot lose being, which, put differently, is also to say that they have no potential whatever for nonbeing. This is a piece of broadly Aristotelean metaphysics."[41]

But there is also a positive answer. Thomas gives as the nineteenth in *Quaestio disputata de anima*: "Furthermore, everything that comes from nothing is capable of returning to nothing. But the human soul is created out of nothing, and is therefore capable of returning to nothing. And so it follows that the soul is corruptible."[42]

Thomas then asks whether the LORD is able to return any creature to nothing, and answers that the Lord's freedom means that he could at any time take any creature out of existence. Thomas then goes on to ask whether as a matter of fact anything is brought to nothing. And the answer to this is no, so far as rational creatures are concerned. The only condition that could bring this about lacks *convenientia*, it is, that is to say, something the LORD would not do, something inappropriate to his nature.[43]

Griffiths sees a contradiction in Aquinas's position here. On the one hand "creatures possess intrinsically a tendency toward nonexistence," and on the other hand "they have no potential for nonexistence." This is the dominant Western position. Griffiths' counter position is that the turn

---

40. Ibid., 137–38.
41. Ibid., 139.
42. Ibid., 140.
43. Ibid., 140–41.

towards nothingness "is a property that belongs to all creatures just because they were created out of nothing; they— we all— remain uneasily in being, hovering over the void from which we came."[44]

It's possible to understand sin as simply damaging. However, "the position preferred here is that sin is typically proliferative: turning oneself toward nothing is a habit that ordinarily increases in range, intensity, and depth over time. Such damage, therefore, does not result in a static condition. Once performed it is likely to be performed again and again, with ever-greater intensity."[45] We have here the beginnings of Griffiths teaching about the possibility of annihilation.

"Angels suffer the results of their sin rather than avoid them by ceasing to be. But the opposed position, that the angels can do this and that the LORD does not inevitably keep them in being, is altogether more plausible. This position makes sense of the fundamental grammar of Christian thought much better than its competitor: it takes seriously what creation *ex nihilo* means; it takes sin seriously; and it takes angelic creatureliness seriously. I conclude that— while the speculative question about the possibility of angelic self-annihilation remains open, and is likely to do so—one possible *novissimum* for the fallen angels is annihilation."[46]

Human Annihilation

"Can human creatures have annihilation as their last thing? The speculative position entertained and argued in this section is that they can, that this is both logically and practically possible." It is sin that brings a person to nothing. The LORD creates out of nothing, but "destruction is not what he does." "Sinners seek what is not, they seek their own destruction." "Sinners become progressively less, moving themselves by their sin back toward where they came from, which is nihil."[47]

"Augustine uses strong language about the results of sin, but he resists the conclusion of annihilation. Why? Because in the later tradition, the view is that the human soul is necessarily immortal, no matter what damage it does to itself. The speculative position taken here is that the reductive self-damage that is sin may, in some cases, find its proper terminus, which is the

---

44. Ibid., 142.
45. Ibid., 142–43.
46. Ibid., 143.
47. Ibid., 192–93.

bringing of the person to nothing; that this annihilation may in some cases be permanent, which means that once sinners have gone out of existence, they will not be reconstituted."[48] Griffiths emphasizes that this is a speculative position but "one that Christians would do well to entertain, but it is not entailed or otherwise required by orthodoxy. It has many advantages, and is on the whole preferable to its major competitors."[49]

Griffiths on the immortality of the soul

As we have seen, one of the main contentions of the conditionalists is that natural immortality is not a Christian doctrine but imported from Platonism. It seems that Griffiths gives a Christian interpretation of the doctrine of immortality—or he admits it is a possibility—with which conditionalists could agree.

> Something of what a human creature is must live during the interim between physical death and the flesh's resurrection, and that something must be nonfleshly—which is not, as we shall see, necessarily to say bodiless. "Soul" (anima) is a convenient shorthand for this. *Animae immortalitas*, then, serves at least to indicate the possibility of continuation without flesh. The phrase, however, is negative in form: it denies death to the soul rather than affirming life of it. This is no small thing: it opens a path for speculative thought. The phrase *animae immortalitas* understood in this way is therefore not, properly speaking, one that belongs to talk of the last things. It serves, instead, as an indicator of a condition, that of fleshless quasi-life, which is a preliminary to something else, life eternal in the proper sense.
> Doctrinally speaking, so far as the schema of doctrine about the last things goes, we should not go further than the weaker second position: that the soul is possibly not mortal. And, when united with the resurrected flesh, may enter into *vita aeterna*, the first item in the doctrinal schema.[50]

If I understand Griffiths correctly he is saying that the immortality of the soul that is the content of Christian doctrine is that aspect of the human person that survives after death, but it is not yet a *novissimum*, that is, it is not yet immortal in the sense that it can never die. This state is

48. Ibid., 201–02.
49. Ibid., 202–3.
50. Ibid., 47–48.

"preliminary to something else," some final state that conditionalists would call immortality proper, and that is a gift of God. It seems Griffiths here is making the distinction between the soul as "spiritual," that is, not material, not dying with the body, and "immortal," a real *novissimum* of the human person. I believe this "preliminary" stage is what Pieper means by his words "simplicity," "immateriality," "spirituality," "supertemporality." (above)

6

Hell Recycled

IN THIS *GUIDE TO CI*, the eternal conscious suffering of people—the common understanding of hell—is not seen as a possibility, and thus not formally treated. Following Griffiths for the purposes of this *Guide* there are only two *novissima* for humans, annihilation and heaven. But the theory of annihilation faces many of the same difficult problems as does the view of eternal conscious suffering. How can a good God annihilate one of his creatures? Is not such a withdrawal of existence against the justice and love of God? Is a person capable of such an absolute rejection of the Father's will to warrant extinction? Is annihilation possible for any person?

I call my approach to hell "recycling" because I will apply many of the objections to hell, and the answers to these objections, to annihilation. When we recycle material things we often use the discarded elements for making something quite different. (In Japan they compress garbage and make building blocks out of it. I presume the smell has been treated!) So I will recycle the common difficulties concerning hell and the people "there" and apply them to the theory of A.

For example, what people "in hell" are said to suffer I will apply to the state of those *on the way* to annihilation. Griffiths uses the phrase "to move ad nihilum," to move towards nothingness.[1] As well, the argument that it is possible for someone to make an ultimate decision against God, and thus "go to hell," I will apply to the person who is "on the way," who, at a certain point, has come to such an absolute decision against the Father's plan that leads God to respect that decision and *to withdraw existence* from that person.

"Hell" is understood here, in relation to annihilation, not as a place but as a continuing and increased state of suffering people go through because of their adamant resistance *on the way* to being annihilated. Neither

---

1. Griffiths, *Decreation*, 15.

are the sufferings of such unrepentant people seen as "punishment" except in the sense that these effects are the painful consequences of what follows upon resisting God's plan of love for them. Such consequences are also one way of understanding what is meant by the "wrath of God."

Understandings of Hell

Paul Griffiths

I take Griffiths' approach as my guide for "recycling hell." Keep in mind that he is a Catholic theologian. The ideas in this section and the quotes are his (unless otherwise noted); I will paraphrase. He admits his is a minority opinion but consistent with Catholic orthodoxy. In the following quote he is referring to the Vatican II document, *Lumen Gentium*:

"Christians are divided into three categories in number 49: those who are pilgrims here below, those who are being purified after they have left this life, and those who are already in glory seeing the Lord even now. There is no mention of a fourth category, those who are already damned; and the language of this part of *Lumen Gentium* is, throughout, that of hope.

None of this is to say that *Lumen Gentium* teaches universalism, whether in the indicative or subjunctive mood; neither is it to say that the actuality of damnation for some is ruled out."[2]

Objections to Hell

"Devastation" is Griffiths word for our present earthly, sinful condition. Pain and suffering are part of our space-time world. To say that such states continue is to say that Christ's work is not complete. There is also a problem with eternal physical pain in a time/space similar to ours. Augustine simply says that God is omnipotent and that he can do anything. That God can do it doesn't mean that that is what he does. All Orthodoxy requires is that this is possible; and this condition can be met by annihilation as well as by hell.

"Most of the speculative tradition [takes it] as axiomatic that hell is real and inhabited, and that it must involve fleshly torture. But these speculations are theologoumena and need not be accepted by Christians. In the traditional view of hell "the Lord is not all in all: there remains a realm separated from him even after the general resurrection, a state of affairs

2. Ibid., 249.

that does not change. There are human creatures so reduced that they lack, irreversibly, the capacity for repentance. Lastly, the Lord acts deliberately to maintain the effects of evil in being. . .and indeed to ensure the existence of an entire realm separate from himself."[3]

The speculative picture of hell has greater disadvantages than annihilation.

"It is important, however, to emphasize also what both pictures have in common, which is what makes them both, barely, possibly Christian. They share a seriousness about sin's nature and effects; they share, too, a deep sense of the importance of the flesh for human creatures. They are both, therefore, possible Christian speculative positions, even if one of them appears more beautiful and more fully articulated with the tradition's deep grammar than the other, and even though the endless-torment position suffers from a profound ugliness in the order of knowing."[4]

And here Griffiths indicates how he is reconstructing hell; it is the position I am taking throughout this book.

"The *novissimum* that is hell for human creatures may be understood as permanent and irreversible annihilation. This condition is one of complete and final separation from the Lord. This condition amounts to success at the project of sin, which exactly is a project of self-extrication from the Lord, who is the condition of the possibility of continuing in being for all human creatures."[5] Griffiths thinks we should keep the word "hell" but interpret it in terms of annihilation.

"Are there any people in hell now? The weight of the speculative position answers yes. But if this speculative position is accepted it means that there are those who have come to nothing or who will do so. Not all human creatures, on this view, will enter into eternal life with the Lord. There is no authoritative doctrine on this matter, and it is entirely typical of church teaching on these matters chastely to avoid indicative-mood claims about whether there are (or are not) any who are damned of particular human creatures.[6]

Griffiths concludes with a comment about "subjunctive universalism," that is, a hope for the salvation of all that is subjective, hypothetical, and doubtful.

3. Ibid., 246.
4. Ibid., 247.
5. Ibid.
6. Ibid., 248.

"The position entertained here on this question combines subjunctive universalism with a modest and tentative judgment that *universalism is unlikely*. (emphasis added) That is, universalism's possibility can be entertained by orthodox Christians but only as a possibility rather unlikely to be actualized. We pray for it under the sign of hope in something like the same way that we pray for world peace— that is, as something we do not expect, but which is not in principle impossible. Even Satan may be saved, as may the worst of human sinners. Whether they have been or will be is not known to us, and we have strong reasons for doubting it, though not strong enough to produce certainty."[7]

Jerry Walls on Hell

Walls' book, *The Logic of Damnation*, is one of the most significant contemporary books defending the doctrine of hell. However, I will be referring here to his more brief and recent treatment of hell in *Heaven, Hell, and Purgatory*: "The Christian drama seems to include an element of the tragic that cannot be swept under the rug."[8] Annihilationism provides this element of the tragic although, as we have seen (chapter 4), Walls denies that A is philosophically defensible. In what follows I paraphrase Walls from his more recent book.

One of the main criticisms of universalism is that eventually it does away with any tragic element to the Christian story. The basic logic against hell is that if God is all-powerful and good, he can and will save everyone. An argument against this line of thinking is that if God is all-good and all-powerful, why is there any evil *now*?

The traditional Christian answer is that evil exists because we have free will. "It is fair to say that most philosophers and theologians believe freedom is at least central to whatever reasons God has for permitting evil. If freedom can account for evil *in this world*, the same freedom may explain why hell exists *in the next world*. Some people may use their freedom to resist God forever."[9]

Walls builds one of his arguments concerning the compatibility of hell and God's love precisely on the *love of God*. In the gospel Jesus commands us to love (John 13: 34). This means that we both have the power to love and

---

7. Ibid., 249–50.
8. Walls, *Heaven*, 67–68.
9. Ibid., 69–70.

the power to refuse. "The obedience God wants from us is an obedience that flows out of genuine love. And this is what brings into focus the staggering reality that hell is possible precisely because God is love. For what this text brings to light is that some may choose not to love Jesus or obey his teaching. Hell is possible precisely because God is love."[10]

The greatest opponent of this argument of Walls is Thomas Talbott who argues that God can save all persons without overriding their freedom. "The heart of his case is that there simply is no intelligible motive for anyone to choose eternal hell. Talbott thinks that, strictly speaking, it is logically impossible that anyone will be lost forever."[11] Walls counters that our decisions are very frequently *not based on logic*.

Another argument from Talbott is that "God can present us with powerful evidence that will compel us to repent."[12] Walls counters that in our own experience, and certainly in Scripture, there are many examples of people going against the most obvious evidence. [The miracles of Jesus, and especially the raising of Lazarus, did not convince everyone.]

Walls turns for some of his final arguments to C.S. Lewis in *The Great Divorce*. Lewis articulates attitudes that reveal people who "in one sense remain rebels to the end. Generally speaking, the reason hell can be freely chosen is that it is a distorted mirror image of heaven. There is no righteousness or holiness in hell, but it does offer an alternative of self-righteousness. It offers no real joy or happiness, but it does offer the deformed sense of satisfaction from holding on to bitterness, resentment, and hurt. There is no real fulfillment, but it does offer the illusory triumph of getting one's way, self-destructive though it is. Hell is the empty shell of which heaven is the pulsating, vibrant reality. But the shell is not without its pleasures, miserable though they are."[13]

And now, my recycling comment. Conditionalists would agree with Walls that such an absolute self-centered and permanent attitude on the part of people is possible, but it leads not to hell but to annihilation. When we consider the Lord's words about what is present in the human heart (Mark 7, 21–23), this perversity gives credence to the possibility of an ultimate decision for a self-centeredness that can completely reject the Father's plan.

10. Ibid., 72.
11. Ibid., 76–77.
12. Ibid., 81.
13. Ibid., 89–90.

Anthony Kelly, *Eschatology and Hope*

Kelly is a member of the Catholic Redemptorist Order and professor of theology at the Australian Catholic University. He believes in the reality of hell. He first gives some reasons why a neglect of hell causes its horrors to be projected onto others. There is need for discussion about hell. "When the topic of hell cannot be mentioned, the destructive force of evil is unacknowledged. Repression of either death or "the second death" (Rev 20:14) is not a sign of a living hope."[14]

"There is something to be said, then, for a sober theological approach that keeps hell where it belongs. It is a possibility residing in those depths of human freedom that can be known only to God. Hell is a theological symbol of the sinner's self-chosen fate. It allows for the possibility for any individual to be terminally frozen in the choice of evil. It also has the power to frustrate the patience and mercy of God (2 Pet 3:9). Whether or not such an ultimate fixation on evil occurs, we simply do not know. What we do know, with all the force of the Gospel, is that such a judgment is reserved only to God."[15]

Kelly holds to the possibility of a final decision that is "terminally frozen in the choice of evil." It is a good description of the stage of a person "going ad nihilum," and finally arriving there. Kelly then explores four themes that support his theological position of hell. I "recycle" them and apply them to annihilation instead of hell.

Healthy Fear

It is a common argument against hell that it is a fear motivation for loving God and living rightly. Kelly justifies fear as a legitimate attitude in our relationship with God.

> If Christian preaching speaks of the possibility of suffering the loss of God, it need not be emotionally manipulative. The feeling of fear has its part to play in motivating genuine human freedom, even if such motivation is not the most mature.
>
> Hell is a carrier of wholesome fear. It objectifies the opposite of self-transcendence, namely, the possibility of self-destruction and an ultimate form of self-disclosure. The Christian doctrine of

---

14. Kelly, *Eschatology*, 139.
15. Ibid., 141.

hell presumes that it is a possibility for everyone. It is one aspect of our common experience of the enigma of human liberty. It candidly acknowledges the precariousness of human liberty in a universe that is not a giant automatic salvation machine. It contains the possibility of a terminal self-destruction.[16]

I note his phrase "the possibility of a terminal self-destruction" which is really the thesis of this book.

Judgment

One of the most common arguments against U is "what about Hitler and Mao and Stalin? Will they get off scot-free? Will we have to be in heaven with them?" This objection is usually answered by referring to the great mercy of God. Kelly argues otherwise. He mentions the enormous evils down through the history of the world, not neglecting those of our own century that are too well known to us.

> Then there is another paradox. Put most shockingly, Christians must hope that hell exits. But at once we must add a qualification. We are longing not for the damnation of others but for the final state in which evil will be revealed for what it is and be brought to nothing. The symbol of hell, for all the reserve with which we must explore it, points to a theological reality. It represents God's ultimate judgment on the evil perpetrated by historical human agents. It marks the limit, in this sense, of God's patience with what most contradicts the divine will to save.
>
> There is no question of positively hoping that individual evildoers will be condemned to hell. Nonetheless, it seems essential to authentic hope to pray and work for a final state in which the power of evil is negated once and for all. What conscience has found most hateful and worthy of utter reprobation will have no part in the new creation.
>
> Hope can allow for a certain sense of the eternity of hell, in that all who will live in the eternal light of God will be conscious of the evils from which they are saved, and which they now experience as forever defeated.[17]

I found his emphasis on hoping for "the final *state* in which evil will be revealed for what it is" very helpful. We are not hoping that so and so will

---

16. Ibid., 143–44.
17. Ibid., 145/50.

go to hell. Such an attitude is often accompanied by very unchristian sentiments such as self-righteousness, revenge, satisfaction in others receiving justice, and so on. No. We are hoping that eventually God will be all in all when *no evil at all will exist in contradiction to the Father's plan.*

Kelly touches briefly on what will be the relationship of those in heaven to those "in hell." It seems to me that if people are no longer in existence this will be less of a problem! And when Kelly states that "the final state. . . will. . .be *brought to nothing*," his view corresponds better to that of the conditionalists: *brought to nothing*, not continuing on forever.

Freedom

Kelly, obviously then, is on the side of those who hold to the possibility of making a final act that eventuates in their going to hell.

"The theoretical and practical recognition of freedom must allow the free person to be truly free. Therein lays the possibility of eschatological tragedy: free human agents can opt for themselves against God; and do so definitely. We are talking not of occasional sins or moral impotence but of the self-determining choice into which evildoers have put the whole deliberate weight of their lives. Hell is the possibility of ending—to quote C.S. Lewis—with a heart 'unbreakable, impenetrable, irredeemable.'"[18]

Justice and Mercy

The above ideas of Kelly about hell are very applicable—as I'm seeking to show—to annihilation as well. However, curiously, in the rest of chapter 7 on hell, Kelly relies more on the mystery of God's actions, and even (in my opinion) veers more towards U.

He begins by criticizing former theories of punishment that used human systems and applied them to God's justice. "Are the laws of punitive human justice binding even on God? Human justice can be little more than the culturally embedded despair that has lost hope for any grace beyond its own system."[19] He doesn't try to come up with some system of justice, but points to Gospel texts (Matt 19:26, Mark 10:27, Luke 18:27), and says that "each in its own context invites hope to look beyond the cultural and social

---

18. Ibid., 151–52.
19. Ibid., 153.

structures of any system of human justice and to place no human limits on the possibilities of divine grace and mercy."[20] In a footnote to the above scriptural texts he says: "Note the series of texts [he quotes six] strongly affirming universal salvation."[21]

"The first and last thing is the limitless saving creativity of God. The sinner may be isolated from God, but Christ is not isolated from the sinner. When all theories of human judgments are silenced, the ultimately determining realities are found only in the depths of divine wisdom and the unbounded freedom of God's love. [He mentions many in Christian history who were universalists.] To hope for the ultimate reconciliation of all with God is to find oneself in good company."[22]

Carol Zaleski, *The Life of the World to Come*

The sub-title of Zaleski's book is "*Near-Death Experiences and Christian Hope.*" It is an early (1996) "meditation upon the last things: the encounter with death, the hope for life beyond death, and the vision of the world to come, as distilled in the classical Christian tradition and recent testimony of near-death experience."[23] She had also studied near-death experiences (NDE) in medieval times. One of her conclusions is that although there are similarities in such accounts over the centuries, "such reports invariably portray this experience in ways that *conform to cultural expectations.*"[24] (emphasis added) Of interest for my study is how present day culture conditions near-death experiences as regards the topics of concern to Kelly above.

"Most striking, of course, is the absence from most twentieth-century near-death accounts of postmortem punishment: no hell, no purgatory, no chastening torments or telltale agonies at the moment of death. The life review, when it occurs, is a reassuring experience, modeled on contemporary methods of education and psychotherapy. The possibility for loss is genuine in the medieval accounts—if one botches the second chance, eternal damnation is the likely result. Today it seems that there is scarcely any

---

20. Ibid., 154.
21. Ibid.
22. Ibid., 156–57.
23. Zaleski, *Life of the World*, 3.
24. Ibid., 20.

possibility for loss. Life and afterlife flow together as an unending stream of fresh opportunities for personal growth."[25]

Zaleski's reflections on *judgment* in NDE are especially relevant for my purposes.

"But if notions of sin and punishment are suppressed in the popular accounts [of NDE], there is, nonetheless, plenty of evidence for the persistence—though in camouflaged form—of the notion of judgment. The form in which the motif of judgment persists is in the "life review." Many readers familiar with NDE will be aware that one of the very common features is that one's whole life passes before one's eyes, often instantaneously. "There is no sense of being judged by an external being; rather the emphasis is on self-evaluation, learning and growth. The following example is typical: 'I never before realized that we were responsible and accountable for EVERY SINGLE THING WE DID. That was overwhelming!'[26]

"This much we can say for the judgment scenarios of contemporary dear-death testimony: although they may be excessively privatistic and optimistic, they at least avoid the unbecoming trait of taking satisfaction in contemplating the doom of others. If we step back and take the long view of the history of judgment motifs in Christian eschatology, we can see that modulated by the many—even redundant—media of forgiveness and reconciliation, the anticipation of judgment is part of what gives life meaning and direction. It completes the life story and thus provides the necessary prelude to the consummation of our common life."[27]

Zaleski does not go into the question of whether or not such a life-review can end tragically; it is not one of her concerns. But she is clear that in NDE a judgment does take place: people judge themselves. Of the countless people who die every day, only a few return to complete their lives and tell their stories. For most people, therefore, we have no record of what direction their decisions took or, for that matter, what was the final outcome of their existence. It's a very probable opinion— in keeping with the thesis of this book— that some people *might not choose* for the Loving Light they see after death, and thus suffer some tragic consequence of such a choice.

This becomes even more probable when we consider—which Zaleski notes elsewhere in her book—that some people do have terrible experiences

---

25. Ibid., 32–33.
26. Ibid., 74–75.
27. Ibid., 75–76.

which they term as hell. Is it possible that some people remain in the state that caused such experiences? I think so; and that is the contention of this book.

Joseph Ratzinger, *Eschatology, Death and Eternal Life*

This was an early (1977) work of the then Professor Ratzinger. I quote from his brief section on "Hell." I am especially interested in his belief in the *possibility of making an ultimate choice as regards our fate*. As we've seen, this is one of the central issues for both the hell and annihilation theories. I note that conditionalists would disagree with his first few lines.

> No quibbling here: the idea of eternal damnation, which had taken ever clearer shape in the Judaism of the century or two before Christ, has a firm place in the teaching of Jesus, as well as in the apostolic writings. Dogma takes its stand on solid ground when it speaks of the existence of hell and of the eternity of its punishments. What should we hold on to here? First to the fact of God's unconditional respect for the freedom of his creature. What can be given to the creature, however, is love, and with this all its neediness can be transformed. The assent to such love need not be "created" by man: this is not something which he achieves by his own power. And yet the freedom to resist the creation of that assent, the freedom not to accept it as one's own, this freedom remains.
>
> Christ descends into Hell and suffers it in all its emptiness; but he does not, for all that, treat man as an immature being deprived in the final analysis of any responsibility for his own destiny. Heaven reposes upon freedom, and so leaves to the damned the right to will their own damnation. The specificity of Christianity is shown in this conviction of the greatness of man. Human life is fully serious. The irrevocable takes place and that includes, then, *irrevocable destruction*. (emphasis added) The Christian man or woman must live with such seriousness and be aware of it. It is a seriousness which takes on tangible form in the Cross of Christ."[28]

Nichols Loudovikos, *Hell and Heaven*

Loudovikos is a Greek Orthodox theologian who is concerned that the final states of heaven and hell not be seen as juridical pronouncements by God.

---

28. Ratzinger, *Eschatology*, 215–17.

His thinking in this area is consonant with Ratzinger and many modern theologians that *novissima* are a result of the *relationship* between God and the freedom of the person whom God respects. Final states are not *juridical decrees*. He notes, as others have, that the trend of denying hell might be "regarded as a desperate attempt to overcome the legalism innate in our understanding of the 'last things.'"[29]

We have seen that Froom finds in Irenaeus of Lyon the teaching about annihilation; Loudovikos also find in Irenaeus the doctrine he will elaborate.

> This means that heaven and earth occur through a synergistic co-operation between God and Man, not through a one-sided moral and juridical provision on the part of God. What we have here are processes of *dialogical reciprocity*, profound encounters of the freedom of God with the deiform freedom of rational creatures. The above theses signify above all that hell and heaven can also be related absolutely to ontology, that is, to the full restoration of the created nature of beings and the never-ending evolution of that nature; or, alternatively, to its never-ending ontological fixity or nullification, after the general resurrection. Thus the judicial element is translated into ontological terms, and avoids its alteration into juridical. God's justice is understood as identical to His love, and the adventures of the reception of this love on the part of man.[30]

"This means that at the Last Judgement what will 'weigh' the truth or the falsehood of the personal choice of each of us is the personal or freely chosen preservation of the truth of our nature as participation in God (naturally in Christ), rather than a fearful denial of it. Consequently, paradise is here the freely chosen continuation of the natural dialogical development of created nature by participation (effected in Christ), whereas hell is precisely the freely chosen refusal to allow nature to follow the path of its completion by participation.[31]

> To conclude, according to the Greek patristic tradition, heaven and hell are born from the personal and free ("in accordance with nature" or "contrary to nature") choice alone of creatures, not from created nature which is universally resurrected— and precisely for this reason heaven and hell are active realizations of freedom, not

29. Loudovikos, "Hell and Heaven," 14.
30. Ibid., 16.
31. Ibid., 18–19.

> simply decisions of passive reward or punishment on the part of God. Heaven is the free choice ("in accordance with nature") of the dialogical and participatory development of created nature in Christ, for all eternity, as "ever-moving stasis," according to Maximus, of the creature within God— whereas hell is the free choice ("contrary to nature") of refusal of the dialogical liberation of nature in the absolute meaning of the Incarnation: here God is encountered, with malicious envy and hostility, according to Maximus "in knowledge but not as participation."
>
> This is a peculiar refusal of the Resurrection through the rejection of the participation that would have allowed the Resurrection to be transformed into a full and conscious communion and cooperation with God.
>
> If heaven appears also to be a supernatural judicial reward, this happens because of God's limitless response to the human desire for participation—and if hell also appears to be a punishment—this is mainly on account of the intense bitter resentment that lies in the unparticipated knowledge of God. Thus the judicial element of Christian eschatology can be translated in ontological terms, and avoid its conception as juridical.[32]

And here is Loudovikos' statement, in an earlier work, about the possibility of hell, according to Maximus the Confessor. Quotes are from Maximus.

> It should be observed that well-being is not the only possible outcome of our existential evolution: a perverted movement of the free choice will lead to woe-being. "Depending on whether the operation of the choice uses the power of nature in accordance with nature or contrary to nature, it will find that the outcome is well-being or woe-being." The ultimate climax of such an evolution is eternal woe-being. Maximus describes with the utmost clarity the difference between eternal well-being and eternal woe-being, whereas eternal being is given by God to all: "As to being and eternal being, God will sustain everyone [in those states] by His presence; but as to eternal well-being, he will sustain in a special way those who are holy, both angels and humans, leaving to those who are not [holy] the state of eternal woe–being, as the fruit of their own gnomic will.[33]

---

32. Ibid., 30.
33. Loudovikos, *Ontology*, 81.

Loudovikos fosters several philosophical positions relevant for my study: 1) that a final choice against God is possible; 2) that it results from a person's freedom and is not a "juridical act" imposed by God; 3) that hell is not contrary to God's love. However, it is not clear whether or not he believes in the *eternity* of hell. Above, he uses the phrase "for all eternity" in reference to the choice for heaven, but does not repeat it for the choice opposite.[34]

He seems to be saying that the eternity of hell is being rejected because it no longer is seen as an act of justice, or a juridical act on the part of God. So his article is aimed at giving a dialogical understanding of hell and of heaven. He quotes Maximus the Confessor that a state of "eternal woe-being" is possible. What, therefore, is his final position about the eternity of hell? In the last few paragraphs of his article he seems to say that it *may not be eternal*.

"The question about the eternity of hell thus does not affect God and his love, *because hell will end when the devil wants to end it, when he ceases from his malice against God* (emphasis added)—because if hell is the absolute narcissistic enclosure within oneself, in an imaginary superiority that denies the reality of corruption and the need for the transformation of the created, then this situation becomes in the end the soul's ultimate blindness, its self-condemnation to hell."[35]

Let the reader decide; but Loudovikos seems to be in the escapist camp that in hell there can be an end to one's resistance.

Maximus the Confessor

Maximus the Confessor is important enough in the Christian tradition to emphasize his position on one's ability *to make a final fateful choice*. He is considered the last of the fathers because he had at his fingertips both the Greek and Latin traditions. (For example, he had no theological problem with accepting the Roman understanding of the philioque, that the Holy Spirit proceeds from the Father *and the Son*.) He was considered important enough to be included in the significant Fourth Edinburgh Conference on *Universalism and the Doctrine of Hell*. Although the author's paper was entitled "Universal Salvation in Origen and Maximus," I am only concerned with Maximus. As with so many questions in the history of theology,

34. Ibid., 84.
35. Ibid., 31–32.

not everyone agrees with Norris's conclusion. He follows the opinion of Sherwood.

"Sherwood claims that Maximus held two poles in tension: 'the perfection and universality of God's saving work in Jesus Christ and the reality of unending punishment, that is, the seeming failure of salvation.' A number of texts from Maximus insist on the fact of unending punishment."[36]

"That rejection of an Origenist doctrine of *apocatastasis* is clear in *Ambigua* 42 and 65. With both passages Maximus compares the different but final conditions of human beings. Those who have chosen virtue and movement in harmony with the *Logos* receive well-being; those who have chosen vice and disharmony with the *Logos* receive ill-being. The first participate in joy; the second do not. The second are fairly assigned to 'ever-ill-being.'"[37]

In a very moving description of life apart from God, Maximus says:

"What is more wretched and oppressive than anything else, to speak truly—and if it makes me grieve just to mention it, then how much worse to suffer it (have mercy, O Christ, and save us from this pain!)—is separation from God and his holy powers, and belonging to the devil and the evil powers, a state which lasts forever, without any prospect of our ever being liberated from this dire situation. And more punishing, more severe than any penalty is to be joined forever with those who hate and are hated—even apart from torture, and all the more with it—and to be separated from the one who loves and is loved."[38]

"Maximus does not see God overwhelming the will of humans, either to save them or to condemn them."[39]

Thus the predominant opinion about Maximus is that he believed in the possibility of a tragic end—an "ever-ill-being"; and that a person was able to make such a choice—"those who have chosen vice." The expression "ever-ill-being" could be used as another term for annihilation.

David Bentley Hart

David Bentley Hart is a very significant Christian (Orthodox) thinker of our time. He has an article in the *Oxford Handbook of Eschatology* entitled

---

36. Norris, "Universal Salvation," 63.
37. Ibid., 65.
38. Ibid., 71.
39. Ibid., 72.

"Death, Final Judgment, and the Meaning of Life." His main theme there is concerned with the impact of the Resurrection on our understanding of death: "In the light of Easter, however, that aboriginal anxiety [about death] is transformed into a kind of spiritual ecstasy. For what God raised up on Easter was the deified humanity of Christ; and he thereby revealed that the true story of our humanity is that of a true union between humanity and God, a marriage of the finite to the infinite, a divinization of the creature in Christ."[40]

Then he follows with this sentence that is very relevant for our theme: "That is to say, God's judgment on humanity, as revealed at Easter, is a call to an inexhaustible experience of the intimate presence of God (a call that, inevitably, leaves open the possibility of the soul turning from God's love toward a *correspondingly limitless dereliction*."[41] (emphasis added) As an Orthodox theologian he is clear about the possibility of making a definitive decision *against* God, leading to a "limitless dereliction."

John E. Thiel, *Icons of Hope: the "Last Things" in Catholic Imagination*

His book is not explicitly concerned with the debate concerning CI, Hell, and U. However, although he is treating "the last things" from his perspective as icons of hope, many of his comments relate to our theme. I quote especially his strong view against U and his belief in the possibility of a final fateful decision.

> Earlier in my argument I proposed that the outcome of the Last Judgement remains in a state of suspense even for the blessed dead, and that this suspense is generated by the hope that God's grace is universally efficacious, that all are saved. Matthean sensibilities would be uncomfortable with this graceful efficacy, and understandably so. Universal salvation seems to undercut genuine responsibility for cooperation with God's grace that Trent defines as necessary for justification.
>
> Since even a quick glance at any moment in history reveals sin of overwhelming proportions, the hope for universal salvation suggests that such sin, which in so many instances is blatantly unrepentant, is held to no account at all in the court of divine judgment. A consequence of such apparent disregard for sin, and

---

40. Hart, "Death," 487.
41. Ibid., 487–88.

human responsibility for it, is that the gift of grace that would bring about universal salvation would seem to be an empty parody of justice.

Grace in such a scenario would not be offered to be received by an enacted cooperation but instead, it seems, distributed freely with a complete disregard for the sin that permeated human lives and indeed all of history. If sin matters not, neither, it seems, does grace. If the most terrible sinners could enter eternal life so easily and in spite of their evil deeds, then salvation would come at no cost, with no struggle, and with no acknowledgement at all of the remarkable differences between an accomplished saintly life and a horrendously sinful life.[42]

Universalists generally believe that there can be, and probably is, some kind of suffering and purification for sinners after death before their final restoration. So they do not get off scot-free! But Thiel is very clear about not only the possibility of an ultimate choice against God, but perhaps even its necessity.

John Kronen and Eric Reitan, *God's Final Victory*

This book is one of the most insightful philosophical/theological critiques *against* the doctrine of hell that I have yet come across. (Curiously, I have not found it commented upon by present day conditionalists.) Its main thesis defends U against *any form* of the doctrine of hell: "Of course, there are alternatives to DH [the Doctrine of Hell] and DU [the Doctrine of Universalism]—most notably Annihilationism (DA), according to which the unregenerate will eventually cease to exist. *For all we know,* based on Scripture and reason, DH, DU, or perhaps even DA, might be true. But we think our arguments for favouring U over Hell offers a template for a similar case favouring U over A."[43]

It's the authors' contention that their arguments against DH are also valid against what we are specifically concerned with here, A. To repeat again: my general approach is to take what authors say about hell and the state of those "in hell," and apply it to A and those "on the way" to A; and

---

42. Thiel, *Icons*, 179–80.
43. Kronen and Reitan, *Victory*, 2.

using their arguments *for* hell *for* CI (A). In an article in an earlier book[44] these authors agree that A is a *species* of hell, and Griffiths would agree.

Freedom

Freedom, as I've often mentioned, is one of the major issues in our whole discussion. The authors of *God's Final Victory* state: "In recent centuries, arguably the most significant theological development concerning DH [the Doctrine of Hell] has been a shift away from defending it in terms of God's justice and towards defending it in terms of God's respect for creaturely freedom— God either cannot or will not (for moral reasons) override creaturely freedom on this matter."[45] We turn to *Victory* for a discussion of freedom in relation to A. I will recycle the arguments the hellenists present for this creaturely freedom in favor of A.

The first argument of the universalists is that God can give an efficacious grace to everyone, understood as a grace that converts people without violating their freedom; and it is not morally wrong for God to do this. Using intricate arguments from Aquinas and Talbott the authors conclude that "God doing this [granting efficacious grace] certainly is *metaphysically possible*, and hence within God's power; and if (as Aquinas maintained) free acts are not random but motivated, it follows that any rational creature presented with the vision of God will freely but inevitably respond affirmatively to the promise of loving union."[46]

However, critics might say that because of a person's bad habits, she or he may not be able to "see" God and thus be open to conversion. No, say the universalists, a free act is still possible: "Even if we can decide to block the vision of God by, as it were, deliberately averting our gaze, the notion of the creature as ordered to God, coupled with God's infinite causal power, seems to entail that it is within God's power to override such resistance."[47] The authors admit that their arguments may not be convincing. Can we ever see God completely? Maybe not. But "what is essential is that the creature be able to experience the divine in a manner suitable to the creature's nature

---

44. Kronen and Reitan, "Species," 216.
45. Kronen and Reitan, *Victory,* 127.
46. Ibid., 136.
47. Ibid., 138.

and sufficient to produce an unambiguous appreciation of the reality of God."[48] But isn't the granting of such a grace immoral?

One argument of Aquinas was that God can reveal to the unregenerate that he is their *summum bonum;* and that he can eliminate any affective states that prevent their acceptance of this truth. On the other hand, he held that it is still possible to freely reject God. But the authors, following Talbott, hold that "if efficacious grace involves establishing the conditions for free choice, then, a fortiori, it cannot override free choice."[49]

Walls concedes that if the unrepentant choose to resist grace they are not free. But— and here is the main difference about freedom for our purposes—"What Walls rejects is the claim that God could therefore save the damned without overriding their freedom. In brief, Walls looks in turn at both ignorance/deception and bondage to desire and argues that both states could be freely chosen by the damned. Walls thinks "their ignorance might be *wilful,* resulting from freely chosen self-deception. We can imagine that someone freely chooses to become a slave to sinful desires because he did not want to exercise the discipline necessary to impose order on his desires."[50]

The authors counter: "It seems unlikely that anyone actually *chooses*— freely or otherwise— to be in bondage to desire. We may still ask why anyone would make such a choice."[51]

N.T. Wright, *Surprised by Hope*

Wright is considered one of the foremost New Testament scholars in the Anglican Church. Before looking at his views on hell—"one of the darkest theological mysteries"—which are especially relevant for our topic, I first note that he agrees with the conditionalists that the doctrine of the "immorality of the soul" is not in the Scriptures.

> Do we have immortal souls, and if so, what are they? Again, much Christian and sub-Christian tradition has assumed that we all do indeed have souls that need saving and that the soul, if saved, will be part of us that goes to heaven when we die. All this, however, finds minimal support in the New Testament, including the

48. Ibid., 139.
49. Ibid., 142.
50. Ibid., 142–43.
51. Ibid., 145.

> teaching of Jesus, where the word *soul*, though rare, reflects when it does occur underlying Hebrew or Aramaic words referring not to a disembodied entity hidden within the outer shell of the disposable body but rather to what we would call the whole person or personality, seen as being confronted by God. As to immortality, 1 Tim 6:16 declares that only God himself has immortality, and 2 Tim 1:10 declares that immortality has only come to light, and hence is presumably only available, through the gospel. In other words, the idea that every human possesses an immortal soul, which is the "real" part of them, finds little support in the bible.[52]

And now, as to his understanding about hell, his first caution is against taking the words of Jesus in the gospels about the afterlife too literally.

> The point is that when Jesus was warning his hearers about Gehenna, he was not, as a general rule, telling them that unless they repented in this life they would burn in the next one. As with God's kingdom, so with its opposite: it is *on earth* that things matter, not somewhere else. It is therefore only by extension, and with difficulty, that we can extrapolate from the many gospel sayings that articulate this urgent, immediate warning to the deeper question of a warning about what may happen after death itself. We cannot therefore look to Jesus' teaching for any fresh detail on whether there really are some who finally reject God and, as it were, have that rejection ratified. All the signs, of course, are that he went along with the normal first-century Jewish perception: there would indeed be such people, with the only surprise being the surprise experienced by sheep and goats alike, at their fate and at the evidence on which it was based.[53]

Wright comes down on the side of those who believe in the *possibility of a tragic ending* for some people. After enumerating several of the major atrocities of the last century, he says: "Opinion in many quarters has, rightly in my view, come to see that there must be such a judgment. Judgment— the sovereign declaration that *this* is good and to be upheld and vindicated, and *that* is evil and to be condemned— is the only alternative to chaos."[54]

He comments briefly on the three possibilities for "those who spurn God's salvation, who refuse to turn from idolatry and wickedness"— hell, U, and CI. Only the third concerns us.

---

52. Wright, *Surprised*, 28.
53. Ibid., 176–77.
54. Ibid., 178.

> A middle way is offered by the so-called conditionalists. They propose "conditional immortality": those who persistently refuse God's love and his way of life in the present world will simply cease to exist. Immortality, such theories point out, is not (despite the popularity of Platonism!) an innate human characteristic; it is something that, as Paul says, only God possesses by right and hence is a gift that God can choose to bestow or withhold. According to this theory, then, God will simply not confer immortality on those who is this life continue impenitently to worship idols and thereby to destroy their own humanness. This view is therefore sometimes known as annihilationism; such people will cease to exist. That word, however, is too strong, suggesting that such people are actively destroyed rather than merely failing to receive a gift that had been held out to them and that they consistently rejected.[55]

I like his alternative to the word "annihilate": the person's refusal of the gift of immortality held out to her. However, he seems to reject the conditionalist view since he ultimately comes up with his own proposed explanation of the final state of the unrepentant:

"My suggestion is that it is possible for human beings so to continue down this road [of idolatry] so to refuse all whisperings of good news, all glimmers of the true light, all promptings to turn and go the other way, all signposts to the love of God, that after death they become, at last, by their own effective choice, *beings that once were human but now are not*, creatures that have ceased to bear the divine image at all. Such people continue to exist in an ex-human state, no longer reflecting their maker in any meaningful sense."[56]

This view is Wright's attempt to preserve a kind of hell with judgment, but to avoid both U and A. People continuing in an "ex-human state" is surely a novel idea in the Christian tradition.

"The last thing I want is for anyone to suppose that I (or anyone else) know very much about all this. Nor do I want anyone to suppose I enjoy speculating in this manner. But I find myself driven, by the New Testament and the sober realities of this world, to this kind of a resolution to one of the darkest theological mysteries. I should be glad to be proved wrong but not at the cost of the fundamental claims that this world is the good creation of

---

55. Ibid., 181.
56. Ibid., 182–83.

the one true God and that he will at the end bring about that judgment at which the whole creation will rejoice."⁵⁷

He opts again here for "some kind of tragic end" for the unrepentant. Because he is a New Testament scholar I was hoping for comments on the basic scriptural position of the conditionalists, namely, that the words used in the Scripture which refer to the "end of the wicked" mean extinction and total destruction and not his novel ex-human state. However, I didn't find any. Perhaps he addresses this issue elsewhere.

John W. Wenham (1913-1996)

Wenham was the former Vice Principal of Tyndale Hall, Bristol, and Warden of Latimer House, Oxford. He went through an evolution in his understanding of CI. He was one of the twentieth-century scholars to ultimately take a positive attitude towards this theory. In his book *The Goodness of God* (1974), having briefly surveyed the basic pros and cons of CI, he wrote:

"A study of the literature reveals a remarkable failure by the 'traditional orthodox' to get to grips with the solid arguments put up by the conditionalists. It needs to be stressed that our summary of the debate in this brief encompass provides no basis for decision on so grave and complex an issue. As far as the thesis of this book is concerned, we shall consider ourselves under no obligation to defend the notion of unending torment until the arguments of the conditionalists have been refuted."⁵⁸

In 1991 he was asked to give a paper at the Fourth Edinburgh Conference in Christian Dogmatics whose theme was *Universalism and the Doctrine of Hell*. As his topic he chose "The Case for Conditional Immortality." He outlines his faith journey from a belief in hell to CI, and how he tentatively began to teach the latter. He came to believe that in both the Old and New Testaments the destiny of the wicked described

> are words of destruction rather than words suggesting continuance in torment or misery. The teaching of the New Testament is to be sharply contrasted with the Greek notion of the immortality of the soul. The ultimate contrast is between everlasting *life* and everlasting *death*, and this clearly shows that it is not simply synonyms but also antonyms with which we have to reckon. I was drawn to Conditionalism by Scripture rather than by a horrified

57. Ibid., 183.
58. Wenham, *Goodness*, 40–41.

recoil from the other doctrine. But I do plead guilty to a growing horror at the thought of millions in endless distress, which I find exceedingly difficult to reconcile not only with the goodness of God, but also with the final supremacy of Christ. If there are human beings alive suffering endless punishment it would seem to mean that they are in endless opposition to God, that is to say, we have a doctrine of endless sinning as well as of suffering. How can this be if Christ is all in all?

I have thought about this subject for more than fifty years and for more than fifty years I have believed the Bible to teach the ultimate destruction of the lost, but I have hesitated to declare myself in print. I regard with utmost horror the possibility of being wrong. We are all to be judged by our words (Matt 12:37) and teachers with greater strictness (Jas 3:1). *Whichever side you are on, it is a dreadful thing to be on the wrong side in this issue.* Now I feel that the time has come when I must declare my mind honestly. I believe that endless torment is a hideous and unscriptural doctrine which has been a terrible burden on the mind of the church for many centuries and a terrible blot on the presentation of the gospel. I should indeed be happy if, before I die, I could help in sweeping it away. Most of all I should rejoice to see a number of theologians (including some of the very first water) joining Fudge in researching this great topic in all its ramifications.[59]

This last statement by Wenham is one of the most frequently quoted by conditionalists.

---

59. Wenham, *"Case for Conditional,"* 190–91. This article is also included in *Re-Thinking Hell*.

6

Catholic Teaching

The Doctrinal Schema

IN AN INTRODUCTORY SECTION entitled "The Doctrinal Schema" Griffiths states: "The Christian doctrine about the novissima can be briefly set out under five headings: life eternal (*vita aeterna*), immortality of the soul (animae immortalitas), resurrection of the flesh (*carnis resurrectio*), restoration of the world (*renovatio mundi*), and beatific vision (*visio beatifica*)."[1]

"It is striking that the doctrinal schema shows almost no interest in the *inglorious last things* (emphasis added) of human creatures. The teaching church did come, with time, to teach, emphatically, that an inglorious last thing is possible for human creatures—that we may enter hell, that a glorious last thing is not our only possibility. But that is a matter of secondary interest, largely absent from the confessions of faith formulated at the ecumenical councils, and receiving much less speculative attention than questions about our glorious last thing."[2]

My *Guide* is concerned exclusively with the possibility that one of these inglorious last things could be annihilation. At the present time the inglorious last things are receiving a great amount of speculative attention and many of the studies concern what the following article by Gonzalez-Ruiz calls a "demythologizing of dogma." The last things are not so much being denied as reinterpreted and explained in a different way. (As an example, the catholic teaching on indulgences refers to a spiritual truth, but many present-day explanations use centuries-old words that are no longer

---

1. Griffiths, *Decreation*, 45.
2. Ibid., 53.

understandable by modern people. The present theological language seeking to explain indulgences needs to be demythologized.)

Jose-Maris Gonzalez-Ruiz and De-mythologizing the Separated Soul

In the prestigious Catholic series *Concilium* there was a volume called *The Problem of Eschatology*. One of the articles was entitled "Should We De-Mythologize the Separated Soul"? The author begins with an introduction about the nature of myth and the need to restore the transparency of myths. He starts with these reflections because much of our eschatological language is mythological, in the good sense. But this is not my main concern.

I begin this chapter with this article because of this statement by the author: "Should we be undertaking the task of 'demythologizing' our formulations, even the dogmatic ones? I think this is essential. If we are agreed on the importance of serious work on the demythologizing of the Bible, why should we resist the inevitable de-mythologizing of dogma?"[3]

His article on the separated soul is an example of what he means by demythologizing doctrinal formulations. Modern eschatology is very much involved in *demythologizing dogmas and doctrinal statements about the last things*. Gonzalez-Ruiz writes:

"I want to examine the old Christian myth of the immediate eschatology of the individual— the "separated soul." It can hardly be doubted that there has been a real "mythologization" of the myth— valid in itself— of the individual's encounter with God beyond the limits of personal life. I shall therefore try to follow the biblical thread, to discover the content of the myth in order to give it back its transparency and at the same time its authentically religious value."[4]

"For a correct understanding of the biblical myth of individual eschatology one has to start from the presupposition that for all the authors of the bible— the Old as well as the New Testament— there is no such thing as the "soul" in the sense in which it is found in Greek thought. The biblical man is one unit. But what is even more important to emphasize is that, according to the Bible, there is no divine element in man which guarantees the survival of human personality after death."[5]

3. Gonzalez-Ruiz, Maria, "De-Mythologize," 94–95.
4. Ibid., 85–86.
5. Ibid., 87.

"For the biblical writers, there is nothing divine or immortal in man: he is all mortal. God alone, through his saving power, can offer man the opportunity to overcome his innate mortality. The God who as a matter of *fact* made himself known to the minds of believers is a God who offers life over and above innate human mortality.[6]

The "myth" the author is seeking to restore to transparency, and which is probably the belief of most Christians, is the Greek understanding of the innate immortality of the soul that he treats in the beginning of his article.

"An outline of Greek thought on the subject of immediate personal eschatology is useful for an understanding of the religious content of the myth. In Platonic metaphysics, as is well known, the soul is not only immortal but eternal. It is a spark of the divine life, which knew the world of sovereign ideas "before," and which later— for reasons that are not always very clear in the Platonic tradition— was cast down from the heights and encased in a human form, where it is a prisoner and an exile, though without losing its imperishable nature."[7]

The author then gives what he considers the correct Judaeo-Christian understanding of "soul" as outlined above. It is generally the contention of the conditionalists that most Christians believe the soul is naturally immortal. The author de-mythologizes this myth. Some of his concluding comments are relevant to our topic, and perhaps especially to Catholic theology. He calls for the *demythologizing of ecclesial formulations of the faith.*

> What happens between the moment of individual death and the full realization of the divine promise with regard to the overcoming of death? There is no denying that in our Christian tradition and in successive ecclesial formulations of our faith we have built up a whole structure of theological imagery (cf. Dante) to give us some sort of answers to our anguished questions. Are these questions valid? Should we be undertaking the task of "demythologizing" our formulations, even the dogmatic ones? I think this is essential. If we are agreed on the importance of serious work on the demythologizing of the Bible, why should we resist the inevitable de-mythologizing of dogma?[8]

The author says that because of our faith in the church we should give her a "blank check" if she comes up with new dogmatic formulations. Such

---

6. Ibid., 92–93.
7. Ibid., 86.
8. Ibid., 94.

demythologizing is not a denial of dogmas but an attempt to define the core of dogmas and give them a new expression and interpretation. The present *Guide* can be seen as an attempt to present to readers some of the new developments in demythologizing the "dogma" *about the final state of a person who no longer desires to accept the will of the Father.* (Note: Hell is not a dogma of the church but a teaching.)

Official Catholic Teaching

The Benedictus Deus of Benedict XII and its Relevance for Annihilationism

In Catholic eschatological discussions the Constitution of Benedict XII *Benedictus Deus* (1336) is often included. First, let us put this teaching in an historical context.

Benedict's predecessor, Pope John XXII, even before becoming pope, "argued that those who died in the faith did not see the presence of God until the Last Judgment. He considered this a legitimate question for the speculation of theologians. He never included this teaching in any official documents, and eventually backed down from his position, and agreed that those who died in grace do indeed immediately enjoy the beatific vision."[9] Pope John died in 1334. Pope Benedict's Constitution is seen as a correction to Pope John's views. Griffiths considers sections of *Benedictus Deus* relevant for A.

This is the passage in *Benedictus Deus* clearly refuting the opinion of John XII: "Moreover we define that according to the general disposition of God the souls of those who die in actual mortal sin go down into hell immediately *(mox)* after death and there suffer the pain of hell. Nevertheless, on the day of judgment, all men will appear with their bodies "before the judgment seat of Christ" to give an account of their personal deeds, "so that each one may receive good or evil, according to what he has done in the body." (2 Cor 5.10)[10]

Since Griffiths' thinking about A is rather unique among Catholic theologians, he is especially interested in the relevance of *Benedictus Deus* to this theory. He says:

---

9. Wikipedia, *Benedictus Deus*.
10. Griffiths, *Decreation*, 204.

Such magisterial teaching has, however, not usually made a clear distinction between the thesis that every soul is necessarily incapable of coming to nothing, on the one hand, and the thesis that every soul is possibly incapable of coming to nothing, on the other.

Prominent among magisterial texts of this latter kind is Benedict XII's 1336 Constitution, *Benedictus Deus*. Benedict's central purpose in this text was to exclude the possibility that the saved are elsewhere than heaven and the damned elsewhere than in hell during the intermediate period between their deaths and the day of the final and general judgment.

Benedict's interest here is not in the possibility (or impossibility) of annihilation; it is only in emphasizing the importance of thinking, first, that everyone's final end is set at their death; that there is no lag between death and the experiential beginning of that end; and that among the possible ends is endless enfleshed suffering. This last point does not contradict my suggestion that annihilation is possible; it would do so only if the categories into which Benedict divides human beings were exhaustive, which the Constitution does not say. It does not contradict the view that the only two last things possible for us are the beatific vision and annihilation; but since the Constitution does not say that as a matter of fact anyone meets the conditions for eternal enfleshed suffering, it remains compatible with the view that, first, annihilation is possible, and, second, that no one in fact suffers eternally. But the question of magisterial teaching on the possibility of hell's emptiness is not the central issue here, for every position on that question is neutral to the question of whether annihilation for some is possible.[11]

Griffiths mentions a few other doctrinal statements about the immortality of the soul: the Fifth Lateran Council stated as a pernicious error that the rational soul is mortal; the Catechism of the Catholic Church (no. 366) is explicit in its support of the claim that the soul is immortal; Paul VI's *Professio Fidei* merely says that human beings are created by God with spiritual and immortal souls (no. 8); and *Gaudium et Spes* from Vatican II uses the same phrase. Griffiths' evaluation:

"These texts, while explicit and clear and most naturally read to rule out the possibility that any human soul can come to nothing, are, once again, *obiter dicta*. Their claims about the soul's immortality (and again, *the distinction between the soul's necessary mortality and its possible or*

---

11. Ibid., 204–05.

conditional mortality is not made) (emphasis added) occur, by the way, in contexts in which the argumentative focus is elsewhere."[12]

"There is, then, *little conciliar teaching of direct relevance to conditional immortality* [emphasis added]; and what little there is has other concerns. Other magisterial teaching is somewhat more expansive, but even here, although there is considerable interest in rejecting the view that immortality is impossible for humans and in affirming the view that damnation is possible, there is not much that speaks directly to annihilation as a form of (or as coextensive with) damnation. It remains possible for a Catholic thinker to speculate along these lines, and to affirm, speculatively, the view that resurrection is only for life [and not for damnation]."[13]

The Council of Trent (1545-63)

In any historical discussion of Catholic doctrine, the Council of Trent looms large. In the light of the Reformation it reemphasized and clarified Catholic teaching. From the Tridentine Catechism:

> Turning next to those who shall stand on His left, He will pour out His justice upon them in these words: *Depart from me, ye cursed, into everlasting fire*, prepared for the devil and his angels.
>
> The first words *depart from me* express the heaviest punishment with which the wicked shall be visited, their eternal banishment from the sight of God, unrelieved by one consolatory hope of ever recovering so great a good. This punishment is called by theologians the *pain of loss* because in hell the wicked shall be deprived forever of the light of the vision of God.
>
> The next words *into everlasting fire* express another sort of punishment, which is called by theologians *the pain of sense*. Moreover, when we reflect that this torment is to be eternal, we can see at once that the punishment of the damned includes every kind of suffering.[14]

This is Augustine's teaching, and it remains the basic doctrine of the Catholic Church to this day.

---

12. Ibid., 206.
13. Ibid., 208–09.
14. *Catechism*, 85–86.

The Sermon of St. Leonard of Port Maurice (1676–1751) on The Little Number of Those Who are Saved.

Before going on to the modern period of Catholic teaching it may be instructive to refer to one of the outstanding sermons of the Catholic tradition. Often in books on hell by Evangelicals the famous sermon of Jonathan Edwards, "Sinners in the Hands of an Angry God" is cited. He allows his imagination to run riot describing the terrors of hell.[15] This sermon by St. Leonard is the Catholic equivalent! I haven't read Edwards' entire sermon, but from the excerpts cited it seems he spent a great deal of time describing the horrors of hell. Very little of this sermon of St. Leonard is occupied with such descriptions: he emphasizes mostly authorities for his main theme that *few will be saved*.

In popular preaching since Augustine the Catholic Church would have generally taught the immortal soul doctrine along with the traditional understanding of hell. Before most people could read, preaching was the most common and powerful vehicle for the transmition of the faith, as well as dramas, paintings, sculptures, and stain glass windows. As well, puppetry began in the pulpit to teach the faith: "Marionette" means "little Mary."

Recall the graphic paintings of hell in the Sistine chapel! This sermon preached by St. Leonard was one of the most famous about hell in the seventeenth and eighteenth centuries. It was delivered hundreds of times (often outside because of the crowds), and resulted in enormous conversions. It's a good example of the understanding about hell by the theologians at this time, and which would have been the popular teaching about hell for many centuries, both before and after. The quotes are from St. Leonard; I paraphrase the rest.

The main emphasis of this sermon was that the majority of Christians are damned. (Augustine's *massa damnata*.) St. Leonard finds in people a decided "inclination to be damned by their own malice." He says he is only talking about adult Catholics, and not about non-Catholics. He quotes Chrysostom, Augustine, Anselm, Jerome and others who taught that most would not be saved. He quotes Aquinas: "Because eternal beatitude surpasses the normal state, especially since it has been deprived of original grace, it is the little number that are saved." The words of Christ, "Many are called but few are chosen" was one of St. Leonard's favorite texts! Most Catholics die "confessing badly at death, and therefore most of them are

---

15. Walls, *Logic*, 1.

damned." Several "facts" from "private revelations" are quoted —for example, demons speaking about people in hell.

And please don't quote me, the Saint says, about the great multitude in the Book of Revelation! This doesn't apply to Catholic adults. Yes, God wants everyone to be saved, and sufficient grace is given for this. Yes, God keeps giving grace until "the sinner becomes obstinate in evil." There is a long plea for repentance in which the Saint keeps repeating, "Thy damnation comes from thee [the individual person]."

However, there is also a great emphasis on God's mercy which is available to everyone. He closes with a prayer asking for mercy: "Lord, I confess that up till now I have not lived as a Christian. I repent, I deplore, and I detest my infidelity. I ask Thee for one thing only, to save my soul."[16]

Throughout the centuries, how many fire and brimstone sermons have been preached, and how much terrible fear of God has been inculcated! ands of anAngry God" is referenced.

The General Modern Teaching of the Catholic Church

Before turning to some specific Catholic authors of our time whose theology is relevant for A, it may be helpful to give the general teaching of the Church as found in authoritative sources. I quote here from several Catholic publications that would have contained the normal Catholic teaching on hell in the twentieth century. It is this teaching that is now in a state of transition and being "demythologized."

Catholic Encyclopedia, "Hell," 1910

Not surprisingly, this early edition of the Catholic Encyclopedia presents the traditional explanation of hell: "The existence of hell is proved first of all from Scripture. The existence of hell can be demonstrated even by the light of mere reason. Holy Writ is quite explicit in teaching the eternity of hell."[17]

However, I was pleased to see that the author was at least aware of other opinions about hell that are of main concern in my two *Guides*, CI and U: "Many admit the existence of hell but deny the eternity of its punishment. Conditionalists hold only a hypothetical immortality of the soul,

---

16. Our Lady of the Rosary.
17. *Catholic Encyclopedia* (1910), 207–08.

and assert that after undergoing a certain amount of punishment, the souls of the wicked will be annihilated. Many Protestants both in the past and in our own times held this doctrine, especially of late Edward White's "Life in Christ." The Universalists teach that in the end all the damned, at least all human souls will attain beatitude."[18]

Since two of my themes are a re-thinking of the ultimate fate of the unrepentant, and a de-mythologizing of eschatological terms, several passages in this early edition are of note, as the author leaves the door open for development.

> Many believe that reason cannot give any conclusive proof for the eternity of the pains of hell, but that it can merely show that this doctrine does not involve any contradiction. *Since the Church has made no decision on this point* (emphasis added), each one is entirely free to embrace this opinion. We admit that God might have extended the time of trial beyond death; however, had He done so, He would have permitted man to know about it, and would have made corresponding provision for the maintenance of moral order in this life. We may further admit that *it is not intrinsically impossible for God to annihilate the sinner after some definite amount of punishment* (emphasis added), but this would be less in conformity with the nature of man's immortal soul; and secondly, we know of no fact that might give us any right to suppose God will act in such a manner."[19]

His arguments against A are built on 1) the "immortality" of the soul, and 2) that we don't have any facts about it!

The following statement of the author also leaves room for development: "In itself, it is no rejection of Catholic dogma to suppose that God might at times, by way of exception, liberate a soul from hell. [He cites some arguments from the past.] But now theologians are unanimous in teaching that such exceptions never take place and never have taken place, a teaching which should be accepted."[20] (It's amazing what some theologians know about what God has not done and never will do!)

Also, the Catholic Church affirms that liturgy is a theological locus that expresses her faith—*lex orandi, lex credendi*. The author asks the following question in reference to his opinion about souls never leaving hell:

---

18. Ibid., 208.
19. Ibid., 209.
20. Ibid.

> How can the Church pray in the Offertory of the Mass for the dead, *Libera animas omnium fidelium defunctorum de poenis inferni et de profundo lacu?* [Deliver the souls of all the faithful departed from the pains of hell and from the depths of the abyss?]
>
> Sometimes [the Church] refers her prayers not to the time at which they are said, but to the time *for which* they are said. Thus the offertory [prayer] in question is referred to the moment when the soul is about to leave the body, although it is actually said sometime after that moment; and as if he were actually at the death-beds of the faithful, the priest implored God to preserve their souls from hell. But which-ever explanation be preferred, this much remains certain that in saying that offertory [prayer] the Church intends to implore only those graces which the soul is still capable of receiving, namely, the grace of a happy death or the release from purgatory.[21]

In this view people after death can still receive grace, which implies some kind of cooperation and growth. People are not static and immobile after death.

The Catholic Encyclopedia, "Hell," 1960

One example—of many—to which we may apply the need for demythologizing, is taken from the multi-volume Catholic Encyclopedia Series of 1960, Volume 28, *Life after Death*, by Maurice Becque, CSSR and Louis Becque, CSSR. In my early Catholic upbringing this would have been an authoritative source I would have consulted to find authentic Catholic doctrine. The authors' teaching about hell is the *exact opposite* of what the conditionalists are claiming and refuting. Some excerpts from this volume.

> [There is] a bashful silence about the dogma of eternal punishment. The furnace will never be extinguished: so the Church teaches. This fire, as Christ forcefully assures us, will endure for ever. Christ never says in explicit terms that those who undergo these instruments of torture will not be able to escape from them one day. The church, which alone possesses the full meaning of the words of the Lord and Master, in this case interprets them in their full rigour. That hell exists and is endless is a dogma of the Catholic faith. True; but in fact will any men be obliged to suffer the pains of hell? It would be temerarious to deny it. It is at the

---

21. Ibid., 209–10.

> least a certitude, and so is the existence of a torture called the pain of sense, which is something additional to the pain of loss, or the absence of God.
>
> Is hell a place? This is not a matter of faith. That it is a state of soul, a misery, an eternal torture, is what the Church imposes and presents as revealed truth. It must never be forgotten that the dogma of hell springs from the divine justice, which must be feared if men are to love him better. When God the Father sent his Son to die for us on the cross, it was not to deliver us from some milk-and-water hell.[22]

This would have been my Catholic belief for most of my early life. It's interesting that this article (1960) is more dogmatic than the earlier article of the 1910 Encyclopedia.

The New Catholic Encyclopedia, "Hell," (1967)

Six or seven years are not a long time to allow for the development of a teaching. Was there any development in the Catholic understanding of hell between the two editions of the 1960 Encyclopedia and this one of 1967? The presentation in the latter continues to teach the traditional doctrine about hell, although the following is a significant change from the 1960 article: "Although there is no creedal statement of belief in hell, the creedal statement that Christ will return to judge the living and the dead entails the doctrinal statement of belief in the mystery of hell."[23] However, in a brief section entitled "Dogmatic Development" it appears that some attempt was being made to understand the reality of hell from new theological perspectives.

> The category of revelation is increasingly used to integrate the theology of hell and eschatology within systematic theology. This category of revelation introduces into the theology of hell the concepts of the kingdom of God and of unbelief. Both concepts express personal realties and entail a concept of freedom: the freedom in which a person rejects the self-giving that another freely makes. In this context *separation from God is the theological idea of hell.* (emphasis added) And by reference to the divine self-giving manifested now in the Lord Jesus, and to be manifested when God is all in all, this idea of hell as separation from God is worked out.

---

22. Becque, "Life after Death," 95–121.
23. Encyclopedia (1967), 1006.

> The consequence of this separation from God is expressed in the idea of hell as retribution for sin; the theological concepts of damnation and hellfire are used to interpret this consequence. While respecting the mystery of God's dealings with the fact of unbelief, this theology of hell endeavors to make a statement of belief in the mystery of hell that is wider in form than the present doctrinal statement of that belief. But it is aware that the truths its idea of hell interprets cannot be held together in logical equilibrium.[24]

It seems we have here some small beginnings of the de-mythologization of dogmas called for by Gonzalez-Ruiz: "The theological concepts of damnation and hellfire are used to *interpret*. . . ." (emphasis added) Also, understanding that the "theological idea" of hell is *separation from God* is compatible with the conditionalist position of A.

The Catechism of the Catholic Church (1994)

"The teaching of the church affirms the existence of hell and its eternity. Immediately after death the souls of those who die in a state of mortal sin descend into hell, where they suffer the punishments of hell, "eternal fire." The chief punishment of hell is eternal separation from God, in whom alone man can possess the life and happiness for which he was created and for which he longs." (No. 1035)[25]

I note that the existence of hell here is called a "teaching of the Church" and not a dogma. There are very few dogmas and many teachings (theologoumena).

Catholic Authors

M.J. Scheeben (1865)

Scheeben was one of my favorite authors in my early theological reading. His writing was poetic and as such he was a forerunner of Balthasar in making theology beautiful. I still treasure memories of his writings. Griffiths give us a summary of some aspects of Scheeben's theology of hell. I quote him to emphasize the traditional understanding of hell by one of the eminent Catholic theologians in the nineteenth century.

---

24. Ibid., 1007.
25. *Catechism of Catholic Church*, 270.

Scheeben assumes that the LORD's justice means and must mean that he punishes the wicked directly for their sins, that every soul is necessarily immortal, and that the souls of all the damned are rejoined to their resurrected flesh at the general resurrection. The language is very strong: the first of the verbs has the connotation of bringing to nothing. . .and the second connotes consumption without remainder. Language of this kind runs like a dark thread through Scheeben's analysis of the punishments of hellfire. The Lord's punitive power reduces the damned almost to nothing, and brings the body to the edge of annihilation. The Lord must punish the wicked with torments that bring them almost to nothing. Justice demands it. That material fire can do this, torment flesh and soul together endlessly, is, Scheeben thinks, a miracle of God's punitive justice, a mystery of agony, pain, and of fear.

For both Augustine and Scheeben (and on these matters they are representative figures; most of the speculative tradition is with them), it is taken as axiomatic, whether because of Scripture or tradition or both, that hell is real and inhabited, and that it must involve fleshly torture. Neither is convincing.

[Their] axioms do not need to be accepted by Christians; they are themselves speculations, as much as any of the positions entertained in this work; they are theologoumenal, we might say, rather than properly theological.[26]

George Panneton, *Heaven or Hell* (1955)

If inquirers in the mid-twentieth century wanted to know the Catholic teaching about hell—besides being referred to encyclopaedias—they might have been handed this book of 360 pages. The following quotations show that the Catholic doctrine about hell at this time was the same as what we found in the encyclopaedias, and what the conditionalists call "traditional," that is, everlasting suffering. It is this doctrine they have been opposing for several centuries now, and which forms the main part of my presentation. It is significant that there is no awareness of CI in this book. (This is to emphasize once again the lack of Catholic familiarity with this topic.) The universalist "heretics" are given one line. The following quotes express the *exact opposite* of what the conditionalists believe.

---

26. Griffiths, *Decreation*, 244–46.

Catholic Teaching

What is Hell? Definition. Hell is a place of punishment where those who die in mortal sin are deprived forever of the sight of God, and suffer terrible and eternal torments.

Those merit Hell, according to the Gospel, who reject the faith of Christ and the light of the Gospel (Mark 16:16; John 3:18–19; and according to the parables, "the foolish virgins" (Matt 25:1),"the wicked rich man" (Luke 16:19), the man who failed to make use of his talents (Matt 25:30), the man who did not show charity toward his neighbor (Matt 25:41–46), the one who had not on his wedding garment, which signifies the state of grace (Matt 22:11–13).

They also merit Hell, the apostle St. Paul tells us, who are impious, idolaters, unjust, thieves, covetous, drunkards, impure, adulterers, and so forth (1 Cor 6:9–10). To these one might add blasphemers, apostates, sacrilegious, militant atheists, murderers, suicides, scandalmongers, maligners, and so on.

A person who dies with the stain of mortal sin upon his soul, even of a single mortal sin for which he has no contrition, merits Hell. Immediately after death the soul enters into eternity. It quits the life of earth (the transitory state) and is fixed forever in happiness, if saved, in misery and hatred of God, if damned.[27]

The pain of loss, loss of God, is for the damned the most terrible pain of all: that is a truth of faith defined as such by the Council of Trent (1545). This truth is based upon the teaching of the Gospel. Indeed, in the scene of the Last Judgment, our Lord represents the sovereign Judge as saying: "Depart from me, you cursed, into everlasting fire!" (Matt 25:41) At the end of the parable of the ten virgins, the Bridegroom, who represents Christ, says to the foolish virgins: "I know you not!" and shuts the door upon them (Matt 25: 10–12). There is the same gesture on the Master's part toward the "workers in iniquity (Luke 13:25). Lastly, in the parable of the king who made a marriage feast for his son, a symbol of the Kingdom of Heaven: "When the marriage was filled with guests, the king went in. . .and he saw there a man who had not on a wedding garment. Then the king said to the waiters: Bind his hands and his feet, and cast him into the exterior darkness; there shall be weeping and gnashing of teeth (Matt 22:2–13).

Now the wedding garment symbolizes the state of grace; the man who has been deprived of this is, therefore, in a state of mortal sin

---

27. Panneton, *Heaven or Hell*, 177–78.

and has been thrown into exterior darkness, which signifies Hell and the pain of loss.[28]

A. Tanquerey, *A Manual of Dogmatic Theology* (1959)

Thousands of Catholic seminarians in the twentieth century would have studied this Manual. It is indicative of Catholic text books used for the formation of clergy. All the "proofs" from Scripture about the final fate of the unrepentant are totally traditional, that is, all are interpreted as referring to everlasting punishment without any other alternative even being considered.

The Existence and Eternity of the Pains of Hell

Errors. All those deny the existence of hell that reject the immortality of the soul or the necessity of some sanction. Arnobius, who, following Zoroaster and the Agnostics, thought that the reprobate are annihilated; this error some Liberal Protestants brought back to life, for example, the Socinians, Rothe, White, and the Origenists, who teach that all angels and men are finally recovered. [Note: the Socinians, Rothe and White were conditionalists. (above)]

Thesis: The devils and those men who die in the state of mortal sin are punished with everlasting sufferings. This is *de fide* [of the faith].

Proof from Scripture. From the time of the Prophets, the existence and eternity of the punishments of hell for the reprobate is clearly evidenced. In the New Testament this dogma is lucidly proclaimed, both in regard to reprobation in general and in regard to the eternity of the punishments.

Proof from Tradition. Many of the Fathers, from the third to the fifth centuries, in spite of Origen's power and authority, assailed these errors.

From the Councils. In the Athanasian Creed the eternity of the punishments is enunciated; also the Councils of Lateran IV in 1215, of Lyons II, of Florence and of Trent.

Proof from Reason. Certainly the existence of punishments by means of which the wicked are punished in another life, for some time at least, can be proved. However, reason cannot apodictically demonstrate the eternity of the punishments, but can

28. Ibid., 263–64.

only persuade by means of probable arguments, on the part of the sinner and on the part of God.[29]

This last statement concerning the limited power of reason as regards the eternity of hell is the only opening for any development in Tanquerey's presentation. For the most part he offered Catholic seminarians an absolutely traditional understanding of hell.

Ludwig Ott, *Fundamentals of Catholic Dogma* (1952)

Another text book used by innumerable seminarians—including myself—was Ott's *Fundamentals*. For my purposes it suffices to say that Ott gives very detailed references to the reality and eternity of hell in tradition and the teaching of the church. His presentation is identical with that of Tanquerey's. He has no doubts and does not present any other possible alternatives: "Hell is a place or state of eternal punishment inhabited by those rejected by God." He does, however, have the following short statement which shows his awareness of other views: "The reality of hell is contested by those sects which teach the total annihilation of the godless after death or after the General Judgment, and also by all who deny personal immortality."[30]

The following two Catholic theologians are mentioned by Froom whose views he considered relevant to his historical study of CI.

Claude Tresmontant, OP (1925–1997) on the Immortality of the Soul

Tresmontant, a Dominican Priest, was educated at the Sorbonne in philosophy and Hebrew, and specialized in New Testament and Palestinian Judaism.

> The idea has obviously gained ground even among certain Roman Catholic scholars that the traditional concept of natural immortality is not grounded in Holy Scripture. Rehearsing the familiar Innate Immortality postulate found in the mystery religions— with its soul set free from the body—Tresmontant presents the contrasting biblical resurrection teaching of Scripture, the salvation

---

29. Tanquerey, *Manual*, 435–40.
30. Ott, *Fundamentals*, 479.

of the whole man, and the error of aspects of the traditional view. Tresmontant:

> "The Jewish doctrine of the resurrection of the dead was still more incomprehensible (if that were possible) to a Greek philosopher than the idea of creation. The mystery religions had done something in those days to make the idea of an immortality of the soul familiar: the soul set free from the body to which it had the misfortune to be bound. But the Judaeo-Christian teaching on the resurrection is quite a different matter. *It does not mean that a part of man— his soul— will be freed by discarding the other part— his material body; biblical teaching implies that the whole man will be saved.*"[31]

Y.B. Tremel, OP

The following excerpt is taken from an article written by this French Dominican in 1955.

> *The New Testament obviously does not conceive of man's life after death philosophically or in terms of the natural immortality of the soul.* Here the sacred writers do not think of life to come as the term of a natural process. On the contrary, for them it is always the result of salvation and redemption; it depends on the will of God and on the victory of Christ.
>
> The New Testament links the resurrection of the dead with the glorious coming of Christ at the end of time to judge all mankind. Christ's resurrection and his entrance into glory at the right hand of the Father are, according to the apostles, a guarantee and a pledge of this second coming. For St. Paul, the victory of the First Born among the dead will not be complete until it overcomes death itself and reveals itself in the risen bodies of those who have been *asleep in death*.[32]

Joseph Ratzinger, Eschatology, "Death and Eternal Life."

For our purposes the then Professor Ratzinger (1977) has a very long and important chapter in this book entitled "The Immortality of the Soul and the Resurrection of the Dead." We are mostly interested in his understanding

---

31. Froom II, 919–20.
32. Ibid., 921–22.

of immortality and how one achieves it. As I've mentioned, the thesis of the conditionalists does not essentially depend on whether the soul is *naturally* immortal or not: God can withdraw existence anytime since he freely gave it. However, the question of immortality is a very important factor for the conditionalists because they believe the doctrine of hell emerged when the soul philosophically was considered naturally immortal. Therefore, any punishment for the unrepentant after death must be immortal because "the soul cannot die."

As we shall see, Ratzinger does not consider the A argument, but his understanding of immortality can serve as a case for the conditionalist position. "Substantial" and "substantialistic" are his words for the soul being naturally immortal, a view he rejects. He also teaches that immortality essentially flows from a relationship with God, another essential position of the conditionalists. Ratzinger's conclusions on this latter point is similar to that of a number of other philosophers and theologians.

His teaching that concerns us is "The Dialogical Character of Immortality." He has spent, in the first part of this chapter, a great deal of time on matters related to immortality, for example, the nature of the soul, and he has now arrived at his conclusions about immortality.

> The challenge to traditional theology today lies in the negation of an autonomous, "substantial" soul with a built-in immortality, in favor of that positive view which regards God's decision and activity as the real foundation of a continuing human existence. Paul Althaus: "Whether believers or no, it is God who makes us endure. He it is who enables us to persist, through all the reality of death in which we are lost to ourselves. He makes us endure and, in resurrection, gives us back to ourselves once more so that we may stand before his judgment seat and live."
>
> It might be said that, as soon a one begins to speak of a soul one renders immortality "substantialistic," in a theologically inappropriate manner. However, in none of the great theological teachers have I found a purely substantialistic argument for immortality. Not even Plato argues on this basis.[33]

Ratzinger then refers to a homily of Gregory of Nyssa who quotes the gospel, "Blessed are the pure of heart, for they shall see God," and comments, "This is eternal life, that they may know you...." But then Gregory notes that the Scripture tells us no one can see God: "If God be Life, then

---

33. Ratzinger, *Eschatology*, 150–51.

anyone who does not see God does not see life. However, the prophets and the apostle testify: no one can see God."[34] Ratzinger then uses the story of Peter walking on the waters to explain how seeing God becomes possible.

> Only the Lord's outstretched hand can save sinking Peter, that is, humankind. That hand reaches out for us in the saying "Blessed are the pure in heart, for they shall see God." Philosophical understanding remains a walking on the waters: it yields no solid ground. Only God incarnate can draw us out of the waters by his power and hold us firm. Only he can make us stand up straight on the breakers of the sea of mortality. His promise is that we will attain the vision of God, which is life, not through speculative thinking but by the purity of an undivided heart, in the faith and love which takes the Lord's hand and are led by it.
>
> Here, then, owing to a christological transformation, the Platonist notion of the life which flows from truth is rendered more profound, and made the vehicle of a "dialogical" concept of humanity: man is defined by his intercourse with God. At the same time, this new concept makes absolutely concrete claims about the things which will set us right on the path of immortality, and so changes a seemingly speculative theme into something eminently practical. The "purification" of the heart which comes about in our daily lives, through the patience which faith and its offspring, love, engender that purification that finds its mainstay in the Lord who makes the paradoxical walking on the waters a possibility and so gives meaning to an otherwise absurd existence. This quite basic conception has remained characteristic of Christian thought in the tradition, though it may be presented with a variety of different nuances.[35]

In the section entitled "Immortality and Creation" Ratzinger addresses the following problem: "When immortality is thought of simply as grace [as in the above section] or, indeed, as the special destiny of the pious, then it takes flight into the realm of the miraculous and loses its claim on the serious attention of thinking people." He then proceeds to give immortality a more rational, philosophical justification.

> Man is capable of grasping truth in its most comprehensive meaning; it also belongs intrinsically to his being to participate in life. We agreed earlier that it is not a relationless being oneself that makes a human being immortal, but precisely his relatedness, or

34. Ibid., 151.
35. Ibid., 151–53.

> capacity for relatedness, to God. We must now add that such an opening of one's existence is not a trimming, an addition to a being which really might subsist in an independent fashion. On the contrary, it constitutes what is deepest in man's being. It is nothing other than what we call "soul." A being is more itself the more it is open, the more it is in relationship. Such openness is not a product of human achievement. It is given to man; man depends for it on Another. But it is given to man to be his very own possession. That is what is meant by creation, and what Thomas means when he says that immortality belongs to man by nature.[36]

Ratzinger then turns to the question that has relevance for our consideration of hell and A: "How is it possible for human beings to live in a fashion that goes counter to their own essence: closed off from, rather than open to, the rest of being?"[37]

> An existence in which man tries to divinize himself, to become "like a god" in his autonomy, independence and self-sufficiency, turns into a Sheol-like existence, a being in nothingness, a shadow-life on the fringe of real living. This does not mean, however, that man can cancel God's creative act or put it into reverse. The result of sin is not pure nothingness. Like every other creature, man can only move within the ambit of creation. Just as he cannot bring forth being of himself, so neither can he hurl it back into sheer nothingness. What he can achieve in this regard is not the annulment of being, but lived self-contradiction, a self-negating possibility, namely "Sheol." The natural ordination towards truth, towards God, which of itself excludes nothingness, still endures, even when it is denied or forgotten.
>
> The Christian teaching on eternal life takes on, once again, a thoroughly practical character at this point. Immortality is not something we achieve. Though it is a gift inherent in creation it is not something which just happens to occur in nature. Immortality rests upon a relationship in which we are given a share, but by which, in sharing it, we are claimed in turn.[38]

I don't know if Ratzinger anywhere in his writings treats of the possibility of annihilation as we are considering it here. He mentions above that man "cannot bring forth being of himself, so neither can he hurl it back into sheer nothingness." But he doesn't seem to treat the question of

36. Ibid., 154–55.
37. Ibid., 155.
38. Ibid., 156–57.

whether or not God actually *may* hurl a person back into nothingness if she is trying to divinize herself. Of course, he would agree that God *can* do this, but he seems to say that the person enters a Sheol-like existence, leaving it undefined what exactly that would be. Is it another way of speaking about hell? It seems close to the option Wright offers (above, chapter 7), a kind of non-person state of the unrepentant.

The following theologians may not specifically treat, or agree with, CI, but their thinking is relevant for our topic.

Peter Phan

Peter Phan is a prominent Catholic theologian on eschatology. He writes:

> Second, the belief in the resurrection does not entail the belief that immortality is a natural, innate attribute of the soul. It may be taken to be an additional gift of God to humans. In other words, one may think that when a person dies, the whole person, that is, both the soul and body perish. In this case, resurrection may be understood to mean the raising to life of the entire human person, of *both* body and the soul, after their death, by a gracious act of God.
>
> Third, we may not be able, nor is it required by the Christian faith, to prove by rational argument the immortality of the soul; rather we may accept this truth on the basis of faith. One may simply hold that the immortality of the soul is not a truth that can be known by means of unaided reason but a truth that has been revealed by God.
>
> Perhaps most significantly it must be noted that what the Bible means by the resurrection of the dead goes far beyond what philosophers mean by the immortality of the soul. A careful reading of Scripture will reveal that the central focus of the Christian message is not the immortality of the soul, though this is not excluded, but eternal life.[39]

> While it is to be acknowledged that in Christian Tradition the eternity of hell has been repeatedly affirmed, especially following Saint Augustine and Saint Thomas, there are also in the early church two other views that argue that hell is not eternal. The first expounded by the second-century Saint Irenaeus, affirms that God alone is eternal and that eternal life or immortality is a gift of God, and not

---

39. Phan, *Living*, 37–38.

a natural attribute of any creature, including humans. The implication of this view, known as "conditional immortality," is that if no creature is naturally eternal, so too is hell [not eternal]. It follows then that by nature hell cannot last forever but will only last as long as evil lasts, and since evil will ultimately be conquered by God, hell will also be destroyed.[40]

That "hell will be destroyed" seems to support the conditionalist view.

John E. Thiel, *Icons of Hope: the "Last Things" in Catholic Imagination*

His book is not explicitly concerned with the debates concerning CI, Hell, and U. However, in his treatment of "the last things" from his perspective as "icons of hope" many of his comments relate indirectly to our theme. Especially is this true of chapter 1, "Imagining the Last Judgment." His treatment of this topic presupposes that he would be on the side of those who believe that a fundamental act that determines a person's eternal destiny *is possible*. He is concerned that the doctrine of the Last Judgment is almost disappearing from the Catholic consciousness.

> Thus, it seems more likely that the Last Judgment's loss of suspense is attributable to a contemporary Catholic belief that virtuous and sinful agency account for little in the drama of salvation. These two beliefs are clearly related. The reason that the Last Judgment has become a foregone conclusion in the faith of contemporary Catholics is that the utterly predictable end has already been revealed in the way grace is imagined to overwhelm human responsibility for virtuous contribution to salvation and for the avoidance of sinful strides to perdition.
>
> As Hans Urs von Balthasar has argued eloquently, it is not at all contrary to Catholic belief to hope that all are saved—that the Last Judgment will have a graceful singularity about it that would simply dash the eschatological imagination of our medieval artists, accustomed as they were to the divisive juxtaposition of the saved and the damned. It is, however, utterly contrary to Catholic belief to maintain that human responsibility exercised in words and deeds matters little in the face of God's grace, even if the motivation for that belief is a deep appreciation for the infinity of God's love and mercy. For nearly all of eternity, then, heaven and hell

---

40. Phan, *Living*, 90.

would be embodied places where entire persons would enjoy or suffer the consequences of how they enacted the entirety of their personal existence in time.[41]

Universalists have no problem with the free choices of people having consequences for their final state. However, their position is that negative resistance cannot last forever. Thiel's last sentence seems to place him on the side of the conditionalists as regards the *possibility of an ultimate choice*—"would enjoy or suffer the consequences. . . ." In any case, the passages quoted are warnings of a belief that goes beyond *hoping* for the salvation of all that would foster a "self-satisfied complacency" in the love and mercy of God.

Ratzinger on Purgatory

Does Ratzinger's teaching about purgatory have any relevance for CI? I think it does because the theology of purgatory admits of further purification and spiritual growth after death. Some conditionalists allow for this. Ratzinger sees the teaching of Clement of Alexandria as one of the starting points for the Catholic understanding of such post-mortem purification which eventually developed into the Catholic teaching about Purgatory.

> In Clement as in the Western writers, the penance imposed by the Church is a concrete process which can and often must continue beyond the gate of death. For him as for them, this process points up the difference between someone's valid fundamental decision, whereby he is accepted in grace, and the defective permeation of the effects of that decision throughout the being of the whole person. More clearly at Alexandria than in the Western tradition. . .the real frontier runs not between earthly life and not-life, but between being with Christ, on the one hand, and, on the other, being without him or against him. The decisive step is taken in baptism: while the fundamental option of the baptismal candidate becomes definitively established with death, its full development and purification may have to await a moment beyond death, when we make our way through the judging fire of Christ's intimate presence in the companionable embrace of the family of the church.[42]

---

41. Thiel, *Icons*, 137–40.
42. Ratzinger, *Eschatology*, 226–27.

Of special relevance for our topic is Ratzinger's expression "fundamental option/decision," and "the defective permeation of the effects of that decision." As I understand the conditionalists, a person becomes "immortal" after she has made this fundamental decision for God. This can be made in this life; this would also be the Catholic position. But such a person can still have some kind of "defective permeation" in her being that needs to be purified. This takes place after death; this is Purgatory, not a place but a temporary state. (St. John Paul II said that purgatory could even be instantaneous.)

Another comment from Ratzinger leads to a further insight for our purposes. He defines Purgatory as "the inwardly necessary process of transformation in which a person becomes capable of Christ, capable of God, and thus capable of unity with the whole communion of saints."[43]

The word "capable" reminds me of how the conditionalists refer to the natural soul as "immortalizable," "capable of becoming immortal." And the person becomes *actually* immortal when this fundamental choice for God is made. Catholic theology would agree that the natural soul is *capable* of Christ, and of God. (Aquinas says somewhere that the soul is almost infinite—*anima est quasi infinita*.) Traditionally, Purgatory has been understood as the state where a person has made this fundamental choice and only needs to be further purified; her eternal destiny has been assured. It's not part of the traditional understanding of Purgatory that people there can ever be lost: they are assured of heaven; they have made the fundamental choice. The possibility of such a choice in this life seems implied in the doctrine of Purgatory since, because of such a choice in our earthly life, the person only needs to be further purified in the next.

Would conditionalists agree that someone who has made this fundamental choice and is "in Purgatory" and thus has "become immortal" can go back on her choice? Some would agree and others not. All agree that God can withdraw existence whenever—in a mutual relationship with the person—he decides the chosen state of the person is without hope. But many conditionalists have a strong belief that once a person has made a definitive choice for God, it is probable that she or he will remain constant in such a decision. And this would be in harmony with the Catholic view that someone in Purgatory who has made the choice for God is safe forever.

---

43. Ibid., 230. Cf. *Purgatory* by Jerry Walls for a unique evangelical approach to this topic.

What if someone has not made such a fundamental choice before death? Is such a definitive choice *against God* in this life possible? Can one have full knowledge and freedom to do so? We have just said that one can make a fundamental decision *for God* in this life, and so enter Purgatory because such a choice has been made. But if someone hasn't made such a choice, and does not go to Purgatory, where do they go? Traditionally the Church has said they go to hell, and no longer have any chance of making a decision for God.

But there is a growing opinion favoring *post-mortem conversion.* And does not the doctrine of Purgatory imply that *people continue to change after death?*

Garrigou-Lagrange, OP, *Life Everlasting and the Immensity of the Soul*

As mentioned above, Lagrange was one of the foremost Thomistic Catholic scholars of the twentieth century and, as such, his views on the topics with which we are concerned are, as expected, *extremely traditional.* To repeat: for the purposes of this study, hell is not being considered as a possibility. I am following Griffiths that there are only two *novissima*, annihilation and heaven. However, there are sections in Lagrange on hell, annihilation, and purgatory that are relevant for our consideration. Lagrange admits, in his treatment of hell,

> that this eternity of suffering cannot be demonstrated apodictically. The mysteries of iniquity and wickedness, and their consequences, are more obscure than the mysteries of grace. They are obscure, not only to us, but even in themselves. Final impenitence, of which hell is a consequence, is the darkest of all mysteries. Just as we cannot demonstrate apodictically either the possibility for the existence of the Holy Trinity, of the redemptive Incarnation, of eternal life, so similarly we are unable to demonstrate apodictically the eternity of the sufferings of hell.[44]

He then goes on to give the traditional arguments for the eternity of hell's sufferings. However, it is this admission, on Lagrange's part and on the part of others, of the *impenetrability of the mysteries connected with final impenitence* that encourages modern scholars to speculate freely about the last things. And then, turning to some objections to the eternity of

---

44. Lagrange, *Life Everlasting*, 85.

the sufferings of hell, he has these reflections on annihilation which were somewhat of a surprise to me: few Catholic theologians spoke about A.

> But, if what religion tells us is true, *then divine justice demands the annihilation of the sinner* (emphasis added), whose ingratitude cancels the benefit of existence. Divine revelation alone can enlighten us here. Revelation says, not that the damned are to be annihilated, but that they are to be punished eternally. God could of course annihilate, but He does not. What He created, He also preserves. He raises the body to life. Further, if every mortal sin were punished by annihilation, all sins would be equally punished. St. Thomas says: "He that sins against God who gives him existence merits indeed to lose that existence. Nevertheless, if we consider the disorder, more or less grave, of the fault committed, and then the affliction due to it, we find that the proper punishment is not the loss of existence, because this is presupposed for merit or demerit, and therefore is not to be corrupted by the disorder of sin."[45]

This is an interesting—but unconvincing—argument of Aquinas against annihilation: if someone is destroyed then he can no longer be meriting or demeriting. In hell one can be punished continually for sin, and thus punishment can be apportioned properly! If all are annihilated, there would be equal punishment and thus it would not really be just! Lagrange admits that the answer must come from revelation. The conditionalists believe that this is exactly what revelation reveals—annihilation.

Lagrange then quotes from a sermon by the great Lacordaire. As with the sermon of St. Leonard (above), it's an example of how *preachers* dealt with the possibility of annihilation.

"The obstinate sinner wishes his own annihilation because annihilation would deliver him from God, the just judge. God would be thus constrained to undo what He has done, and that which He has made to last forever. The universe is not meant to perish. Shall, then, a soul perish simply because it does not wish to acknowledge God? No. A soul, the most precious work of the Creator, will live on forever. You can soil that soul, but you cannot destroy it. God, whose justice you have challenged, turns even the lost souls into images of His law, into heralds of His justice."[46]

Lacordaire argues that the soul has been made to "last forever," that is, the soul is naturally immortal. He follows the traditional argument derived

---

45. Ibid., 89.
46. Ibid., 90.

from the Platonic influence on the Scriptures. And he seems to be following Aquinas (above): people in hell forever are "heralds of His justice." The punishment of hell is more just than annihilation.

Lagrange on Purgatory

For very many years I have thought that our common understanding of the Greek "immobile state" of people after death was wrong: as long as people are alive there must be movement, either growth or decline in fulfilling the Father's plan. Gregory of Nyssa speaks of going from "glory to glory" in the afterlife. The traditional "static" understanding is exemplified in Lagrange's traditional teaching that at the moment of death there is the particular judgement: "This instant terminates merit and demerit, covers their entire terrestrial life, and is therefore definitive."[47]

But what if people have died in *venial* sin? How are these forgiven if they can no longer merit? Lagrange comes up with a very complicated scholastic answer: "Such sins are remitted to them by the act of charity and contrition which they make immediately after death, at the moment of the particular judgment. This act is no longer meritorious. But it is an act of charity and contrition which suffices to remit venial sins. This doctrine is very probable"[48] It is not clear, however, how acts of charity and contrition can be "non-meritorious."

The most important point of Lagrange for our discussion is that personal growth is possible "in purgatory," in the after-life. But for those who do not believe in purgatory, cannot such growth be applied to other states?

"Souls in purgatory can grow in virtue, at least those which are in the faculties purely spiritual, as, for instance, prudence and justice. The souls in purgatory do [also] perform intense acts of faith, hope, charity, religion, and hence it seems that infused virtues, too, would increase, not indeed by repetition of acts. . .but because God, in mercy, would grant this growth without any new merit. This is not in harmony with the traditional doctrine. St. Thomas says, "After death there is no way to acquire grace or to increase it."[49]

---

47. Ibid., 139–40.
48. Ibid., 141.
49. Ibid., 145–46.

It seems this opinion of Lagrange could be extended and applied to "mortal sins" and to those who chose against God in their lifetimes; it can be therefore applied to the possibility of post-mortem conversions.

Joshua R. Brotherton, *Universalism and Predestinationism: A Critique of the Theological Anthropology that Undergirds Catholic Universalist Eschatology*

As the title indicates, the author is critiquing what he understands as the anthropology undergirding the universalist position, which is that all human beings are likely to be saved. His conclusion is that this anthropology "undermines the natural integrity of human freedom."[50] I will briefly try and summarize the author's the view that a final tragic choice is possible for persons. It is not necessary, for my purposes, to enter into all the complexities of his argumentation. He mostly critiques Balthasar's theology of grace and freedom which he finds defective. Balthasar has a "proclivity towards universalism."[51] "He [Balthasar] does not take seriously enough the reality of moral evil."[52]

"Universalism presupposes predestinarianism. By 'predestinarianism' is meant a competitive understanding of the relationship between divine grace and created freedom such that freedom is authentic only if grace *overcomes* its capacity for sin."[53] "Human freedom was created by God with the real potential for rejecting its full actualitzation, for contradicting its own deepest desire, and for refusing the higher freedom offered as a divine reward."[54] "It is also important not to turn a blind eye to the terrible reality that God (presumably, for a greater good) ordinarily permits free creatures the enduring power to resist grace, however defective such a 'power' may be."[55] "Affirming that God cares for every free creature with infinite compassion in Christ, does not imply, however, that God will not allow human beings to reject the offer of glory on their own accord."[56]

---

50. Brotherton, "Universalism," 603.
51. Ibid., 619.
52. Ibid., 609.
53. Ibid., 604.
54. Ibid., 610.
55. Ibid., 611.
56. Ibid., 613.

The author sees in Jacques Maritain's "eschatological proposal a more promising path than Balthasar's subjunctive universalism."[57] "Maritain's position [is] that it is more proper to the nature of our freedom for God to allow for 'nihilation. . . ."[58] "Maritain's eschatological proposal is precisely that the pain of loss and remorse of conscience eternally suffered by the damned is mitigated by an ever-growing natural knowledge and love of God granted by divine mercy following final judgment."[59]

Some conclusions of the author after he critiques other views:

"God may truly desire that all human beings cease from resisting divine grace, but God permits some to persist in resisting its efficacy."[60] "It is clear that it is both fitting that God respect perseverance in sin and that it be possible for God to become 'omnia in omnibus' (1 Cor 15:28) without saving every human being from eternal pain of loss."[61] "Certainly all things will be reconciled to the Father in Christ by the spirit, but the particular form that reconciliation takes need not be the salvation of all human beings ,and universal salvation appears to be an especially doubtful proposal."[62]626

I quote Brotherton as another witness to the possibility of making a final fateful decision.

Recent Doctrinal Statements

Letter on Certain Questions Concerning Eschatology, Sacred Congregation for the Doctrine of the Faith, 1979

I present only some aspects of this brief Letter that are relevant for our topic. The Letter is concerned with the article of the Creed concerning life everlasting, and so everything in general after death. The Letter says "there is no question here of restricting or preventing the theological research that the faith of the Church needs and from which it should profit. The Sacred Congregation, whose task is to advance and protect the doctrine of the faith, here wishes to recall what the Church teaches in the name of Christ, especially concerning what happens between the death of the Christian and

---

57. Ibid., 620.
58. Ibid., 621.
59. Ibid., 622.
60. Ibid., 624.
61. Ibid., 626.
62. Ibid.

Catholic Teaching

the general resurrection." The Letter lists, then, '"what the Church considers to pertain to the essence of the faith."(No.6)

1. The Church believes in the resurrection of the dead.
2. The Church understands this resurrection as referring to the whole person.
3. The Church affirms that a spiritual element survives and subsists after death, the human self. The Church uses the word "soul."
4. The Church's prayers are *loci theologici* and are not to be rendered meaningless.
5. The Church looks for the glorious manifestation of our Lord, Jesus Christ.
7. The Church believes in the happiness of the just who will one day be with Christ. She believes that there will be eternal punishment for the sinner, who will be deprived of the sight of God, and that this punishment will have a repercussion on the whole being of the sinner. She believes in the possibility of a purification for the elect before they see God, a purification altogether different from the punishment of the damned. This is what the Church means when speaking of Hell and Purgatory.[63]

Griffiths Comments on No. 7 in the Letter

These phrases, especially "eternal punishment for the sinner," can be read in such a way as not to contradict the view that the ordinary meaning of damnation is annihilation. What, after all, could be more punishing for a being made for the eternal happiness of the *visio Dei* than to eternally lack that delight? Such lack would certainly be entailed by annihilation. And this interpretation is certainly compatible with the phrase [also in the document] "this punishment will have a repercussion on the whole being of the sinner." However, it must be admitted that the reading just suggested is unlikely to be the one the congregation had in mind. It is much more likely that the term "punishment," thrice repeated in the paragraph quoted, was intended to imply that the damned continue to exist and to suffer, not that they go out of existence.

---

63. *Letter on Certain Questions*, 3–4.

However, the plain sense of the text does not immediately rule out the view that some human beings may go out of existence. The Letter certainly does not make the distinction between conditional and necessary immortality necessary for full discussion of this topic.[64]

"The view presented and defended here, according to which one possible end of humans is self-caused and permanent annihilation, such that those who suffer it do not emerge from the intermediate state, is speculative. It is one that Christians would do well to entertain, but it is not entailed or otherwise required by orthodoxy."[65]

"There is, then, little conciliar teaching of direct relevance to conditional immortality, and what little there is has other concerns. Other magisterial teaching is somewhat more expansive, but even here, although there is considerable interest in rejecting the view that immortality is impossible for humans and in affirming the view that damnation is possible, there is not much that speaks directly to annihilation as a form of (or as coextensive with) damnation. It remains for a Catholic thinker to speculate along these lines, and to affirm, speculatively, the view that resurrection is only for life."[66]

In conclusion the Letter states:

"Neither Scripture nor theology provides sufficient light for a proper picture of life after death. Christians must firmly hold the two following essential points: on the one hand they must believe in the fundamental continuity, thanks to the power of the Holy Spirit, between our present life in Christ and the future life. On the other hand they must be clearly aware of the radical break between the present life and the future one. Our imagination may be incapable of reaching these heights, but our heart does so instinctively and completely."[67]

What I found very significant about the Letter is the *extreme restraint* of this concluding statement compared to the dogmatism of the encyclopedia articles cited above. In the late twentieth century Catholic theology has come a long way in de-emphasizing dogmatic statements about the afterlife. Presently, there is a much wider scope for speculation in eschatology, and the road has been taken to de-mythologize dogmatic statements.

---

64. Griffiths, *Decreation,* 207–08.
65. Ibid., 203.
66. Ibid., 208–09.
67. *Letter on Certain Questions,* 4.

Esteban Deak makes this significant comment about Vatican II's treatment of eschatology: "However, by examining the documents of this council, we can be justifiably surprised, for they do not at all reflect the traditional features of a dualistic eschatology. The terms, such as 'hell,' 'condemnation,' 'eternal torments,' 'eternal punishment' (and all their synonyms) do not occur in any document of this Council, whether pastoral or dogmatic. The idea of last judgment appears only twice."[68]

Some Current Questions in Eschatology, the International Theological Commission, 1992

This forty-six page document is one of the most extensive contemporary treatments of eschatological questions by the Catholic Church. I mention only one aspect most relevant to our topic: *the document seems to identify the spirituality of the soul with immortality.* This is the traditional Catholic understanding, but not that of the conditionalists. I submit my interpretation of this Letter to professional theologians. Here are the statements.

> The Second Vatican Council teaches: "Though made of body and soul, man is one. Through his bodily composition he gathers to himself the elements of the material world; thus they reach their crown through him, and through him raise their voice in free praise of the Creator. Now, man is not wrong when he regards himself as superior to bodily concerns, and as more than a speck of nature or a nameless constituent of the city of man. For by his interior qualities he outstrips the whole sum of mere things. He plunges into the depths of reality whenever he enters into his own heart. God, Who probes the heart, awaits him there; there he discerns his proper destiny beneath the eyes of God. Thus, when he recognizes in himself a spiritual and immortal soul, he is not being mocked by a fantasy born only of physical or social influences, but is rather laying hold of the proper truth of the matter. (Vatican II, The Church in the Modern World, 14)
>
> By these words the Council acknowledged the value of the spontaneous and elemental experience through which people perceive themselves to be superior to all other earthly creatures and indeed capable by knowledge and love of possessing God. The basic difference between people and these other creatures appears in the innate desire for happiness which causes man to reject and abhor the idea of the total destruction of his person; "he rebels

---

68. Deak, *Apocatastasis*, 336.

> against death because he bears in himself an eternal seed which cannot be reduced to sheer matter." Because this immortal soul is spiritual, the Church holds that God is its creator for every person. (Paul VI, *Credo of the People of God*, 8. Also Pius XII, Encyclical *Humani Generis*).
>
> This anthropology makes possible the already noted eschatology of the twofold phase. This Christian anthropology includes a duality of elements (the "body-soul" schema) which can be so separated that one of them ("the spiritual and immortal soul") subsists and endures separately.[69]

I may be mistaken, but it seems that this document equates the spirituality of the soul with its immortality—"a spiritual and immortal soul," "this immortal soul," "eternal seed," "the spiritual and immortal soul." If so, this recent document is a witness to the traditional understanding of the Catholic view, that the soul is naturally immortal. On the other hand, Carol Zaleski says: "The wording of the Letter appears to me to leave the question open, however, rather than warrant the rejection of immortality language."[70]

I note that in the encyclopedia articles and in all the above sources the traditional understanding of "forever" is simply taken for granted— unending duration of time. The conditionalist argument is that eternal suffering is not in the Scriptures, and that it is an interjection from Platonism.

---

69. *Some Current Questions*, 5.1.
70. Zaleski, *Life of the World*, 94.

Afterword

AFTER WRITING THESE TWO *Guides* the reader may wonder what my personal conclusion is about our final destiny. (Of course any conclusion is only another theological opinion, a theologomenon.) Until a few years ago I had never heard of CI. However, I had been somewhat familiar with Origen's Universalism: the word apocatastasis kept appearing in the tradition, but I never thought it was a legitimate "Catholic" option. I was very happy, however, to learn that these two alternatives to the traditional doctrine of hell were serious theologoumena found in the tradition. For most of my life I was reluctant to accept hell, but did accept it, as many still do, as "the teaching of the Church." I no longer believe in hell as the existence of a state of conscious suffering forever for those who refuse the Father's plan. For a brief period I was a universalist. However, I have come to the conclusion that CI is the more probable answer to the question of the fate of those who remain adamant in their refusal to love.

The main reason for my preference for CI is that U does not really give a convincing answer to the tragic possibility of the denial of God as presented in the Scriptures and, indeed, in most religious traditions. Revelation must provide the final answer to this question, not philosophy. And because the great Plato is often quoted on the side of both the universalists and the conditionalists, the following comment by Pieper is extremely significant:

"According to Plato, "this" world and the "other" world are separated not only by death, but by the *Judgment* (emphasis added); and that no form of existence in the beyond is conceivable which would not be a disposition granted after divine judgment. According to Plato, that is, life beyond death as an object of human hope could certainly not be a mere continued existence of the soul. Socrates says it clearly: for one who does not desire the good, immortality is a terrible danger— because "those who are thought

Afterword

to be incurable because of the greatness of their crimes" are hurled into Tartarus "whence they never come out." In Plato's opinion "true bliss" exists for the good. Plato, therefore, thought there would be some kind of tragic fate for those "incurable in their crimes." [1]

That the great Plato believed in the possibility of a "tragic fate" is an enormous supportive philosophical argument for the conditionalists. It seems the majority of the Christian tradition missed this element of Plato's understanding of the "immortality of the soul."

I am also convinced that CI was the most ancient belief in the early years of Christian reflection, that of the Apostolic Fathers and the Apologists. This was followed, however, by the theological opinion of U with the Alexandrians; and then the teaching of eternal torment propagated mostly by Augustine. My theory now is that we are involved in a reversal of this historical trend: eternal torment has been and is now the predominant belief for most Christians; U has been rising in a very pronounced but still very marginal way; and now CI is returning. I believe that, eventually, CI will assume its original predominant place and become the main view of Christians. Both U and CI have always been minor movements throughout Christian history, and in our time hell is being both denied and re-evaluated by many Christians. CI is one of those major re-evaluations that has very solid biblical and philosophical foundations. Throughout my studies I've kept in mind statements from the Church and theologians about *just how little we know of life after death*. They are reminders of our human limitations and are safeguards against presuming too much about what God can and cannot do. Stephen Davis: "I do not think we know much about the future life." [2] Balthasar: "Concerning the whereabouts and circumstances of the dead, we know nothing." [3] N. T. Wright: "Neither Scripture nor theology provides sufficient light for a proper picture of life after death."[4] Vatican document: "All our language about future states of the world and of ourselves consists of complex pictures that may or may not correspond very well to the ultimate reality." [5] And Lagrange gives us what may be the

---

1. Pieper, *Death*, 103.
2. Davis, "Hell," 102.
3. Balthasar, *Descent*, 401.
4. Wright, *Surprised*, xiii.
5. Letter.

greatest reason for humility on this topic: "Final impenitence, of which hell is a consequence, is the darkest of all mysteries." [6]

Quoting these reminders about the great limitations upon our knowledge of the novissima, I was reminded of Augustine's similar humility about the life of the blessed:

> Now let us see, as far as the Lord deigns to help us to see, what the saints will be doing in their immortal and spiritual bodies. And yet, to tell the truth, I do not know what will be the nature of that activity, or rather of that rest and leisure. I have never seen it with my physical sight; and if I were to say that I had seen if with my mind—with my intellect—what is the human understanding, capacity or quality, to comprehend such unique perfection. And we do not know what new qualities the spiritual body will have, for we are speaking of something beyond our experience.
>
> And so, when there are some things which are beyond our understanding, and on which the authority of Holy Scripture offers no assistance, then we must needs be in the state described in the Book of Wisdom, in these words: "The thoughts of men are timorous and our foresight is uncertain." (Wis 9, 14)[7]

Isn't it extremely curious—and very unfortunate— that Augustine did not apply this scepticism to his understanding about hell!

But I do not wish to end on this strong agnostic note which would allow for any and every possible theory. I conclude with a reflection from Pope Emeritus Benedict XVI that I had vaguely come to believe even before I read it in his encyclical *Spe Salvi*. He expresses both something of the hope of the universalists while allowing, unlike them, for a possible final fatal choice of some people who would be

> beyond remedy and the destruction of good [in them] would be irrevocable: this is what we mean by the word *Hell*. There can be people who have totally destroyed their desire for truth and readiness to love, people for whom everything has become a lie, who have lived for hatred and have suppressed all love within themselves. This is a terrifying thought, but alarming profiles of this type can be seen in certain figures of our own history.
>
> On the other hand there can be people who are utterly pure, completely permeated by God, and thus fully open to their neighbors—people for whom communion with God even now gives

---

6. Lagrange, *Life Everlasting*, 48.
7. Augustine, *City of God*, 1081, 1085.

direction to their entire being and whose journey toward God only brings to fulfillment what they already are.

Yet we know from experience that neither case is normal in human life. For the *great majority of people* (emphasis added)—we may suppose—there remains in the depths of their being an ultimate interior openness to truth, to love, to God. What happens to such individuals when they appear before the Judge? [He then quotes the famous text from Paul (1 Cor 3:12–15) "each man's work will be revealed with fire." He interprets this fire as Christ himself.]

In the pain of this encounter, when the impurity and sickness of our lives become evident to us, there lies salvation. His gaze, the touch of his heart heals us through an undeniably painful transformation 'as through fire.' But it is a blessed pain, in which the holy power of his love sears through us like a flame, enabling us to become totally ourselves and thus totally of God.

If it were merely grace, making all earthly things cease to matter, God would still owe us an answer to the question about justice—the crucial question that we ask of history and of God. If it were merely justice, in the end it could bring only fear to us all. The incarnation of God in Christ has so closely linked the two together—judgment and grace—that justice is firmly established: we all work out our salvation "with fear and trembling" (Phil 2:12). Nevertheless grace allows us all to hope and go trustfully to meet the Judge whom we know as our "advocate," or parakletos (cf. John 2:1).[8]

In these few lines the Pope harmonizes, in one comprehensive vision, most of the major elements of theologians writing about the last things. The universalists place absolute emphasis on Benedict's view "that there remains in the depths of their being an ultimate interior openness to truth, to love, to God." One of the attractions of the universalists for me was the unlimited hope of grace they placed in everyone's "ultimate interior openness," so that *everyone* will ultimately be overcome by grace and arrive at the heavenly banquet. To modify this view the Pope suggests that most people—"*the great majority*"—always retain openness to God in the depths of their being, *but possibly not everyone*. This is my final hope as well, that the *majority* of people will eventually be overcome by the grace of God, remain open, and eventually be overwhelmed by "the touch of the heart of Christ." But there is still "the question of justice."

---

8. Benedict XVI, *Saved in Hope*, Nos. 45, 47.

Afterword

Benedict's vision is neither the terrible *massa damnata* of Augustine as expressed in the sermon of St. Leonard of Port Maurice and in countless "hell and damnation" sermons throughout the ages, nor that of the universalists where no fatal final choice is even possible. He tends decidedly towards the wonderful spectacle from the Book of Revelation: "After this I had a vision of a great multitude, which no one could count, from every nation, race, people, and tongue. They stood before the throne and before the Lamb. . . (6: 9). Of course, this text can be interpreted in a universalist sense—the multitude includes *everyone*; but it could also mean that "the great majority of people" will be saved.

As argued by the conditionalists, I believe that people have the power of making a final fatal choice to refuse the Father's plan, and that some will so choose. God then accepts the finality of that decision and withdraws existence since they no longer desire to fulfil the purpose for which they were created. Since existence was a totally free gift, it is not unjust to remove it. I believe this scenario may be most applicable to angels who have both more awareness and more power of resistance than us poor mortals. So I can more readily understand the annihilation of fallen angels. There is a place for much more hope for God's mercy for *us*, weak and stupid as we are, since our earthly preparation leaves much to be desired as we come into the presence of the Judge. I close, then, with the vision of Revelation "of a great multitude," while mourning that some of my sisters and brothers will "suppress all love within themselves," even that of the heart of Christ. Their existence will then be taken from them. May this number be extremely few!

Bibliography

Augustine, Saint. *The City of God*. Translated by Henry Bettenson. London: Penguin Books, 1972.
Balthasar, Hans Urs von. *Dare We Hope That All Men Be Saved?* Translated by David Kipp. San Francisco: Ignatius, 1988.
———. *Explorations in Theology*: I: *The Word Made Flesh*. Translated by A.V. Littledale with Alexander Dru. San Francisco: Ignatius, 1964.
———. "Eschatology in Outline." In *Explorations in Theology. I: Spirit and Institution*. San Francisco: Ignatius Press, 1995. V
———. "Descent into Hell." Translated by Edward T. Oakes, SJ. In *Explorations in Theology*. IV. San Francisco: Ignatius, 1995
Beauchemin, Gerry, and D. Scott Reichard. *Hope Beyond Hell*. With D. Scott Reichard, The Trilogy. Olmito, Texas: Malista, 2016.
Becque, Maurice, CSSR, and Louis Becque, CSSR. *Life after Death*. Catholic Encyclopedia 28. New York: Hawthorn Books, 1960.
Benedictus Deus. *On the Beatific Vision of God*. Constitution Issued by Pope Benedict XII in 1336. www.papalencyclicals.net/Ben12bdeus.html.
Benedict XVI. Encyclical Letter, *Saved in Hope (Spe Salvi)*. Boston: Pauline Books & Media, 2007.
Bonda, Jan. *The One Purpose of God: An Answer to the Doctrine of Eternal Punishment*. Grand Rapids: Eerdmans, 1998.
Boruff, John. "John Calvin on Hell." www. John Boruff, Wesleygospel.com
Brotherton, Joshua R. "*Universalism and Predestinationism: A Critique of the Theological Anthropology that Undergirds Catholic Universalist Eschatology*." Theological Studies 77(3) (2016) 603–26.
Buckareff, Andrei and Allen Plug. "Value, Finality, and Frustration: Problems for Escapism?" In *The Problem of Hell, A Philosophical Anthology*, edited by Joel Buenting, 77–90. Farnham, England: Ashgate Publishing Limited, 2010.
Buenting, Joel, ed. *The Problem of Hell, A Philosophical Anthology*. Farnham, England: Ashgate Publishing Limited, 2010.
Cain, James. "Why I am Unconvinced by Arguments against the Existence of Hell." In *The Problem of Hell, A Philosophical Anthology*, edited by Joel Buenting, 133–44. Farnham, England: Ashgate Publishing Limited, 2010.
Cameron, Nigel M. de. S, ed. *Universalism and the Doctrine of Hell: Papers Presented at the Fourth Edinburgh Conference on Christian Dogmatics, 1991*. Carlisle, UK: Paternoster, 1992.

Bibliography

Catechism of the Council of Trent. Translated by James A, McHugh, OP and Charles J. Callan, OP. 1923. Rockford, IL: Tan Books and Publishers, Inc., 1982.

Catechism of the Catholic Church. Liguori, Mo: Liguori Publications, 1994.

Catholic Encyclopedia. *An International Work of Reference on the Constitution, Doctrine, Discipline, and History of the Catholic Church.* Vol. VII. New York: The Encyclopedia Press, Inc., 1910.

Cullman, Oscar. *Immortality of the Soul or Resurrection of the Dead? The Witness of the New Testament.* New York: The MacMillan Company, 1958.

Daley, Brian E. *The Hope of the Early Church. A Handbook of Patristic Eschatology.* Grand Rapids, MI: Baker Academic, 2010.

Date, Christopher M., Gregory Stump, and Joshua W. Anderson, eds. *Rethinking Hell, Readings in Evangelical Conditionalism.* Eugene, OR: Cascade, 2014.

Davis, Stephen T. "Hell, Wrath, and the Grace of God." In *The Problem of Hell, A Philosophical Anthology,* edited by Joel Buenting, 91-102. Farnham, England: Ashgate Publishing Limited, 2010.

Deak, Esteban. "Apocatastasis: The Problem of Universal Salvation in the Twentieth Century Theology." PhD diss., University of St. Michael's College, 1977.

Dyer, George J. *Limbo, Unsettled Question.* New York: Sheed and Ward, 1964.

Fackre, Gabriel. "Divine Perseverance." In *What About Those Who Have Never Heard?* Edited by John Sanders, 71–95. Downers Grove, IL: IVP Academic, 1995.

Froom, Leroy Edwin. *The Conditionalist Faith of Our Fathers. The Conflict of the Ages over the Nature and Destiny of Man.* 2 Vols. Washington, D.C.: Review and Herald, 1965-66.

Fudge, Edward William. *The Fire That Consumes. A Biblical and Historical Study of Final Punishment.* Huston, Texas: Providential, 1982.

Fudge, Edward William and Robert A. Peterson. *Two Views of Hell. A Biblical and Theological Dialogue.* Downers Grove, IL: InterVarsity, 2000.

Gonzalez-Ruiz, Maria. "Should We De-Mythologize the Separated Soul"? In *Concilium, The Problem of Eschatology,* eds. Edward Schillebeeckx, OP and Boniface Willems, OP, Vol. 41. New York, NY: Paulist, 1969.

Griffiths, Paul J. *Decreation. The Last Things of All Creatures.* Waco, Texas: Baylor University, 2014.

Harmon, Kendall, S. "The Case against Conditionalism: A Response to Edward William Fudge." In *Universalism and the Doctrine of Hell: Papers Presented at the Fourth Edinburgh Conference on Christian Dogmatics,* 1991, edited by Nigel M. de S. Cameron, 193–224. Carlisle, UK: Paternoster, 1992.

Hart, David Bentley. "Dream-Child's Progress." *First Things,* April 2016, Number 262, 31–38.

———. "Death, Final Judgment, and the Meaning of Life." In *The Oxford Handbook of Eschatology,* edited by Jerry L. Walls, 476–88. New York: Oxford University Press, 2008.

International Theological Commission. *The Hope of Salvation for Infants Who Die Without Being Baptised.* Rome, January, 2007. www.vatican.va/roman_curia/congregations/cfaith/cti_documents/re_con_cfaith_doc.

Jerome Biblical Commentary. Englewood Cliffs, NJ: Prentice-Hall, Inc., 1968.

Kelly, Anthony. *Eschatology and Hope.* Maryknoll, New York: Orbis Books, 2006.

Bibliography

Kershnar, Stephen. "Hell and Punishment." In *The Problem of Hell, A Philosophical Anthology*, edited by Joel Buenting, 115-32. Farnham, England: Ashgate Publishing Limited, 2010.

Kropf, Richard W. *Searching for Soul: Teilhard, de Lubac, Rahner, and the Evolutionary Quest for Immortality*. Teilhard Studies Number 69, Fall, 2014. American Teilhard Association.

Kronen, John and Eric Reitan. "Species of Hell." In *The Problem of Hell, A Philosophical Anthology*, edited by Joel Buenting, 199-218. Farnham, England: Ashgate Publishing Limited, 2010.

———. *God's Final Victory: A Comparative Philosophical Case for Universalism*. New York: Continuum, 2011.

Kvanvig, Jonathan L. *The Problem of Hell*. New York: Oxford University Press, 1993.

———. *Destiny and Deliberation, Essays in Philosophical Theology*. New York: Oxford University Press, 2011.

Lagrange, Reginald Garrigou. *Life Everlasting and the Immensity of the Soul. A Theological Treatise on the Four Last Things: Death, Judgment, Heaven, Hell*.

Letter on Certain Questions Concerning Eschatology, Sacred Congregation for the Doctrine of the Faith, May 17, 1979. www.vatican.va/.../rc_con_cfaith_doc_19790517_escatologia_en.htm.

Levering, Matthew. *Jesus and the Demise of Death. Resurrection, Afterlife, and the Fate of the Christian*. Waco, Texas: Baylor University, 2012.

Loudovikos, Nicolaos. *A Eucharistic Ontology. Maximus the Confessor's Eschatological Ontology of Being as Dialogical Reciprocity*. Brookline, Mass: Holy Cross Orthodox Press, 2010.

———. "Hell and Heaven, Nature and Person. Chr. Yannaras, D. Staniloae and Maximus the Confessor." In International Journal of Orthodox Theology, 5:1 (2014) 3-86.

MacDonald, Gregory. *The Evangelical Universalist*. Eugene, OR: Cascade, 2006.

McKenzie, John L. SJ. *Dictionary of the Bible*. New York: MacMillan Publishing Co., Inc., 1965.

Martin, Jennifer Newsome. *Hans Urs von Balthasar and the Critical Appropriation of Russian Religious Thought*. Notre Dame: University of Notre Dame Press, 2015.

New Catholic Encyclopedia. New York: MaGraw-Hill, Catholic University of America Press, 1967. Vol. VI.

Norris, Frederick W. "Universal Salvation in Origen and Maximus." In *Universalism and the Doctrine of Hell: Papers Presented at the Fourth Edinburgh Conference on Christian Dogmatics, 1991*, edited by Nigel M. de S. Cameron, 35-72. Carlisle, UK: Paternoster, 1992.

Ott, Ludwig. *Fundamentals of Catholic Dogma*. Translated by Patrick Lynch. Rockford, IL: Tan Publishers, Inc., 1974.

Our Lady of the Rosary, Prospect, KY.

Petavel, E. *The Problem of Immortality*. Translated by Frederick Ash Freer. London: Elliot Stock, 1892.

———. *The Extinction of Evil: Three Theological Essays*. Boston: Charles H. Woodman, 1889.

Phan, Peter. *Living Unto Death. A Christian Theology of Death and Life Eternal*. Hobe Sound, FL: Lectio Publishing, 2014.

Pieper, Josef. *Death and Immortality*. Translated by Richard and Clara Winston. South Bend, Ind: St. Augustine's, 2000.

Bibliography

Rahner, Karl. *Hominisation, The Evolutionary Origin of Man as a Theological Problem.* Translated by W.T. O'Hara. Frieburg: Herder, 1965.

Ramelli, Ilaria. *The Christian Doctrine of Apocatastasis: A Critical Assessment from the New Testament to Eriugena.* Leiden: Brill, 2013.

Ratzinger, Joseph. *Eschatology. Death and Eternal Life.* Translated by Michael Waldstein. Washington, DC: Catholic University of America, 1988.

Saint Leonard of Port Maurice: *The Little Number of Those Who are Saved.* Prospect, KY: Our Lady of the Rosary Library, 2012.

Sanders, John, ed. *What About Those Who Have Never Heard? Three Views on the Destiny of the Unevangelized.* With Gabriel Fackre and Ronald H. Nash. Downers Grove, Il: IVP Academic, 1995.

Some Current Questions in Eschatology. The Catholic International Theological Commission, 1992. Published with the approval of His Eminence Joseph Cardinal Ratzinger, President of the Commission. www. Some Current Questions in Eschatology.

Storm, D. Anthony. *The Sickness Unto Death.* http: sorenkierkegaard.org/sickness-unto-death.html.

Talbott, Thomas. "Grace, Character Formation, and Predestination unto Glory." In *The Problem of Hell, A Philosophical Anthology*, edited by Joel Buenting, 7–27. Farnham, England: Ashgate Publishing Limited, 2010.

Tanquerey, A. *A Manuel of Dogmatic Theology.* Translated by Rt. Rev. Msgr. John J. Byrnes. New York: Desclee, 1959.

Thiel, John E. *Icons of Hope, the "Last Things" in Catholic Imagination.* Notre Dame: University of Notre Dame Press, 2013.

Travis, Stephen. "The Nature of Final Destiny." In *Rethinking Hell, Readings in Evangelical Conditionalism,* edited by Date, Christopher M, Gregory Stump, and Joshua W. Anderson, 44–47. Eugene, OR: Cascade, 2014.

Tugwell, Simon, OP. *Human Immortality and the Redemption of Death.* Springfield, Il: Templegate, 1991.

VanArragon, Raymond J. "Is It Possible to Freely Reject God Forever?" In *The Problem of Hell, A Philosophical Anthology,* edited by Joel Buenting, 29–43. Farnham, England: Ashgate Publishing Limited, 2010.

Varghese, Roy Abraham. *The Wonder of the World, A Journey from Modern Science to the Mind of God.* Fountain Hill, AZ: Tyr Publishing, 2003.

Walker, D.P. *The Decline of Hell. Seventeenth-Century Discussion of Eternal Torment.* Chicago: University of Chicago Press, 1964.

Walls, Jerry L. *The Logic of Damnation.* Notre Dame, Ind: University of Notre Dame Press, 1992.

———. *Purgatory, The Logic of Total Purification.* New York: Oxford University Press, 2012.

———. *Heaven, Hell, and Purgatory. A Protestant View of the Cosmic Drama.* Grand Rapids, MI: Brazos, 2015.

Walls, Jerry L and Claire Brown. "Annihilationism: A Philosophical Dead End?" In *The Problem of Hell, A Philosophical Anthology,* edited by Joel Buenting, 45–64. Farnham, England: Ashgate Publishing Limited, 2010.

Wenham, John W. *The Goodness of God.* London: Inter-Varsity, 1994.

Bibliography

Wenham, John W. "The Case for Conditional Immortality," in *Universalism and the Doctrine of Hell: Papers Presented at the Fourth Edinburgh Conference on Christian Dogmatics,* edited by Nigel M. de Cameron, 161–91. Carlisle, UK: Paternoster, 1992.

Wild, Robert. *A Catholic Reading Guide to Universalism.* Eugene, OR: Wipf and Stock, 2015.

Wright, N.T. *Surprised by Hope. Rethinking Heaven, the Resurrection, and the Mission of the Church.* New York, N.Y.: Harper Collins, 2008.

Zaleski, Carol. *The Life of the World to Come.* New York: Oxford University Press, 1996.

Subject Index

absolute decision, 36. *See also* final decision
act of God, annihilation as, 88
ad nihilum, person on the way, 112
adaptation, of arguments about hell, 4–5
Against Heresies (Irenaeus), 49
agent, freely doing wrong, 83
Agnostics, 156
alternative destinies, theological, 4
Althaus, Paul, 159
angels, annihilation of, 114–16, 179
animae immortalitas, 117
annihilation (A)
    arguments against, 94–95, 150
    conformable with God's moral perfections, 89
    consistent opinion among the Apologists and the Apostolic Fathers, 8
    criticisms about, 97
    as a definite possibility, 114
    "ever-ill-being" as another term for, 133
    everlasting nature of, 5
    as a form of damnation, 147
    Griffiths on, 114–17
    as more in keeping with God's goodness, 89
    as more merciful than eternal punishment, 31
    more serious than eternal damnation, 105
    as a natural end to human existence, 95
    no "natural process" leading to, 88
    not a natural consequence, 5–6
    not a "natural" progression leading to zero, 95
    as not a possibility, 99
    not a punishment, 55
    as a *novissimum*, 15
    objections to the possibility of, 104
    as ordinary meaning of damnation, 171
    as our end, 95
    permanent in some cases, 117
    philosophical arguments against, 94
    as philosophically unmotivated, 87, 90
    as possible, 8, 146
    proponents of, 9
    reasoning disproving, 104
    reflections on by Lagrange, 167
    relating Davis's comments to, 93
    reverent skepticism about, 41
    as scriptural, 9
    self-caused and permanent, 172
    of the sinner, 150
    as a species of hell, 136
    used instead of Conditional Immortality (CI), 4
    as utter limit of Hell, 72
    by way of omission, 98
    of the wicked, 47
annihilationism, 9–15
    Davis on, 33
    denying that anyone is in hell, 97
    designating theories, 12
    philosophical arguments against, 87
    proper, 12

Subject Index

annihilationism *(cont.)*
    providing an element of the tragic, 122
    Socinians and, 55
"Annihilationism: A Philosophical Dead End?" (Brown and Walls), 87–91
Anonymous Christian, 109
apocatastasis rejection of an Origenist doctrine of, 133
Apocrypha, 22
Apologists, 8, 44, 48–52, 176
Apology (Athenagoras), 52
Apostolic Fathers, 8, 44–47, 176
Aquinas, Thomas, 77
    on acquiring grace after death, 168
    argument against annihilation, 167
    commentary on Aristotle's *Metaphysics*, 78
    on God revealing he is *summum bonum*, 137
    on human cognition, 110
    on intellectual substance, 115
    intricate arguments from, 136
    number on the saved, 148
    positing the spiritual soul, 110
    on sins against God, 167
    on the soul as almost infinite, 165
Aristotelean metaphysics, 115
Aristotle, 53, 78
Arnobius of Africa, 51–52, 156
Athanasian Creed, 156
Athenagoras, 49, 52
Augustine
    doctrine of hell, 3, 51, 52
    eternal torment propagated by, 176
    hell as real and inhabited, 154
    humility about the life of the blessed, 177
    massa damnata of, 179
    on omnipotence, 120
    on results of sin, 116
    teaching of, 147
Augustinianism, errors of, 63
Australian Catholic University, 124
Averroes, 53

Balthasar, Hans Urs von, 7, 163
    criticized by Brotherton, 169
    on the dead, 176
    greatest Catholic mind of the twentieth century, 34
    on judgment, 38
    not a universalist, 34
    on philosophy's unique contributions to human understanding, 73
    on possibility of final choice in the scriptures, 34–38
baptism, 65, 164
baptismal instruction, manual for, 46
Barlow, Professor, 70
Bayle, Peter, 53
beatific vision (*visio beatifica*), 142
beatitude, all human souls attaining, 150
Beauchemin, Gerry, 42–43
Becque, Louis, 151
Becque, Maurice, 151
Beecher, Edward, 47
Beet, Dr., 30
behavior patterns, casually open to revision, 101
believers, as the children of the resurrection, 49
Benedict XII, Constitution of, 145
Benedict XVI, 177
Benedictus Deus, 145
beneficent being, opting for annihilation, 94
Beneficent-Character Principle, 94, 95
Berdyaev, N., 42
St. Bernard of Clairveau, 16
bible teaching, general trend of, 30
biblical hermeneutic, call for, 18
biblical images, suggesting annihilation, 13
biblical man, as one unit, 143
Biblical teaching, harmonies and benefits of, 66
Book of Revelation, great multitude in, 149, 179
Book of Wisdom, 177
Boros, 86–87
Bradshaw, Timothy, 72
Brotherton, Joshua R., 169–70
brought to nothing, as the final state, 126

Subject Index

Brown, Claire, 87–91
Buckareff, Andrei A., 91–92
Buenting, Joel, 14, 87–96
burning bush, miracle of, 71

Cain, James, 95–96
Calovius, 55
Calvin, John, 54
Calvinism, errors of, 63
capacity for indestructibility, 79
"capacity for truth," 79
"The Case for Conditional Immortality" (Wenham), 140
Catechism of the Catholic Church, 87, 146, 153
Catholic authors, 3–4, 153–70
Catholic biblical commentaries, 28–31
Catholic Church
    Catechism of, 87, 146, 153
    on innate immortality of the soul, 4
    modern teaching of, 149–53
Catholic Encyclopedia, on "Hell," 149–51
Catholic International Theological Commission, 2
Catholic positions, on a final decision, 85–96
Catholic Redemptorist Order, 124
Catholic teaching, 142–74
    official, 145–49
Catholic theology, about the afterlife, 172
Catholics, Conditional Immortality (CI) almost totally unknown among, 1
causal impossibility, 100, 101
character formation, process of, 101
chastisement, of the wicked as eternal, 49
choice, consequences of, 82, 84
choice of Heaven, as no longer possible, 101
choosing
    against God, 107
    lost ability for, 100
    not to survive, 5–6
Christ
    affirming bodily death without annihilation, 111
    as "the constant source of our life," 45
    giving life eternal, 69

"Many are called but few are chosen," 148
    as only source of immortality, 65
    saving people wherever they are, 93
    sharing the natural fear of death, 39
    as the source of all life, 49
    spoke often of hell, 23
    on the terrible fate awaiting those who reject God's mercy, 23
Christ Will Come Again: Hope for the Second Coming of Jesus (Travis), 13
Christian conditionalist, position of, 8
Christian doctrine
    not "lifted" straight from the text of Scripture, 18
    of the Resurrection, 39
"Christian Universalism," 42–43
Christians
    categories of, 120
    majority of damned, 148
Christ's redemptive work, saved through, 18
church doctrine, status of, 2
Clement of Alexandria, 92, 164
Clement of Rome, 44–45
cognition of truth, "seeing," 79
"coming to one's senses," never, 109
conciliar teaching, Conditional Immortality (CI) and, 147, 172
Conditional Immortality (CI), 12, 139
    conciliar teaching and, 147, 172
    conclusions about, 3
    as the dominant teaching of the Christian Church until Athenagoras, 49
    hell not eternal in, 163
    hypothesis of, 76
    introduction to, 2
    main questions connected with, 6
    as a minority view, 4
    as the most ancient belief, 176
    as not scriptural, 41
    objections to, 7
    opinions on, 7
    as possibility, 2
    subject of, 1

Subject Index

Conditional Immortality *(cont.)*
    support for, 13, 175
    in the writings of the earliest Fathers of the Church, 65
conditionalism
    as the basis of the belief in Annihilationism, 12
    harmonizing Scripture with Scripture, 60
    lifted out of the assigned category of heresy, 59
    as a return to the primitive Gospel, 65
conditionalist eventual extinctionism, 14
The Conditionalist Faith of Our Father (Froom), 3
conditionalist positions, 8, 66–71
conditionalist uniresurrectionism, 14
conditionalist views, 3
conditionalists
    on absolute self-centered and permanent attitude, 123
    Apostolic Fathers as, 44–47
    arguments of, 87
    on attaining the beatific vision, 19
    basic argument from tradition, 44
    bible for, 64–66
    on "biblical majority report as misguided," 90
    on a final irremediable act of a person is possible, 88
    scriptural positions of, 42
    understanding the wrath of God, 32
    on words in scripture describing the end of the unrepentant taken literally, 43
consciousness
    of eternal sufferings, 95
    of an infinite self, 113
Constable, Henry, 62–63
Constitution of Benedict XII, 145
constrained liberty (U), 75
"consuming fire," God as, 26–27
continuance of life, as conditional, 51
corruption, as contrary to the definition of an intellectual substance, 115
corruption argument, facing serious problems, 88

Council of Trent, 147
Councils, proof from, 156
created beings, returning to nothingness, 78
creatio ex nihilo, Christian doctrine of, 103
creation
    calling back to life the whole man, 39
    God's guidance of, 56
creation *ex nihilo*, taking sin seriously, 116
creative power, conferring existence, 74
creatura, universe as, 78
creature. *See also* man
    experiencing the divine, 106
    incapable of maintaining itself, 78
cross, as being "to us salvation and life eternal," 45
Cullman, Oscar, 39–41
cultural expectations, conforming to, 127

Daley, Brian, 48
damnation, 35, 37–38
damned, 129, 171
"damned ghost," being, 102
Dare We Hope That All Men Be Saved? (Balthasar), 7, 34–36
"darkness outside," 103
Davis, Stephen T., 32–34, 92–94, 176
day of judgment
    deciding on, 91
    having confidence in, 38
    "before the judgment seat of Christ," 145
day of wrath, 35
de Lubac, 112
dead
    already living with Christ, 40
    sleep of, 47
Deak, Esteban, 173
death
    as cessation of functions, 65
    destruction of, 71
    as extinction or cessation, 61
    as the last enemy of God, 39
    meaning the end of existence, 31
    as a natural "transition," 40

Subject Index

as the ontologically privileged place, 86
popular definition of, 61–62
topics of, not treated, 4
"Death, Final Judgment, and the Meaning of Life" (Hart), 134
death and destruction, Beauchemin on, 43
Death and Immortality (Pieper), 77
decisions, eventuating in eternal separation from God, 82
The Decline of Hell, Seventeenth-Century Discussions of Eternal Torment (Walker), 54
decomposition, in the Old Testament, 21
decreation, of Paul Griffiths, 7–9
"defective permeation," needing to be purified, 165
demise of death, Jesus and, 110–11
demons, asking not to be destroyed, 68
demythologizing, of dogma, 142
denizens of hell, accepting God's grace and leaving hell, 91
"depart from me," 147
dereliction, 134
desire, being in bondage to, 106
despair, not to will to be oneself, 112–13
Destiny and Deliberation (Kvanvig), 100, 106
destroying fire, consignment to, 103
destruction
    aspects of, 21
    evidence for the wicked's final total, 11
    meaning the unmaking, or cessation, of the destroyed, 102
    of the unrepentant, 20
    of what is worthless, 30
"devastation," 120
devil, deceit of, 19–20
"The Dialogical Character of Immortality" (Ratzinger), 159
"dialogical" concept, of humanity, 160
dialogical reciprocity, processes of, 130
Dictionary of the Bible (McKenzie), 28
The Didache, 46
disobedience, God's patience with, 108

divination, 111
divine authority, recognizing but resenting, 90
Divine Being, faith in the justice of, 62
divine justice
    demanding annihilation of the sinner, 167
    dogma of hell springing from, 152
Divine Perseverance, Fackre and, 109–10
"The Doctrinal Schema" (Griffiths), 142–43
doctrinal statements
    about the immortality of the soul, 146
    recent, 170–74
Doctrine of Hell (DH), 105
    arguments against, 135
    imbedded in the NT, 96
doctrine of Purgatory, 166
dogmas
    defining the core of, 145
    de-mythologizing of, 143
    demythologizing of, 142
    status of, 2
"Dogmatic Development," 152
Donne, John, 42

ecclesial formulations of the faith, demythologizing of, 144
Edwards, Jonathan, 148
"efficacious grace," 37
elect, enrolled for eternal life, 50
"elimination," less frequently for annihilation, 5
"end of the wicked," 140
endless cycles, far-Eastern theories of, 93
endless extinction, 67
endless sinning, 141
endless suffering, 95
endless torment
    doctrine of, 31, 60
    as hideous and unscriptural doctrine, 141
ends and means pattern, 57
Ephesians, letter of Ignatius to, 45
Epistle of Barnabas, 47
Epistle of St. Jude, 28
Epistle to the Magnesians, 45–46

escapism, satisfying the universalist, 92
"escapist theory," of hell, 91
eschatological exclusion, from Christ's presence, 42
eschatological judgment, of God, 41
eschatology, 4, 173
Eschatology, Death and Eternal Life (Ratzinger), 85–86, 129
"Eschatology in Outline" (Balthasar), 38
"eternal," meaning of the word, 27
eternal banishment, from the sight of God, 147
eternal conscious punishment, 80
eternal damnation, 104, 129
eternal farewell, 28
"eternal fire," 28, 153
eternal hell. *See also* hell
 intelligible motive for anyone to choose, 123
 as a kind of metaphysical dualism, 90
 not destroyed, 70–71
 symbolic form of, 29
eternal joy, depriving a creature of, 104
"eternal judgment," 27–28
eternal life
 as central focus of the Christian message, 162
 Christian teaching on, 161
 as the gift of God through Jesus Christ, 30
 not all human creatures entering into, 121
 renewal of, 45
 through perseverance in good works, 32
eternal misery, motive for choosing, 107
eternal physical pain, in a time&slash,space similar to ours, 120
eternal punishment
 as an act of judgment, 13
 versus "conditional immortality," 13
 consisting in a gradual destruction, 28
 described, 66
 not in the Scriptures, 3
 Petavel on, 27

 philosophical arguments against, 94
 predictions foretelling, 66
 projected into the Scriptures, 41
 references to, 13
 for the sinner, 171
 suffering, 49
 as unjust, 70
"eternal redemption," obtained by Jesus, 27
eternal torment
 living forever in, 9
 man could never have invented, 68
 out of paganism, 20
 powerful preachers proclaimed, 70
 serving no useful purpose, 13
 teaching of propagated mostly by Augustine, 176
 weight of the evidence against, 30
Eternal Torment of the non-repentant non-elect, dogma of, 54
eternity, applying to the result of the act, 27
"eternity of evil," as "not a doctrine of the bible," 63
eternity of evil (hell), 75
eternity of hell
 Holy Writ explicit in teaching, 149
 hope allowing for, 125
 question about, 132
The Eternity of Hell Torments (Whiston), 58
eternity of hell's sufferings, arguments for, 166
Ethics (Spinoza), 78
"ever-ill-being," Maximus on, 133
everlasting fire, into, 147
everlasting life, versus everlasting death, 140
"everlasting punishment," 48
everlasting torment. *See* eternal torment
"ever-moving stasis," according to Maximus, 131
everything, coming from nothing capable of returning to nothing, 115
evidence, people going against the most obvious, 123
evil

Subject Index

down through the history of the world, 125
existing because of free will, 122
final extinction of, 60
ingenious answer to the problem of, 56
relation to non-existence, 75
revealing for what it is, 125–26
tending towards its own extinction, 75
as a thing of time, 63
evil action, choosing to perform, 84
evil and evil doers, eternal existence of, 69
ex-human state, existing in, 139
existence
    being deprived of the benefits of, 49
    God withdrawing, 5
    not totally free gift, 179
    removal of a person's, 5
    removal of as a mutual affair, 6
existence "by nature," always primary, 79
existence of hell, 32, 149
ex-man, being, 102
The Extinction of Evil: Three Theological Essays (Petavel), 10, 27, 66–71
extinction of the sinner, constituting the punishment, 67

"face to face encounter," 82
Fackre, Gabriel, on "The Divine Perseverance," 109
faithful, given eternal life as a gift, 11
fallen angels, 115
Farrar, Frederic William, 63–64
Father of Orthodoxy, Irenaeus as, 49
fear, as a legitimate attitude in our relationship with God, 124–25
few will be saved, as main theme, 148
Fifth Lateran Council, on rational soul as mortal, 146
final choice against God, as possible, 132
final decision. *See also* absolute decision; ultimate decision
    Catholic positions on, 85–96
    determining ultimate fate, 9
    against God, 98

"terminally frozen in the choice of evil," 124
time of making, 86
final destruction, texts indicating, 20
final end, set at their death, 146
final fatal choice, 177, 179
final judgement, not treated, 4
final negative choice, can be willed, 110
final tragic choice, possible for persons, 169
final tragic decision, possibility of making, 114
finality, idea of, 103
finally impenitent, falling into non-existence, 11–12
fire, destructive effects of, 30
The Fire That Consumes (Fudge), 11, 71
first death, distinguished from the final death, 51
first-order desires, versus second-order desires, 91
flaming fire, taking vengeance, 58
"forever," understanding of, 174
forgiveness, accepting from God, 93
free choice, necessary condition for, 83
free negative choice, as possible, 82
freedom, 105–7
    allowing possibility of eschatological tragedy, 126
    concept of, 152
    to decide whether or not we exist, 89–90
    God "overriding" human, 105
    God's respect for, 84, 105, 129, 136
    having the power making choices for ever, 87
    human created by God, 169
    issue of a person's, 91
    Kvanvig on, 106–7
freely rejecting God forever, 83
Freer, Frederick Ash, 64
Froom, Leroy Edwin, 2–4
    on the Apologists, 48
    on Apostolic Fathers, 44, 47
    on Conditionalism, 10–11
    conditionalist interpretations of, 19
    on Farrar, 63

Subject Index

Froom, Leroy Edwin *(cont.)*
   on Immortal-Soulism, 10–11
   on Irenaeus, 130
   on Justin, 48
   on latter half of the nineteenth
      century, 58–59
   on *The Problem* and Petavel, 10
   scriptural evidence attesting to the
      destruction of the unrepentant,
      17
   theologians mentioned by, 157–58
fruits, reaping of our actions, 57
Fudge, Edward, 11, 20, 41
"fundamental option/decision,"
      Ratzinger's expression of, 165
Fundamentals of Catholic Dogma (Ott), 157
future punishment, 30, 62

Gaudium et Spes, from Vatican II, 146
Gehenna of unquenchable fire, 28, 51, 138
getting one's way, triumph of, 123
gift of immortality, receiving, 95
gift of life, 46
Gladstone, William, 61–62
glorious *novissimum*, 114
God. *See also* Lord
   absolute right to annihilate, 55
   allowing harm caused by our misuse
      of freedom, 107–8
   annihilating a person, 79
   annihilating rather than consigning
      to hell, 94
   annihilating some of his creatures, 90
   attributes manifest in all His acts, 19, 56
   bringing an end to all He has begun, 21–22
   in the business of saving people, 5
   complying with the person's decision
      to no longer love him, 5
   as a consuming fire, 71
   correcting cognitive errors, 107
   created the universe out of nothing, 103
   creating and maintaining the
      universe, 56
   creating us in his image, 89
   decision to reject, 86
   desiring to destroy evil, 32
   desiring union with, 91
   drawing us out of the waters, 160
   facilitating a sinner's perpetual
      rejection of him, 85
   frustrating the patience and mercy
      of, 124
   granting efficacious grace, 105
   granting immortality, 6
   image of, 67
   as immortal, 19
   liberating a soul from hell, 150
   limitless saving creativity of, 127
   making some persons immortal, 97
   mercy of, 149
   never giving up on anyone, 108, 109
   not taking away a person's freedom, 84
   as omnipotent, 103
   permission of sin, 57
   permitting free creatures to resist
      grace, 169
   possible to freely reject, 106
   producing everything according to
      simple, unchanging laws, 57
   providential ends and means pattern, 57
   removing obstacles to a free choice, 91
   respecting freedom of the creature to
      resist his love, 38
   respecting perseverance in sin, 170
   victory over sin and death, 81
   withdrawing existence from a person, 9, 119
God in Christ, linked together judgment
      and grace, 178
God's Final Victory (Kronen and Reitan), 17, 104, 105, 135–37
God's love, relating the permanent
      separation from God with, 96
God's throne of judgment, responsibility
      of each man before, 35

Subject Index

God's wrath. *See* wrath of God
Goethe, on mind, 78
"going ad nihilum," Kelly's description of, 124
Gomorrha, 28
Gonzalez-Ruiz, Jose-Maris, 143–45
The Goodness of God (Wenham), 140
grace
  after death, 151
  allowing us all to hope, 178
  converting people, 105, 136
  given to those too hardened to profit by it, 57
  of God, 32
  imagined to overwhelm human responsibility, 163
  unlimited hope of, 178
  winning over resistance of all creaturely wills, 81–82
"Grace, Character Formation, and Predestination unto Glory" (Talbott), 81–82
grace of repentance, not accepting, 92
"grand theological narrative," of the conditionalists, 19
The Great Divorce (Lewis), 123
Greek thought, on immediate personal eschatology, 144
Gregory of Nyssa, 159–60, 168
Griffiths, Paul J., 1, 7, 15
  on annihilation, 114
  on *Benedictus Deus*, 145–46
  on the Christian doctrine about the *novissima*, 142–43
  comments on Letter on Certain Questions, 171–73
  as guide for "recycling hell," 120–22
  on immortality of the soul, 117–18
  theology about the last things, 7–9
  on two *novissima*, 166
guarantee, of being saved, 105
Guillebaud, Harold E., 29–31
guilt, Christian theory based on, 93

Hades
  Christ's descent into, 92
  duration of the flames of, 68
  the intermediate abode, 70–71
Handbook of Anglican Theologians, 72
"handmaid of theology," philosophy as, 73
happiness, innate desire for, 173
happiness of the just, 171
Harmon, Kendall S., 7, 14, 41–42
Hart, David Bentley, 133–34
heathen dualism, infiltration of, 65
heaven
  as a free choice, 131
  not treated, 4
Heaven, Hell, and Purgatory (Walls), 122
heaven and hell, as active realizations of freedom, 130–31
Heaven or Hell (Panneton), 154–56
Hebrew tongue, affirming complete destruction, 20
hell. *See also* eternal hell
  as another word for annihilation, 97
  arguments against, 80
  as a carrier of wholesome fear, 124
  cast into the lake of fire, 70–71
  as a choice by the person rather than a punishment, 98
  defined, 155
  denoting what becomes of a person, 15
  disadvantages of the speculative picture of, 121
  a domain of "remains" of persons, 103
  ending when the devil wants it to end, 132
  as exact opposite of what the conditionalists are claiming and refuting, 151
  existing and endless, 151
  existing and populated for eternity, 91
  as a failed and inglorious *novissimum*, 114
  as fear motivation, 124–25
  as freely chosen, 130, 131
  Griffiths reconstructing, 121
  Jerry Walls on, 122–23
  Kvanvig and the problem of, 97–100
  as loss of being, 72

hell *(cont.)*
    as a metaphorical description, 104
    milder views proposed, 89
    need for discussion about, 124
    not a dogma of the church but a teaching, 145
    as not a punishment from God unilaterally imposed, 5
    not contrary to God's love, 132
    not made for men, 103
    not taught in the Scriptures, 19
    objections to, 120–22
    pain and suffering in, 5
    parallel to heaven, 103
    people choosing to be in, 33, 92
    as permanent and irreversible annihilation, 121
    as a place or state of eternal punishment, 157
    as possible because God is love, 123
    pro and con arguments to support Conditional Immortality (CI), 5
    as a punishment, 131
    reconciling people going to, 56
    recycled, 119–41
    in relation to annihilation, 119–20
    representing God's ultimate judgment, 125
    as retribution for sin, 153
    as a symbol of the sinner's self-chosen fate, 124
    teaching of, 3
    as "the teaching of the Church," 175
    themes supporting theological position, 124
    those meriting, 155
    traditional explanation of, 149
    traditional view of, 120
    as ultimately a mystery, 85
    understanding of provided by God out of love, 91
    understandings of, 120–41
    as unjust, 56
"Hell, Wrath, and the Grace of God" (Davis), 32, 92–94
Hell and Heaven (Loudovikos), 129–32
"Hell and Punishment" (Kershnar), 94–95
"hell will be destroyed," supporting the conditionalist view, 163
Hellenists, on freedom, 90, 105
hellfire, punishments of, 154
"heralds of His justice," people in hell as, 168
Hick, John, 7
historical man, debasement of Creation by, 78
Hocking, William E., 76–77
Holy Spirit, 26, 40
Hope Beyond Hell (Beauchemin), 42–43
human annihilation, 116–17
human beings. *See also* man
    freely choosing where consequences extend forever, 83
    living in a fashion going counter to their own essence, 161
    some going out of existence, 172
    suffering endless punishment, 141
human creatures. *See also* man
    capable of both a glorious and an inglorious *novissimum*, 114
    importance of the flesh for, 121
    lacking the capacity for repentance, 121
human defiance, resisting to the end, 37
human freedom. *See* freedom
human immortality. *See* immortality
human justice, 126
human liberty, 125
human rebellion, 31
human self, surviving and subsisting after death, 171
human soul. *See also* soul(s)
    capable of returning to nothing, 115
    not inherently immortal, 51
    philosophic theory of the indestructability of, 10
    ultimately independent of the body, 78
"hypothesis of a final decision," 86

"I know you not!" 155
"icons of hope," 163

Subject Index

Icons of Hope: the "Last Things" in Catholic Imagination (Thiel), 134–35, 163–64
Ignatian Spiritual Exercises, Balthasar's commentaries on, 36
St. Ignatius, 36
Ignatius of Antioch, 45–46
ignorance, sin as, 113
imagery, details of the afterlife disclosed in, 29
"Imagining the Last Judgment" (Thiel), 163
"immobile state," of people after death, 168
immortability, 77
"immortable" soul, 6, 9
"immortableness"
    of the conditionalists, 110
    of the soul, 80
immortal life, 47
immortal soul, as spiritual, 174
immortalist eventual extinctionism, 14
immortality, 79
    according to the Old and New Testament, 65
    as an additional gift of God, 162
    asserted to be peculiar to the redeemed, 47
    to be acquired, 59
    belonging to man by nature, 161
    bestowed at the resurrection, 49
    Christian understanding of, 41
    claims about the soul's, 146
    as conditional, 45
    demanding a dogmatic study, 65
    as exemption from death and annihilation, 50
    flowing from a relationship with God, 159
    forfeited by man through his transgression, 50
    as a gift, 50, 161
    as a gift of God, 118
    God free to eliminate, 12
    for God's redeemed alone, 62
    making capable of, 80
    man's entire nature created for, 49
    as a natural quality of man, 72
    not a natural gift, 10
    not a teaching of the Scriptures, 3
    not an innate human characteristic, 139
    as not natural, 12
    not natural but a gift through faith, 40
    as only a negative assertion, 39–40
    only God having, 30, 138
    Plato's views on, 77
    question, aspects of, 64–71
    question of, 159
    rational, philosophical justification of, 160–61
    Ratzinger's conclusions about, 159
    Sacrament as medicine of, 45
    for the saved in Christ, 46
    Simon Tugwell on, 110
    of the soul, 6
    soul capable of, 6
    truly conquering death, 80
    of the unsaved, denying, 49
"Immortality and Creation" (Ratzinger), 160
immortality of individual souls, as indefensible, 66
"The Immortality of Man" (Cullman), 39
immortality of the individual spirit, coming from Greek philosophy, 75
"The Immortality of the Soul and the Resurrection of the Dead" (Ratzinger), 158–59
immortality of the soul (*animae immortalitas*), 142
    Catholic understanding of, 77
    coming from Plato's philosophy, 9
    derived from Greek philosophy, 13
    Greek conception of, 39
    Griffiths on, 117–18
    metaphysical doctrine of a natural indefeasible, 62
    as misleading, 77
    as a misunderstanding, 39
    not in the Scriptures, 137–38
    not one word by Apostolic Fathers, 47

Subject Index

immortality of the soul *(cont.)*
    not taught in Scripture, 61
    as not yet immortal, 117–18
    as Platonic theory, 73
    proving by rational argument, 162
    question of, 2
    regarded as a gift or endowment, 61
    taught by Athenagoras, 52
    as truth revealed by God, 162
    viewed by science, 65
The Immortality of the Soul or the Resurrection of the Dead? (Cullman), 39
"immortalizability," of the human spirit, 111
"immortalizable," natural soul as, 165
impenitence, 88, 166
impenitent sinners, 67, 75
indestructibility of the soul, 77–78, 79, 80
individual eschatology, 14, 143
indulgences, 143
infernalists, 34, 35, 84
Infinite Negative Well-Being Thesis, 95
inglorious last things, of human creatures, 142
inherent immortality, pagan concept of man's, 60
innate immortality of the soul
    as myth, 144
    not a teaching of the Scriptures, 3
    presumption of, 51
    vs. scriptural witness of immortality as a gift, 3
inner man, continuing to live with Christ, 40
Innnate Immortality, found in mystery religions, 157
"intermediate period" between death and the final resurrection, 4
Irenaeus, 49–50, 130, 162–63
irrevocable destruction, as possible, 129
"Is it Possible to Freely Reject God Forever?" (VanArragon), 82–85

Jerome Biblical Commentary, on the fate of the wicked, 28

Jesus and the demise of death, Matthew Levering on, 110–11
Jesus Christ. *See* Christ
St. John Paul II, on purgatory, 165
judgment
    anticipation of, 128
    Balthasar on, 38
    of God, 125
    in near-death experiences (NDE), 128
    persistence of the notion of, 128
juridical decrees, final states not, 130
justice
    demands of, 105
    of God evaluating every being, 57
    mercy and, 126–27
    punishment not exceeding, 94
    question of, 178
    retributive, 104
Justin Martyr, 48

Kareth, as worst of all punishments, 53
Kelly, Anthony, 124–27
Kershnar, Stephen, on "Hell and Punishment," 94–95
Kierkegaard, Soren, 112–14
"kingdom" of resistance, 90
Kirundi dialect of Rwanda, 29
kolasis, meaning mutilation, 67
Koran, hell of endless torment, 53
Kronen, John, 104–5, 135–37
Kronen and Reitan, 17–18
Kropf, Richard W., 111–12
Kvanvig, Jonathan L., 15
    on C.S. Lewis, 102–4
    on freedom, 106–7
    on "Losing Your Soul," 100–102
    objections raised by, 93
    problem of hell and, 97–100
    syllogism of, 89

Lacordaire, sermon by, 167–68
Lagrange, Garrigou, 29, 166, 168–69, 176–77
Last Judgment, 134, 155, 163
"the last things," 134, 142, 163

Subject Index

Leibnitz, 56
St. Leonard of Port Maurice, 148–49, 167, 179
Letter on Certain Questions Concerning Eschatology, Sacred Congregation for the Doctrine of the Faith, 170–73
Letters of Ignatius, considered to be authentic, 45–46
Levering, Matthew, 110–11
Lewis, C.S., 102, 123, 126
liberty
    constrained, 75
    human, 125
life after death, 172, 176
Life after Death (Becque and Becque), 151
"life and death," meaning of, 30
life apart from God, description of, 133
life beyond death, 175
life eternal (*vita aeterna*), 142
Life Everlasting and the Immensity of the Soul (Lagrange), 166–68
Life in Christ (White), 59, 60, 150
The Life of the World to Come (Zaleski), 127–29
life review, 127, 128
"limitless dereliction," 134
limits, on divine grace and mercy, 127
liturgy, Catholic Church on, 150
living soul, conforming to the law of God, 27
logic, decisions frequently not based on, 123
The Logic of Damnation (Walls), 122
Logos, virtue and movement in harmony with, 133
Lord. *See also* God
    brought angels into being from nothing, 115
    ensuring the existence of an entire realm separate from himself, 121
Lord's Super, as symbol of immortality, 65
losing one's soul, 100, 101–2
loss of soul theory, 100
lost abilities, idea of, 100

Loudovikos, Nichols, on *Hell and Heaven*, 129–32
love of God, 122–23
Loving Light, people not choosing, 128
Lumen Gentium, 15, 120

MacDonald, Gregory, 18
Macquarrie, John, 72
magisterial teaching, on annihilation, 172
Magnesians, letter of Ignatius to, 45–46
Maimonides, Moses, 53
majority, retaining openness to God, 178
Malebranche, Nicholas, 56–57
man. *See also* creature; human beings; human creatures
    becoming "like a god," 161
    as mortal, 144
    no divine element in, 143
    placed upon too lofty a pedestal, 67
    setting limits to salvation, 86
A Manual of Dogmatic Theology (Tanquerey), 156–57
Marcus Aurelius, 52
Maritain, Jacques, 170
Marshall, Chris, 31
massa damnata, Augustine's, 148
material, producing concepts beyond, 79
Matthew, 24–25, 67
Maximus the Confessor, 131, 132–33
McKenzie, John L., 28–29
means and ends, of God, 56
mercy
    of God giving the Prodigal Son time, 108
    God's available to everyone, 149
    justice and, 126–27
metaphysical capital punishment, 97
"metaphysical suicide," committing, 14
Methaphysics, Aristotle's, 78
Middle Ages, non-Christian witnesses, 53
miracles, as extraordinary acts of God, 57
moral beings, destroying, 68
moral character, wholly a work of God within, 81
moral equilibrium, of the world, 33, 92
moral evil
    END of, 71

Subject Index

moral evil *(cont.)*
    explanation of, 57
    not simple deprivation of being, 75
moral relativism, 92
mortal sin
    dying with, 145, 155
    as a radical possibility of human freedom, 87
mortality
    of the human soul, 53
    putting on immortality, 110
    of the soul, 9
Murphy, on humans' metaphysical composition, 111
Murray, Michael, 17–18
myths, restoring the transparency of, 143

"natural deterioration," 88
natural immortality of the soul, 3, 4, 6
natural mortality, view of, 71–72
natural soul, 165
nature, nothing ever annihilated in, 67
"Near-Death Experiences and Christian Hope," 127
near-death experiences (NDE)
    in medieval times, 127
    people relating, 82
    twentieth-century, 127
Necessary Universalism, 107
neural pathways, 111
New Catholic Encyclopedia, on "Hell," 152–53
New Testament (NT)
    dealing with final punishment, 24–25
    man's life after death and, 158
    references to "eternal punishment," 13
    teaching of, 23, 24
    as ultimate Word of God in Jesus Christ, 36
Newton, Isaac, 58
nihil, "nothing," 11
nihilation, allowing for, 170
no turning back state of soul, 109
nonexistence
    no potential for, 115
    preferable to dependence of God, 98

non-survival, emphasizing a person's choice, 98
Norris, Frederick W., on Maximus, 133
not being, incapable of, 78
nothingness, 98, 116, 119
novissima
    balanced theological view of, 37
    final states for human persons, 8
    for humans, 119
    only two, 92
    questions about, 80
    as a result of the relationship between God and the freedom of the person, 130
novissimum
    definition of, 15
    Griffiths defining, 114
    for the unrepentant, 93
nullification, after the general resurrection, 130

obedience, flowing out of genuine love, 123
obstinate sinner, wishing his own annihilation, 167
Offertory of the Mass, praying for the dead, 151
Old Testament
    abode of the dead, 20
    describing final fate of the wicked, 21
    on the destiny of the unrepentant, 19
    historical books of, 21
    teaching a resurrection of the wicked for divine judgment, 24
Oliphant, 27
omissions, easier to justify than commissions, 99
On the Resurrection of the Dead (Athenagoras), 52
"on the way *ad nihilum*," 113
"on the way to nihilum," 112
ontology, hell and heaven related absolutely to, 130
Origen, 62–63
Origenism, 49
Origenists, 50, 156
Ott, Ludwig, 75–76, 157

Subject Index

The Oxford Handbook of Eschatology, 11
    Griffiths on "Purgatory," 8
    Hart in, 133–34

paganism, as source of idea of immortality of the soul, 9
pain of loss, 147
pain of sense, 147, 152
pains of hell, existence and eternity of, 156–57
Panneton, George, 154–56
parables, teaching eternal suffering, 67–68
paranesis (catechetical pedagogy), 38
pardon, unaccompanied by repentance, 75
Parry, Robin, 31–32
Paul
    on destruction of death, 71
    on "each man's work revealed with fire," 178
    on God allowing time for people to repent, 108
    on God's grace, 81
    on humans undergoing bodily death without annihilation, 111
    on immortality, 139
    "resurrection" as replacement, 112
    speaking of eternal suffering, 69
    on those meriting Hell, 155
    victory of the First Born among the dead, 158
    "the wages of sin is death," 30
penance, imposed by the Church, 164
people
    having power to make a final fatal choice, 179
    in hell now, 121
    judging themselves, 128
    perceiving themselves to be superior to other earthly creatures, 173
perdition, not imposed by Christ, 86
"perishing," for the wicked, 45
permanent annihilation, as a *novissimum*, 15
person, being free to choose nonexistence, 98

personal belief, inseparability of personal salvation from, 109
personal growth, possible "in purgatory," 168
person's wish, not to survive, 6
perversity, 123
Petavel, Emmanuel, 10, 64–66
    on the Apostolic Fathers, 47
    on destruction of the unrepentant, 17
    on eternal punishment, 27
    philosophical approaches to Conditional Immortality (CI), 74
    on scriptural arguments, 25–28
Peter, walking on the waters, 160
2 Peter, on immortality of the soul, 67
Phaedrus (Plato), 77
Phan, Peter, 162–63
philioque, Roman understanding of, 132
St. Philip Neri, 56
philosophers, of the Nineteenth Century, 74–80
philosophical reflection, 18
philosophy, using to understand Scripture, 73
physical death, 14
picture-language, New Testament language as, 13
Pieper, Josef, 77–80, 118, 175
Pinnock, Clark H., 11–12
Plato, 77, 175, 176
Platonic philosophical viewpoint, 112
Platonism, 52, 60
Plato's philosophy, as source of idea of immortality of the soul, 9
Plug, Allen, 91–92
Pope John XXII, 145
possibilities of fate, for those continuing to resist God's will, 2
possibility
    of a final decision against the Father's will, 85
    of making a final fateful decision, 34
    of a tragic ending for some people, 138
    of an ultimate choice, 35
    of the withdrawal of existence, 8
post-mortem conversion, 93, 166

Subject Index

post-mortem conversion theory, 110
post-mortem suicide, wicked attempting, 89
preachers
    dealing with the possibility of annihilation, 167
    making great mistakes, 70
"predestinarianism," 169
preexistence of souls, 74
Principle of Alternative Possibilities (PAP), 107
The Problem of Eschatology, 143
The Problem of Evil (Kvanvig), 89
The Problem of Hell, A Philosophical Anthology (Buenting), 80–85, 87–96
The Problem of Immortality (Petavel), 10, 64–66, 74
Prodigal Son, parable of, 108
Professio Fidei, of Paul VI, 146
"proofs," from Scripture about final fate of the unrepentant, 156
prophets, combining moral principle with historical fate, 21
Protestant clergy, courage of, 3
Protestants, study of Conditional Immortality (CI), 1–2
proud, ruin of all, 68
Proverbs, affirming moral principles, 21
Psalms, affirming moral principles, 21
pseudepigrapha literature, documenting the sinner's total extinction, 22
psychological point of view, making a final decision from, 102
psychological possibility, 101
punishment
    as eternal fire, 48
    as infinite, 71
    Jesus threatened sinners with terrible, 66
    not exceeding justice, 94
    proof from Scripture, 156
    as punitive, 50
    as purgative, 50
    of the rejected, 47
    setting forth with clearness, 70
    supreme, 65
    as unjust, 95
puppetry, teaching the faith, 148
pure mortality, 12
Purgatory, 4, 164–66, 168–69
purification, for the elect, 171

Rahner, Karl, 37, 112
Ramelli, Ilaria, 27
Ramsey, A. M., 23
rational suicide argument, for annihilation, 89
"rationality principle," of Kvanvig, 98
Ratzinger, Joseph, 158–62
    on Eschatology, Death and Eternal Life, 129
    on the hypothesis of a final decision, 85–87
    on Purgatory, 164–66
real possibility, of eternal ruin, 36
reason, proof from, 156–57
rebellion, deleterious effects of, 31
rebellious in hell, 90
recycling, common difficulties concerning hell, 119
redemption, fruits of the work of, 70
Reformation, Calvin the major theologian of, 54
Reitan, Eric, 104–5, 135–37
rejecting God, 82
    forever, as possible, 85
Renouvier, 74
repentance
    cut off at death, 23
    grace of, 92
    human creatures lacking the capacity for, 121
    unaccompanied by pardon, 75
repression, of death or "the second death," 124
resistance
    considering as a possibility, 91
    removing examples of, 90
Restitutionism (U), 62
restoration of the world (*renovatio mundi*), 142
resurrection
    Christian doctrine of, 39

Subject Index

impact on our understanding of death, 134
Judaeo-Christian teaching on, 158
loss of the gift of, 41
as a positive assertion, 40
receiving the gift of, 80
referring to the whole person, 171
Resurrection for the Judgment, 79
resurrection of life and judgment, 36
resurrection of the body, 4, 39
resurrection of the dead, Jewish doctrine of, 158
resurrection of the flesh (*carnis resurrectio*), 142
Rethinking Hell (Date), 8–9
retribution, of the wicked, 47
retributive justice, 104
righteous, salvation of, 26
The Righteous Judge (Guillebaud), 30
risen bodies, of those asleep in death, 158
Romanism, errors of, 63
Rothe, Richard, 59, 156
Ruar, Martin, 55

salvation, 35, 37, 60
sanctification, 111
Satan, may be saved, 122
Scheeben, M.J., 153–54
scientific law, 103
scriptural arguments, comments about, 25–28
scriptural opposition, to Conditional Immortality (CI), 17
scriptural texts, speaking of the death and destruction of the sinner, 18
scriptural witness, on the possibility of a final refusal of the Father's plan, 34
Scripture
　as ambiguous on the fate of the wicked, 30
　biblical resurrection teaching of, 157–58
　relevant, 17–43
　teaching the withdrawal of existence, 19

Searching for Soul: Teilhard, de Lubac, Rahner, and the Evolutionary Quest for Immortality (Kropf), 111
second death, 30, 51, 65
Secretan, M., 75
"see" God, not being able to, 105
self-deception, ignorance resulting from, 137
self-destruction, 75, 124
self-evaluation, emphasis on, 128
self-preservation, instinct of, 69
self-righteousness, alternative of, 123
separation from God, 152, 153
sheep and goats, division of mankind into, 38
Sheol, 20, 161
Sheol-like existence, person entering, 162
Sherwood, on Maximus, 133
"Should We De-Mythologize the Separated Soul"? 143–45
Sickness unto Death (Kierkegaard), 112
sin
　apparent disregard for, 134
　bringing a person to nothing, 116
　capable of damaging cognitive abilities, 88
　despair over one's, 113
　enslaving, 84
　persistence in, 113
　result of not pure nothingness, 161
　as self-extrication from the Lord, 121
　as simply damaging, 116
　Socratic definition of, 113
　as typically proliferative, 116
　wages of as death, 75
　in the will, 113
sinful acts, 84
sinful desires, becoming a slave to, 106
sinners
　enabling to freely reject God forever, 85
　rewarded according to deeds, 46
　terminating existence, 14
"Sinners in the Hands of an Angry God" (Edwards), 148
"sinning forever," possibility of, 84

Subject Index

Sistine chapel, graphic paintings of hell in, 148
Socinians, 55–56, 156
Socrates, 39, 175–76
Sodom, 21, 28
Some Current Questions in Eschatology, International Theological Commission, 173–74
"Some Current Questions in Eschatology," 2
Soner, Ernst, Socinian account of A, 55–56
soteriological problem of evil, 109
soul(s). *See also* human soul
    ceasing to exist at death, 12
    destroying, 69
    destruction of, 103
    enduring as long as God wills, 50
    growing in virtue in purgatory, 168
    immortal and eternal in Platonic metaphysics, 144
    immortal or immortable, 9
    immortality of, 2, 6
    Judaeo-Christian understanding of, 144
    made to "last forever," 167–68
    as mortal, 74
    of a neutral character, 51
    persisting in existence, 12
    as possibly not mortal, 15, 117
    rendering immortality "substantialistic," 159
    as "spiritual," 111, 118
    as a substance, 74
    ultimate death of, 27
Spe Salvi, 177
"Species of Hell" (Kronen and Reitan), 104–5
Spinoza, *Ethics*, 78
spiritual body, qualities of, 177
spiritual soul, 111
spirituality of the soul, 79, 173, 174
state
    of grace, 155–56
    hopeless, 5
Storm, D. Anthony, 112
"strong view of hell," 97

subjunctive universalism, 121–22, 170
submission to God, rebelling against, 99
substantialistic argument, for immortality, 159
suffering
    endured in hell, 59
    finite nature of, 96
    not approaching a limit, 94
    over the course of one's afterlife, 96
    punishment with everlasting, 156
    resulting from natural punishments, 95
    through eternity, 61
"sufficient grace," rejected by the sinner, 37
summum bonum, God as, 106, 137
Surprised by Hope (Wright), 137–40
survival, conditional possibility of, 77
Systematic Theology (Tillich), 71–72

Talbott, Thomas, 81–82, 107, 123, 136
Tanquerey, A., 156–57
teaching, of the modern Catholic Church, 149–53
The Teaching of the Twelve Apostles, 46
Teilhard, 112
teleological view, of no independence from God, 99
terminable existence, of the wicked, 48
terminal self-destruction, possibility of, 125
Tertullian, 51, 52
Tertullian Augustinianism, 63
theologomenon, any conclusion as, 175
theologoumenal positions, rather than theological, 154
theologumena, 2
Theopedia, definition of annihilationism, 9–10
Thiel, John E., 134–35, 163–64
St. Thomas. *See* Aquinas, Thomas
thoughts, of God, 109
Tillich, Paul, 71–72
total eradication of being, 100
Tradition
    ancient and modern, 44–72
    proof from, 156

Subject Index

traditional theology, on interminable tortures, 69
"tragic fate," possibility of, 176
transition, into eternity, 41
Travis, Stephen, 13
Tremel, Y.B., 158
Tresmontant, Claude, 157–58
Tridentine Catechism, 147
Tugwell, Simon, 16, 110

ultimate choice, possibility of, 164
ultimate decision. *See also* final decision
making against God, 119
unending punishment, Maximus on, 133
unfallen man, in his first estate in Eden, 49
universal reconciliation, without divine coercion, 92
Universal Restitution, 62
universal salvation
as an empty parody of justice, 135
as an especially doubtful proposal, 170
Scriptures affirming, 127
theory of, 66
universal worship, of Christ, 42–43
Universalism (U)
arguments for, 105
Beauchemin rejecting, 42
concepts of, 26
as part of a grand theological narrative, 18
presupposing predestinarianism, 169
recently into the Catholic academic world, 1
studies advocating, 17
as unlikely, 122
Universalism and Predestinationism: A Critique of the Theological Anthropology that Undergirds Catholic Universalist Eschatology (Brotherton), 169–70
Universalism and the Doctrine of Hell, Fourth Edinburgh Conference on, 132, 140
universalist position, Kvanvig attacking, 106

universalist reading of Scripture, 18
"universalist redemption" (*apokatastasis*), 35
universalist statements, threats invalidating, 36
Universalist system, salvation as inevitable, 26
universalists
on anyone being lost, 19
on consequences of free choices, 164
emphasis on interior openness to truth, 178
first argument, 105
on state of hopelessness, 88
unrepentant souls, 3, 106, 140
unsaved, wishing to be annihilated, 89
utter destruction, 20, 66

"Value, Finality, and Frustration: Problems for Escapism" (Buckareff and Plug), 91–92
VanArragon, Raymond J., 82–85
Vatican document, on future states of the world, 176
vengeance, two-sided, 35
venial sin, dying in, 168
vita aeterna, enter into, 117

Walker, D. F., 54–57
Walls, Jerry, 87–91, 122–23, 137
"way of death," 46
"way of life," 46
wedding garment, 155
well-being, 94, 131
Wenham, John W., 23, 140–41
Whiston, William, 58
White, Edward, 59–60, 64, 150, 156
whole man, will be saved, 158
"Why I Am Unconvinced by Arguments against the Existence of Hell" (Cain), 95–96
wicked
attempting post-mortem suicide, 89
as being destroyed for ever, 69
compared to chaff, 58
destiny of as destruction, 140

Subject Index

wicked *(cont.)*
    to die, perish, be destroyed, 47
    doctrine of the destruction of, 69
    everlasting extinction of, 24
    fate of as revealed, 68
    impenitent ceasing to exist, 11
    Maimonides' words on the fate of, 53
    punished in eternal fire, 48
    resurrection of, 55
    "shall cease to exist," 48
    subject to perpetual dissolution, 55
    total, ultimate, everlasting extinction, 11
    ultimate extinction of the personality of, 59
    will vanish, 21
will, being the chief cause of sin, 113
withdrawal of existence, as not unjust, 6
woe-being, eternal, 131
wrath of God
    continuing in the next life, 34
    as God's opposition to human disobedience, 92
    from heaven, 32
    as our only hope, 32–33
    scriptural understanding, 31–43
    understanding, 120
wrath of the Lamb, 26
Wright, N. T., 137–40, 176

Zaleski, Carol, 127–29, 174
zoe aionios, 67
Zoroaster, 156

www.ingramcontent.com/pod-product-compliance
Lightning Source LLC
Chambersburg PA
CBHW060605230426
43670CB00011B/1985